POST OFFICE JOBS

How to Get a Job With the U.S. Postal Service

Dennis V. Damp

BOOKHAVEN PRESS
Moon Township, PA

POST OFFICE JOBS
How to Get a Job With The U.S. Postal Service

By Dennis V. Damp

Copyright © 2000 by Dennis V. Damp

First Printing 1996   Second Printing 1997   Third Printing 2000 (**Revised**)

Printed and bound in the United States of America

Published by
BOOKHAVEN PRESS LLC
P.O. Box 1243
Moon Township, PA 15108

Disclaimer of All Warranties and Liabilities

Library of Congress Catalog-in-Publication Data

Damp, Dennis V.
    Post Office Jobs: How to Get a Job With The U.S. Postal Service /
Dennis V. Damp. -- 2nd ed.
        p.   cm.
    Includes bibliographical references and index.
    ISBN 0-943641-19-5 (alk. paper)
    1. Postal service--Vocational guidance--United States. 2. Postal
service--United States--Employees.   3. Postal service--United States
Examinations, questions, etc.
HE6499.D18   2000
383' . 145' 0973--dc21   99-32727
                                                                      CIP

For information on distribution or quantity discount rates, Telephone 412/262-5578 or write to: Sales Department, Bookhaven Press LLC, P.O. Box 1243, Moon Township, PA 15108. Distributed to the trade by Midpoint Trade Books, 27 West 20th Street, Suite 1102, New York, NY 10011, Tel: 212-727-0190. Individuals can order this title with credit card toll free (ORDERS ONLY) at 1-800-782-7424.

Table of Contents

Introduction

The U. S. Postal Service (USPS) employs 852,285 workers — more than any other Fortune 500 company — and generates more than 60 billion dollars in sales annually. General Motors is a close second, employing 650,000 people worldwide. Each year the Postal Service hires approximately 40,000 new employees to replace those who retire, transfer, or choose to leave for personal reasons.

This book is a one-stop-resource for those interested in working for the Postal Service. It presents what jobs are available, where they are, and how to get one. *Post Office Jobs* dispels the myth that everyone in the postal service is a mail carrier or clerk. Yes, over half of all workers are mail carriers and clerks, the remaining 200,000 + workers are employed in hundreds of occupations; from janitors and truck drivers to accountants, personnel specialists, electronics technicians, and engineers.

The average salary, benefits, and premium pay for career bargaining unit employees in 1996 (excluding corporate-wide expenses) was $44,613 per work year.[1] U.S. Postal Service jobs are considered to be some of the highest paying, benefit loaded, and fundamentally secure positions in the entire federal system.

Post Office Jobs presents eight steps to successfully landing a job and helps Job seekers:

❶ Identify job openings.

❷ Match skills correctly to hundreds of postal job classifications.

❸ Determine when postal exams are scheduled in their area.

---

[1] The United States Postal Service's Comprehensive Statement on Postal Operations - 1997

❹ Prepare for exams and score between 90% and 100%.

❺ Thoroughly complete job applications and resumes.

❻ Prepare and practice for the job interview.

❼ Apply for jobs that don't require written tests.

❽ Pass the pre-employment drug screening test
(**DON'T TAKE DRUGS**).

This book also offers sage advice and detailed practice exams for the largest occupations. Chapter Six was excerpted by permission from Norman Hall's *Postal Exam Preparation Book* and provides sample exams with study tips for the 470 Battery Tests' four key testing areas. Mr. Hall has scored 100% on the United States Postal Exam four times. *Post Office Jobs* is the only career guide and job finder that includes complete position descriptions for 28 Post Office jobs. It also lists all 2,000 Postal Service job classifications including the pay and total number employed in that occupation.

Postal employees are interviewed prior to appointment by the selecting supervisor/manager. No other postal exam book offers detailed guidance on how to successfully handle this often nerve racking face-to-face encounter. The interview chapter guides you step-by-step through the complex interview process and provides answers to sample stress questions that you may encounter.

Many professional and administrative occupations do not require written examinations. Your background, work experience, and education will be used to determine your eligibility for the job. You'll learn how to apply for these positions throughout the country. A comprehensive and updated list of testing centers is provided in Chapter Four.

Job seekers that have a computer with a modem and subscribe to any online service can visit **Federaljobs.Net** (http://federaljobs.net) for up-to-date guidance on all federal employment opportunities. This site guides visitors to hundreds of federal employment web sites including the new Postal Services' employment home page. Federaljobs.net includes extensive assistance for job seekers and covers many topics of value for people interested in securing federal jobs.

If you're looking for good pay with excellent benefits, pursue the postal service job market. Use this book's resources, including the Job Hunter's Checklist in Appendix A, to begin your personal job search.

Chapter One
The U.S. Postal Service

The U. S. Postal Service (USPS) employs 852,285 workers in 300 job categories for positions at 39,000 post offices, branches, stations, and community post offices throughout the United States. Approximately 40,000 postal workers are hired each year to backfill for retirements, transfers, deaths and employees who choose to leave the Postal Service.

Vacancies are advertised internally by the USPS and not by the Office of Personnel Management. In 1971, the Postal Service became independent. Pay scales are determined by the Postal Pay Act and are not a part of the General Pay Schedule.

Pay starts at $22,340 per year for full time career employees at the PS-1-AA pay grade and increases to $43,101 at the PS-10-O top pay grade. The average annual base salary for bargaining unit employees exceeds $33,000 or $15.86 per hour. Adding benefits, overtime, and premiums, the average bargaining unit hourly rate was $21.45, yielding an effective annual compensation rate of $44,613.[1] The PS pay scale is the largest pay system in the USPS and is predominately for bargaining unit employees. There are also Executive and Administrative Schedules for nonbargaining unit employees that range from $20,875 up to $148,400 for the Postmaster General.

Adding benefits, overtime, and premiums, the average bargaining unit hourly rate was $21.45, yielding an effective annual compensation rate of $44,613.

BENEFITS

Postal employees receive the same benefits provided to federal employees.

---

[1]Comprehensive Statement on Postal Operations, 1997 — USPS

Vacation & Sick Leave

All employees receive: 10 paid holidays, 13 days of vacation for the first three years, twenty days of vacation with three to fifteen years service and after fifteen years twenty-six days. Additionally, 13 sick days are accrued each year regardless of length of service. Military time counts toward benefits. If you have three years of military service, you begin with four weeks paid vacation and three years toward retirement.

Health Benefits & Life Insurance

Medical health plans and the *Federal Employees' Group Life Insurance* (FEGLI) programs are available to all employees. The medical plan is an employee-employer contribution system and includes HMO and Blue Cross and Blue Shield programs. There are hundreds of plans to choose from. The FEGLI program offers low cost term life insurance for the employee and basic coverage for the family. FEGLI offers up to five times the employee's salary in death benefits.

One of the primary benefits of Postal Service employment is the satisfaction you experience from working in a challenging and rewarding position. Positions are available with the level of responsibility and authority that you desire.

Retirement

The Postal Service retirement system was significantly changed for individuals hired after January 1, 1984. Social Security is withheld and a new employee contribution system is fashioned after a 401k defined contribution plan. You can elect to contribute up to 3 percent of your salary into a *THRIFT savings 401k plan*. The government will match your contribution up to 5 percent. This is effectively a 5 percent pay increase. Your contributions are tax deferred and reduce your taxable income by the amount contributed. The retirement benefit is determined by the amount that has accumulated during the employee's career. This includes the interest earned and capital gains realized from the retirement fund.

There are many withdrawal options including lump sum and various fixed term annuities. The contribution plan payout is in addition to the social security benefits that you will be eligible for at retirement. Postal workers pay considerably less for their health benefits than competitive federal civil service employees due to their negotiated union contracts.

EMPLOYEE CLASSIFICATIONS

Initial appointments are either casual (temporary) or Part-Time Flexible (Career). Hourly rates for Part-Time Flexible employees vary depending upon the position's rate schedule. Some positions are filled full-time such as the Maintenance (Custodial) classification.

Full-Time and Part-Time Flexible (career) employees comprise the *Regular Work Force*. This category includes security guards. Part-Time Flexible employees are scheduled to work fewer than 40 hours per week and they must be available for flexible work hours as assigned. Part-Time Flexible employees are paid by the hour. Hourly rates vary from $10.99 for MH Grade 4 Step A to $18.02 for MH Grade 6 step O. See Chapter Two for a complete pay scale listing.

A *Supplemental Work Force* is needed by the Postal Service for peak mail periods and offers casual (temporary) employees two 89-day employment terms in a calendar year. During Christmas an additional 21 days of employment can be offered to Supplemental Work Force employees.

College students may be considered for casual (temporary) employment with the Postal Service during the summer months. The rate of pay is $8.81 per hour. Tests are not required and appointments cannot lead to a career position. Apply early for summer work. Contact Post Offices in your area by no later than February for summer employment applications.

QUALIFICATION REQUIREMENTS

Various standards from age restrictions to physical requirements must be met before you can take one of the Postal Service exams.

Age Limit

You must be eighteen to apply. Certain conditions allow applicants as young as sixteen to apply. Carrier positions, requiring driving, are limited to age 18 or older. High school graduates or individuals that terminated high school education for sufficient reason are permitted to apply at age 16.

Entrance Exams

Clerk, carrier and other specific postal job applicants must pass an entrance exam. Specialties such as mechanic, electronic technician, machinist, and trades must also pass a written test. The overall rating is based on the test results and your qualifying work experience and education. Professionals and certain administrative positions don't require an entrance exam or written test. They are rated and hired strictly on their prior work experience and education.

The **NEW 470 Battery examination** covers seven major entry level positions including:

- ✔ **Carrier**
- ✔ **Clerk**
- ✔ **Distribution Clerk, Machine**
- ✔ **Flat-Sorting Machine Operator**
- ✔ **Mail handler**
- ✔ **Mail Processor**
- ✔ **Mark-Up Clerk, Automated**

The *470 Battery Examination* covers the majority of entry level hiring although some offices also maintain custodial registers, which by law, are reserved for veteran preference eligibles. The USPS also maintains *motor vehicle* and *tractor trailer registers* and some highly skilled maintenance positions such as *Building Equipment Mechanic, Engineman, Electronics Technician, and General Mechanic.* All of the skilled maintenance positions require examination 931. A separate announcement, examination number 932, is required for Electronics Technician positions.

Six sample exams are presented in Chapter Five and a sample *470 Battery Test* is included in Chapter Six to help you prepare for this test. The 470 examination and completion of forms will require approximately two hours and fifteen minutes. Jobs with the U.S. Postal Service are highly competitive due to the excellent salary and benefits offered. It's essential that you pass the test with the highest score possible to improve your chances. Applicants scoring between 95-100% have a better chance of being hired. An excellent study guide for the 470 Battery Test is Norman Hall's *Postal Exam Preparation Book.*

Citizenship

Applicants do not have to be U.S. citizens. If you have permanent alien resident status in the United States of America or owe allegiance to the United States of America you can apply for Postal Service Jobs.

Physical Requirements

Physical requirements are determined by the job. Carriers must be able to lift a 70-pound mail sack and all applicants must be able to efficiently perform assigned duties. Eyesight and hearing tests are required. Applicants must have at least 20/40 vision in the good eye and no worse than 20/100 in the other eye. Eyeglasses are permitted.

State Drivers License

Applicants must have a valid state driver's license for positions that require motor vehicle operation. A safe driving record is required and a

Postal Service road test is administered for the type of vehicle that you will operate.

DRUG TESTING (SUBSTANCE ABUSE)

The Postal Service maintains a comprehensive program to insure a drug-free workplace. A qualification for postal employment is to be drug free, and this qualification is determined through the use of a urinalysis drug screen. When you are determined to be in the area of consideration for employment, you will be scheduled for a drug screening test.

APPLICATION PROCEDURES

Positions Requiring Written Examinations

The USPS does not maintain a national directory or register of openings. The Postal Service has a decentralized hiring process for personnel and examination related matters. The examinations are administered by examination center personnel from local Customer District Human Resources offices located in most large cities. A comprehensive listing of Customer Service District offices is provided in Chapter Four.

To apply for postal positions you must contact a Management Sectional Center (MSC), Bulk Mail Center, General Mail Facilities, Customer Service District Office or a Sectional Center Facility to register for the postal workers civil service exam. Contact your local post office to find out where the tests are administered in your area. A complete listing of Postal facilities is available from the USPS in their National Five-Digit Zip Code and Post Office Directory (two volumes) which may be purchased from any post office for $15.00. A copy of this publication is usually available for use in the post office lobby.

A passing score of 70 percent or better on an exam will place the applicant's name on an eligible *register* for a period of two years. Registers are lists of job applicants that have passed an exam or evaluation process. Your score determines your placement on the register. Applicants can write to the Postal Examination office for a one-year extension. Requests for extension must be received between the eighteenth-and twenty-fourth month of eligibility. Most people hired have a score of between 90% and 100%. There is a separate register for each job classification. To improve your chances, test for as many different positions that you can qualify for.

Positions That Don't Require a Written Exam

Vacancies in these positions—generally professional and admin- istrative—are announced (advertised) first within the Postal Service. Postal employees who have the knowledge, education, credentials, and skills may apply for these openings. If there aren't any qualified applicants (called bidders in the federal sector), then the postal service will advertise the vacancies to the general public and accept resumes and applications for rating. All applicants must pass an entrance examination and/or an evaluation process to be placed on a register in numerical score order.

It is generally recommended that job applicants seeking entry level professional and administrative positions take the 470 Battery Exam to get their foot in the door. Once hired, as vacancies open in their specialty such as accounting, budget, and engineering, they will have first crack at the jobs through internal Postal Service job announcements.

Realistically, many professional jobs won't be filled internally. Few postal clerks and non professional employees will have law degrees, engineering credentials, or doctorates for example. Review the list of more than 2,000 job classifications in Chapter Ten to see the scope of available jobs. This list also includes the total number employed and the pay for that occupation.

These job openings will generally be advertised in local papers. You should also contact local Customer Service Districts personnel offices listed in Chapter Four to identify upcoming job vacancies for your speciality.

You will be rated on a point system (maximum of 100 points) even without a written test. Therefore, your resume and *Application For Employment* (PS Form 2591) must be thoroughly completed and include all key information such as degrees, training, credentials, and detailed work experience. Only the top three candidates will generally be referred to the selecting official for consideration.

VETERANS PREFERENCE

Veterans receive five or 10 point preference. Those with a 10% or greater compensable service-connected disability are placed at the top of the register in the order of their scores. All other eligibles are listed below the disabled veterans group in rank order. The Veterans Preference Act applies to all Postal Service positions. Refer to Chapter Eight for detailed information on Veterans Preference.

Custodial exams for the position of cleaner, custodian, and custodial laborer are exclusively for veterans and present employees. This exam is open only to veterans preference candidates.

PAY SCALES

There are several pay schedules in the Postal Service. The Postal Service (PS) pay scale for bargaining unit employees and the Executive and Administrative Schedule (EAS) pay scale for non-bargaining unit employees are presented in this chapter. Special pay scales are also used for rural letter carriers.

The Postal Service also pays extra compensation, overtime, and night shift differential to workers. A Cost of Living Adjustment (COLA) is added to the base salary of employees at the rate of one cent per hour for each increase of a .4 point increase in the Consumer Price Index.

POSTAL SERVICE (PS) Full Time Annual Rates (11/22/97)

PS - GRADE	AA	A	B	C	D	E	F	G	H	I	J	K	L	M	N	O
1	$22,300	$24,666	$26,753	$28,841	$31,948	$31,161	$32,375	$32,587	$32,799	$33,012	$33,225	$33,438	$33,652	$33,861	$34,076	$34,288
2	22,655	25,081	27,158	29,292	32,462	32,692	32,922	33,152	33,385	33,613	33,844	34,076	34,304	34,537	34,767	34,995
3	22,989	25,396	27,589	29,780	33,018	33,266	33,518	33,763	34,014	34,260	34,512	34,759	35,008	35,255	35,504	35,751
4		25,363	28,059	30,313	33,622	33,890	34,161	34,430	34,696	34,965	35,234	35,504	35,775	36,043	36,311	36,578
5		26,844	29,728	32,043	34,276	34,564	34,855	35,142	35,433	35,721	36,010	36,301	36,588	36,879	37,167	37,456
6		28,418	31,498	32,692	34,980	35,295	35,610	35,921	36,237	36,551	36,862	37,178	37,493	37,806	38,123	38,437
7		29,017	32,170	33,399	35,744	36,082	36,419	36,758	37,099	37,434	37,774	38,110	38,448	38,788	39,125	39,462
8				33,990	36,562	36,929	37,295	37,662	38,031	38,396	38,766	39,130	39,498	39,864	40,230	40,599
9				34,816	37,454	37,855	38,249	38,646	39,040	39,435	39,831	40,230	40,624	41,024	41,420	41,816
10				35,687	38,396	38,824	39,250	39,679	40,108	40,534	40,962	41,391	41,817	42,246	42,674	43,101

Step Increases AA-O are awarded on time in service and range from 96 weeks to 24 weeks between increases.

EXECUTIVE & ADMINISTRATIVE STEP SCHEDULE (EAS) 11/22/97

EAS GRADE	MIDPOINT	EAS GRADE	MIDPOINT
1	$23,693.00	15	$41,921.00
2	24,470.00	16	44,366.00
3	25,275.00	17	45,333.00
4	26,295.00	18	48,368.00
5	27,171.00	19	50,660.00
6	28,150.00	20	53,409.00
7	29,304.00	21	56,003.00
8	30,478.00	22	59,333.00
9	31,699.00	23	62,567.00
10	32,837.00	24	65,663.00
11	34,436.00	25	68,929.00
12	36,089.00	26	72,367.00
13	37,773.00		
14	39,745.00		

POSTAL OCCUPATIONS WITH OVER 1,000 EMPLOYEES

OCCUPATION	NUMBER EMPLOYED
Accounting Clerk	1,193
Auto Mechanic	2,762
Bldg. Equipment Mechanic	1,928
Bldg. Maintenance Custodian	1,004
Bulk Mail Clerk	1,350
Bulk Mail Technician	1,864
Carrier City	223,562
Carrier Technician	28,240
Clerk Finance	1,137
Custodian	1,844
Customer Service Manager/Supr.	17,138
Data Collection Technician	1,183
Data Conversion Operator	8,078
District Clerk	36,014
Distribution Clerk	95,706
Distribution Operations Mgr./Supr.	15,520
Electronics Technician	6,467
Flat Sorting Mach. Operator	19,940
General Clerk	3,350
General Expediter	3,747
Human Resource Specialists	2,361
Laborer Custodial	13,134
Mail Handler/Tech/Operator	52,165
Maintenance Control Clerk/Tech	1193
Maintenance Managers/Supervisors	2,447
Maintenance Mechanic/MPE	8,221
Markup Clerk	6,124
Motor Vehicle Operator	3,475
Parcel Post Dist-Machine	9,572
PM/Relief/Replacement	12,951
Postal Police Officer	1,313
Postmaster	26,803
Postal Inspector	1,674
Rural Delivery Carriers	45,049
Sack Sorting Mach. Operator	1,616
Secretary	1,115
Special Delivery Messenger	1,555
Tractor Trailer Operator	4,633
Vehicle maintenance	4,689
Window service Clerk/Tech	8,435

Chapter Two
The Hiring Process

The U.S. Postal Service is an Equal Opportunity Employer. Hiring and advancement in the Postal Service is based on qualifications and performance regardless of race, color, creed, religion, sex, age, national origin, or disability. Applicants do not have to be U.S. citizens. If you have permanent alien resident status in the United States of America or owe allegiance to the United States of America you can apply for Postal Service jobs. The majority of positions require passing a postal exam. Professionals such as doctors, engineers, and others are employed through an interview process.

Postal installation managers are generally appointing officials and are delegated the authority to fill vacancies by transfer, reassignment, reinstatement of a former federal or postal employee, promotion, or from an entrance register of eligibles. Regardless of the recruitment source, the applicant must meet the qualifications of the position, including passing the appropriate examination. Examinations can be either written or a rated application process such as that used for professional positions. Generally, it is a written examination.

EMPLOYEE CLASSIFICATIONS

There are two employee classifications; Regular Work Force (PS) and Supplemental Work Force. The regular work force comprises two groups; full-time and part-time flexible. All new hires except technician positions and professionals start as part-time flexibles. Part-time flexibles are not guaranteed 40 hours per week but generally work five to six days per week and will be required to work up to 50 hours per week during peak periods.

The Postal Service's hiring process comprises four components, the suitability and selection component is separated into three sub groups as specified below:[1]

- ❑ Recruitment
- ❑ Examinations
- ❑ Registers
- ❑ Suitability
  - ✔ Suitability
  - ✔ Selection
  - ✔ Appointment

RECRUITMENT

The deployment of high-technology equipment and the structure and demands of many postal jobs in today's work environment have changed the Postal Service's view on recruitment. Their goal for recruitment is to attract an adequate number of qualified applicants to consider for postal employment. Local management evaluates its hiring needs. Evaluation consists of forecasting future hiring needs, assessing existing applicant pools, considering other hiring options such as special emphasis programs, and reviewing any upcoming Postal Service organizational changes.

EXAMINATIONS

The majority of occupations require entrance examinations. They help identify applicants that meet preestablished qualification requirements for filling vacant positions. Examinations measure or evaluate knowledge, skills, and abilities to predict probable future work performance. Passing examination scores are between 70 and 100. Entrance examinations are offered at locations where hiring is anticipated. Test dates and times are advertised in local papers and at the mail facilities that are actively recruiting. See Chapter Four for a list of Customer Service District Offices that you can call or write for test dates.

REGISTERS

Registers are lists containing applicant names and other information, including an examination rating and/or results of an evaluation process. The names of applicants who pass an entrance examination and/or evaluation process are placed on the register in numerical score order. That is why it is important for applicants to score as high as possible on their

---

[1] Reference the U.S. Postal Service's Self-Instruction Module

entrance exams. Passing grades are between 70 and 100, however, most are hired with scores between 90 and 100.

Eligible applicants are ranked on a register according to final ratings (including veterans preference points - see Chapter Eight) and divided into two groups. The first group is made up of veterans who have a compensable service-connected disability. The second group is made up of everyone else.

It is important for applicants to score as high as possible on their entrance exams.

When it isn't feasible to announce an examination, the general application file, an alternative recruitment source, can be used to fill temporary positions. A general application file is comparable to a one-time use or temporary register. Because no examination is given and to comply with the provisions of the veteran preference, applicants must be considered for employment by priority groups. Persons entitled to 10-point veteran preference who have a compensable service-connected disability are placed ahead of all other persons entitled to veteran preference and then placed ahead of all other applicants on the list.

SUITABILITY

Applicants are screened and evaluated to determine their overall suitability for postal employment prior to selection. This evaluation includes a review of:

✔ The applicant's work history
✔ Criminal conviction history[2]
✔ Personal interviews (See Chapter Seven)
✔ Medical assessment

Medical assessment is an example of suitability screening that occurs after the job offer. The Rehabilitation Act of 1973 prohibits the Postal Service from inquiring into an applicant's medical suitability until a bona fide job offer is made. Medical assessment is done after selecting an applicant who has met all other suitability requirements.

After an applicant is hired, a career employee's job performance is evaluated during the probationary period. Fingerprints are submitted for a special agency check to be performed by the Office of Personnel Management (OPM) to ensure that there is no derogatory information about the individual that has not been discovered in the screening process. Thorough screening is done to ensure that individuals who do not meet Postal Service requirements are eliminated from the hiring process.

---

[2] Because of the critical nature of suitability screening, evaluation activities continue after the job offer and hire.

SELECTION

Selection is the process of identifying the best-qualified applicant for employment. Employing officials make selection decisions based on an evaluation of all information obtained during suitability screening. It is important to understand that a decision to select does not guarantee that the applicant will be appointed to the Postal Service. The applicant's medical assessment, which is completed after selection, or the identification of derogatory information about the applicant, may disqualify the individual before the appointment is effected.

APPOINTMENT

Appointment is the process of placing a selected applicant, who is totally qualified, on the Postal Service rolls. The appointment is made after suitability is confirmed.

GETTING IN THE FRONT DOOR

Getting in is half the battle. If you are qualified as a computer systems analyst and there are currently no openings, take the appropriate entrance exam and apply for entry level positions such as Postal Clerks and Mail Carriers. The Postal Service offers in-service examinations for various specialities and generally advertises jobs in-house first to offer qualified workers opportunities for advancement. You will have a good chance to bid on other jobs if you have the qualifications and a good track record.

There are two things to aim at in life: first, to get what you want; and after that to enjoy it. Only the wisest of people achieve the second.

— **Logan Smith**

INTERVIEWS

The Postal Service conducts interviews as part of the suitability recruitment process. You need to be prepared for these interviews. There are generally a good number of high scoring applicants and the selecting official will use the interview process to determine the best candidates for the jobs. Refer to Chapter Seven for guidance on how to prepare for interviews.

Chapter Three
What Jobs Are Available

This chapter provides detailed occupational descriptions for the largest Postal Service jobs. A list of occupations with more than 1,000 employees is available on page 16. Chapter Nine provides comprehensive job descriptions for 28 diverse occupations and Chapter Ten offers a complete list of all 2,000 Post Office jobs including pay. Use the *Job Hunters Checklist* in Appendix A to assist you with your job search.

To find out when Postal Service exams will be administered in your area, call or write your local Customer Service District office. Customer Service District offices are listed in Chapter Four by area. If you are looking for a professional, administrative, or technical position, that may not require a written exam, ask the personnel specialist at the Customer Service District office when they will be recruiting for those specialties. If jobs are currently open, request an application package. The two primary application forms are the PS 2479-B (Application/Admission Card) and the PS Form 2591 (Application for Employment) a four page document. These forms are printed in Appendix B. Use these forms to draft your application prior to receipt of the job announcement.

Postal recruitment notices are often advertised in national and local newspapers, publications, journals and periodicals. You can also visit **Federaljobs.net** on the internet at http://federaljobs.net for direct links to over 200 federal recruiting web sites. The U.S. Postal Service now has it's own on-line National Job Listings service at http://www.usps.com/hrisp/ or you can call their toll free national vacancies number, 1-800-JOB USPS, local employment number, 1-800-276-5627, or 1-800-NATL VAC for national vacancies.

Individual mail facilities in your area should also be contacted to find out if they intend to recruit in the near future.

Our business in life is not to get ahead of others, but to get ahead of ourselves — to break our own records, to outstrip our yesterdays by our today.

Susan B. Johnson

IMPROVING YOUR CHANCES

The more contacts you make the greater your chances. **Don't get lost in the process.** Too many job seekers pin all their hopes on one effort. They take one exam then forget about the process until they receive a reply. Post Office jobs are highly competitive. The more positions that you apply for and examinations that you take the better your chances.

Good things come to those who
wait, as long as they work like
hell while they wait.

The interviewing techniques' presented in Chapter Seven will help you prepare for the suitability screening process discussed in Chapter Two. Prepare for the interview. The Postal Service requires that each individual be interviewed prior to making an offer of appointment. They use Form 2591, Application for Employment, as a guide during the interview process to verify education, job history, specialized skills, and to clarify reasons for leaving previous jobs. Take time to thoroughly complete the job application. Type the application if possible or print legibly. You can copy and use the sample forms provided in Appendix B to prepare your application.

You aren't locked into the first job or, for that matter, location that you are originally selected for. Once hired, you'll have opportunities to bid for jobs in-house. Post Offices, General Mail Facilities, and District Offices are located throughout the country and you can bid to many locations for future promotions or to enter a related or new career field.

POSTAL SERVICE OCCUPATIONS

POSTAL CLERKS AND MAIL CARRIERS
(The Largest USPS Occupations)

Nature of the Work

Each day, the United States Postal Service receives, sorts, and delivers millions of letters, bills, advertisements, and packages. To do this, it employs 853,300 workers. Almost three out of four of these workers are either mail handlers or clerks , who sort mail and serve customers in post offices, or mail carriers, who deliver the mail.[1]

---

[1] Occupational Outlook Handbook, 1998-99 Edition, U.S. Department of Labor

Clerks and carriers are distinguished by the type of work they do. Clerks are usually classified by the mail processing function they perform, whereas carriers are classified by their type of route, city or rural.

About 350 mail processing centers throughout the country service post offices in surrounding areas and are staffed primarily by postal clerks. Some clerks, more commonly referred to as mail handlers, unload the sacks of incoming mail; separate letters, parcel post, magazines, and newspapers; and transport these to the proper sorting and processing area. In addition, they may perform simple canceling operations and rewrap packages damaged in processing after letters have been put through stamp-canceling machines. They are taken to other workrooms to be sorted according to destination. Clerks operating electronic letter-sorting machines push keys corresponding to the ZIP code of the local post office to which each letter will be delivered; the machine then drops the letters into the proper slots. A growing proportion of clerks operate optical character readers (OCRs) and bar code sorters, machines that can "read" the address and sort a letter according to a code printed on the envelope. Others sort odd-sized letters, magazines, and newspapers by hand. Finally, the mail is sent to local post offices for sorting according to delivery route and delivered.

Postal clerks at local post offices sort local mail for delivery to individual customers and provide retail services such as selling stamps and money orders, weighing packages to determine postage, and checking that packages are in satisfactory condition for mailing. Clerks also register, certify, and insure mail and answer questions about postage rates, post office boxes, mailing restrictions, and other postal matters. Occasionally, they may help a customer file a claim for a damaged package.

Once the mail has been processed and sorted, it is ready to be delivered by mail carriers. Duties of city and rural carriers are very similar. Most travel established routes delivering and collecting mail. Mail carriers start work at the post office early in the morning, where they spend a few hours arranging their mail for delivery and taking care of other details.

Carriers may cover the route on foot, by vehicle, or a combination of both. On foot, they carry a heavy load of mail in a satchel or push it in a cart. In some urban and most rural areas, they use a car or small truck. Although the Postal Service provides vehicles to city carriers, most rural carriers use their own automobiles. Deliveries are made house-to-house, to roadside mailboxes, and to large buildings such as offices or apartments, which generally have all the mailboxes on the first floor.

Besides delivering and collecting mail, carriers collect money for postage-due and C.O.D. (cash on delivery) fees and obtain signed receipts for registered, certified, and insured mail. If a customer is not home, the carrier leaves a notice that tells where special mail is being held.

After completing their routes, carriers return to the post office with mail gathered from street collection boxes, homes, and businesses. They turn in the mail receipts and money collected during the day and may separate letters and parcels for further processing by clerks.

The duties of some city carriers may be very specialized; some deliver only parcel post while others collect mail from street boxes and receiving boxes in office buildings. In contrast, rural carriers provide a wide range of postal services. In addition to delivering and picking up mail, they sell stamps and money orders and accept parcels, letters, and items to be registered, certified, or insured.

All carriers answer customers' questions about postal regulations and services and provide change-of-address cards and other postal forms when requested. In addition to their regularly scheduled duties, carriers often participate in neighborhood service programs in which they check on elderly or shut-in patrons or notify the police of any suspicious activities along their route.

Postal clerks and mail carriers are classified as casual, part-time flexible, part-time regular, or full time. Casual workers help process and deliver mail during peak mailing or vacation periods. Part-time flexible workers do not have a regular work schedule or weekly guarantee of hours; they replace absent workers and help with extra work as the need arises. Part-time regulars have a set work schedule of less than 40 hours per week. Full-time postal employees work a 40-hour week over a 5-day period.

Working Conditions

Postal clerks usually work in clean, well-ventilated, and well-lit buildings. However, other conditions vary according to work assignments and the type of labor saving machinery available. In small post offices, mail handlers use hand trucks to move heavy mail sacks from one part of the building to another and clerks may sort mail by hand. In large post offices and mail processing centers, chutes and conveyors move the mail, and much of the sorting is done by machines. Despite the use of automated equipment, the work of mail handlers and postal clerks can be physically demanding. These workers are usually on their feet, reaching for sacks and trays of mail or placing packages and bundles into sacks and trays.

Mail handlers and distribution clerks may become bored with the routine of moving and sorting mail. Many work at night or on weekends because most large post offices process mail around the clock, and the largest volume of mail is sorted during the evening and night shifts.

Window clerks, on the other hand, have a greater variety of duties, frequent contact with the public, and rarely have to work at night. However, they may have to deal with upset customers, and they are held accountable for the assigned stock of stamps and for postal funds.

Most carriers begin work early in the morning, in some cases as early as 4:00 a.m. if they have routes in the business district. A carrier's schedule has its advantages, however: Carriers who begin work early in the morning are through by early afternoon, and they spend most of the day on their own, relatively free from direct supervision.

Carriers spend most of their time outdoors, and deliver mail in all kinds of weather. Even those who drive often must walk when making deliveries and must lift heavy sacks of parcel post items when loading their vehicles. In addition, carriers always must be cautious of potential hazards on their routes. Wet roads and sidewalks can be treacherous, and each year numerous carriers are bitten by unfriendly dogs.

Employment

The U.S. Postal Service employed 297,000 clerks and mail handlers and 332,000 mail carriers in 1996. About 90% of them worked full time. Most postal clerks provided window service and sorted mail at local post offices, although some worked at mail processing centers. Most mail carriers worked in cities and suburban communities, 48,000 were rural carriers.

629,000 clerks and mail handlers work for the USPS

Training, Other Qualifications, and Advancement

Postal clerks and mail carriers must be U.S. citizens or have been granted permanent resident-alien status in the United States. They must be at least 18 years old (or 16, if they have a high school diploma). Qualification is based on a written examination that measures speed and accuracy at checking names and numbers and ability to memorize mail distribution procedures. Applicants must pass a physical examination as well, and may be asked to show that they can lift and handle mail sacks weighing up to 70 pounds. Applicants for jobs as postal clerks operating electronic sorting machines must pass a special examination that includes a machine aptitude test. Applicants for mail carrier positions must have a driver's license, a good driving record, and a passing grade on a road test.

Applicants should apply at the post office or mail processing centers where they wish to work in order to determine when an exam will be given. Applicants' names are listed in order of their examination scores. Five points are added to the score of an honorably discharged veteran, and 10 points to the score of a veteran wounded in combat or disabled. When a vacancy occurs, the appointing officer chooses one of the top three applicants; the rest of the names remain on the list to be considered for future openings until their eligibility expires, usually two years from the examination date.

Relatively few people under the age of 25 are hired as career postal clerks or mail carriers, a result of keen competition for these jobs and the customary waiting period of 1-2 years or more after passing the examination. It is not surprising, therefore, that most entrants transfer from other occupations.

New postal clerks and mail carriers are trained on the job by experienced workers. Many post offices offer classroom instruction. Workers receive additional instruction when new equipment or procedures are introduced. They usually are trained by another postal employee or, sometimes, a training specialist hired under contract by the Postal Service.

A good memory, good coordination, and the ability to read rapidly and accurately are important. In addition, mail handlers should be in good physical condition. Mail handlers and distribution clerks work closely with other clerks, frequently under the tension and strain of meeting dispatch transportation deadlines. Window clerks and mail carriers must be courteous and tactful when dealing with the public, especially when answering questions or receiving complaints.

Postal clerks and mail carriers often begin on a part-time flexible basis and become regular or full time in order of seniority as vacancies occur. Full-time clerks may bid for preferred assignments such as the day shift, a window job, or a higher level nonsupervisory position as expediter or window service technician. Carriers can look forward to obtaining preferred routes as their seniority increases, or to higher level jobs such as carrier technician. Both clerks and carriers can advance to supervisory positions.

Job Outlook

Those seeking a job in the Postal Service can expect to encounter keen competition. The number of applicants for postal clerk and mail carrier positions is expected to continue to far exceed the number of openings. Job opportunities will vary by occupation and duties performed.

Overall employment of postal clerks is expected to grow more slowly than the average through the year 2005. In spite of the anticipated increase in the total volume of mail, automation will continue to increase the productivity of postal clerks. Increasingly, mail will be moved using automated materials-handling equipment and sorted using optical character readers, bar code sorters, and other automated sorting equipment. In addition, demand for window clerks will be moderated by the increased sales of stamps and other postal products by grocery and department stores and other retail outlets.

Conflicting factors also are expected to influence demand for mail carriers. Despite competition from alternative delivery systems and new forms of electronic communication, the volume of mail handled by the Postal Service is expected to continue to grow. Population growth and the formation of new households, coupled with an increase in the volume of third class mail, will stimulate demand for mail delivery. However, increased use of the "ZIP + 4" system, which is used to sort mail to the carrier route, should decrease the amount of time carriers spend sorting their mail. In addition, the Postal Service is moving toward more centralized mail delivery, such as the use of more cluster boxes, to cut down on the number of door-to-door deliveries. Although these trends are expected to increase carrier productivity, they will not significantly offset the growth in mail volume, and employment of mail carriers is expected to grow about as fast as the average for all occupations.

In addition to jobs created by growth in demand for postal services, some jobs will become available because of the need to replace postal clerks and mail carriers who retire or stop working for other reasons. The factors that make entry to these occupations highly competitive - attractive salaries, a good pension plan, steady work, and modest educational requirements contribute to a high degree of job attachment, so that replacement needs produce relatively fewer job openings than in other occupations of this size. In contrast to the typical pattern, postal workers generally remain in their jobs until they retire; relatively few transfer to other occupations.

Although the volume of mail to be processed and delivered rises and falls with the level of business activity, as well as with the season of the year, full-time postal clerks and mail carriers have, to date, never been laid off. When mail volume is high, full-time clerks and carriers work overtime, part-time clerks and carriers work additional hours, and casual clerks and carriers may be hired. When mail volume is low, overtime is curtailed, part-timers work fewer hours, and casual workers are discharged.

Earnings

In 1996, base pay for beginning full-time postal clerks who operate scanning and sorting machines was $24,599 a year, rising to a maximum of $35,683 after 14 years of service. Entry-level pay for window clerks and clerks in retail outlets was $26,063 a year in 1996 whereas those with 14 years of service earned $36,551 a year. Entry-level pay for full-time regular mail handling clerks ranged from $21,676 to $22,944 a year in 1996.

Experienced full-time, city delivery mail carriers earn, on average, $34,135 a year. Postal clerks and carriers working part-time flexible schedules begin at $12.82 and hour and, based on the number of years of service, increase to a maximum of $18.07 an hour. Rural delivery carriers had average base salaries of $35,000. Their earnings are determined through an evaluation of the amount of work required to service their routes. Carriers with heavier workloads generally receive an equipment maintenance allowance when required to use their own vehicles. In 1996, this was approximately 36.5 cents per mile.

In addition to their hourly wage and benefits package, some postal workers receive a uniform allowance. This group includes workers who are in the public view for 4 or more hours each day and various maintenance jobs. The amount of the allowance depends on the job performed—some workers are only required to wear a partial uniform, and their allowance is lower. In 1996, for example, the allowance for a letter carrier was $277 per year, compared to $119 for a window clerk.

Most of these workers belong to one of four unions: American Postal Workers Union, AFL-CIO; National Association of Letter Carriers, AFL-CIO; National Postal Mail Handlers Union, AFL-CIO; and National Rural Letter Carriers Association.

Related Occupations

Other workers whose duties are related to postal clerks include mail clerks, file clerks, routing clerks, sorters, material moving equipment operators, clerk typists, cashiers, data entry operators, and ticket sellers. Others with duties related to mail carriers include messengers, merchandise deliverers, and delivery-route truck drivers.

Sources of Additional Information

Local post offices and State employment service offices can supply details about entrance examinations and specific employment opportunities for postal clerks and mail carriers.

CUSTODIAN AND CUSTODIAL LABORER

Note: These positions are restricted to veteran preference eligibles.

The Job:

Custodian duties include manual cleaning, housekeeping, and buildings and grounds maintenance. Custodial Laborers perform manual labor in connection with the maintenance and cleaning of the buildings and grounds. All positions may include irregular hours.

General Qualifications:

All applicants will be required to take a written examination. The examination and completion of forms will require approximately one hour and 30 minutes.

Custodial positions require prolonged standing, walking, climbing, bending, reaching and stooping. Employees must lift and carry heavy objects on level surfaces, on ladders and/or stairways. Custodial positions may require the use of hand tools and power cleaning equipment.

A qualification for postal employment is to be drug-free. This is determined through the use of a urinalysis drug screen. Applicants who qualify on the examination and are in the area of consideration for employment will be scheduled for the drug test.

Applicants must have vision of 20/40 (Snellen) in one eye and the ability to read without strain, printed material the size of typewritten characters, glasses permitted.

How to Apply:

Application/Admission Card, (PS Form 2479-A/B), is available from and can be submitted to the hiring postal location(s): (Submit only one application)

Applicants will be notified of the date, time, and place of the examination and will be sent material to prepare for the examination.

Selection Process:

A minimum score of 70 points (exclusive of Veteran Preference) on the examination places the applicant's name on a list of eligibles for two years. Names are placed on the hiring list according to the score on the examination.

DATA CONVERSION OPERATOR

The Job

Data Conversion Operators extract information from source documents, transfer that information to computer input forms, and enter data using a keyboard.

General Qualifications

All applicants will be required to take a written examination. The examination and completion of forms will require approximately two hours.

Applicants must have six (6) months or equivalent of clerical or office machine operating experience, preferably on a data conversion machine. Typing is required.

A qualification for postal employment is to be drug-free. This is determined through the use of a urinalysis drug screen. Applicants who qualify on the examination and are in the area of consideration for employment will be scheduled for the drug-test.

Applicants must have vision of 20/40 (Snellen) in one eye and the ability to read without strain, printed material the size of typewritten characters, corrective lenses permitted. The ability to distinguish basic colors and shades is desirable.

Applicants must be able to hear the conversational voice, hearing aids permitted.

How to Apply

Application/Admission Card, (PS Form 2479-A/B), is available from and can be submitted to the hiring postal location(s): (Submit only one application) Applicants will be notified of the date, time, and place of the examination and will be sent material to prepare for the examination.

Selection Process

Applicants must first attain a minimum score of 70 points (exclusive of Veteran Preference) on the written examination. The applicants' names are then placed, by score, on a hiring list of eligibles for a period of two years. Applicants who qualify on the examination and are in the area of consideration for employment will be scheduled for a job simulated typing performance test.

MAINTENANCE POSITIONS

The Job

Maintenance positions require highly skilled and experienced individuals. All applicants must meet the Knowledge, Skills, and Abilities listed on the job description.

General Qualifications

All applicants will be required to pass a three hours written examination, complete a Candidate Supplemental Application booklet and successfully complete an interview.

A qualification for postal employment is to be drug-free. This is determined through the use of a urinalysis drug screen. Applicants who qualify on the examination and are in the area of consideration for employment will be scheduled for the drug test.

Maintenance positions require prolonged standing, walking, climbing, bending, reaching and stooping. Employees must lift and carry heavy objects on level surfaces, on ladders and/or stairways.

For positions requiring driving, applicants must have a valid state driver's license and a safe driving record. They must be able to obtain a Government Motor Vehicle Operator's Identification Card. Applicants may be required to qualify on industrial powered lifting equipment.

Applicants must have vision of 20/40 (Snellen) in one eye and the ability to read without strain, printed material the size of typewritten characters, glasses permitted. The ability to distinguish basic colors and shades is required.

How to Apply

Application/Admission Card, (PS Form 2479-A/B), is available from and can be submitted to hiring postal location(s): (Submit only one application for all the position(s) listed on this announcement.)

Applicants will be notified of the date, time, and place of the examination and will be sent material to prepare for the examination.

Selection Process

Applicants must first attain a minimum score of 70 points (exclusive of Veteran Preference) on the written examination. They must then complete a Candidate Supplemental Application booklet and successfully complete an interview. The applicants' names are then placed, by score, on a hiring list of eligibles for a period of two years.

VEHICLE OPERATOR/ TRACTOR-TRAILER OPERATOR

The Job:

Motor Vehicle Operators operate mail trucks to pick up and transport mail in bulk. Tractor-Trailer Operators operate heavy duty tractor-trailers either in over-the-road service, city shuttle service or trailer operations. May include irregular hours.

General Qualifications:

Applicants for Motor Vehicle Operator and Tractor-Trailer Operator positions must have at least two years of driving-experience, with at least one year of full-time experience (or equivalent) driving at least a seven-ton capacity truck or 24-passenger bus.

For Tractor-Trailer Operators, at least six months of the truck driving experience must be with tractor-trailers. Only driving experience in the United States, its possessions, territories, or in any United States military installation worldwide will be considered.

At the time of appointment, applicants must have a valid commercial driver's license, with air brakes certification, for the type(s) of vehicle(s) used on the job from the state in which they live. After being hired, applicants must be able to obtain the appropriate certification to operate specific postal vehicles.

Applicants will be required to pass a two hours and 30 minutes written examination and must also complete forms detailing their employment history, driving record, and other qualifying factors, to demonstrate possession of the following abilities: 1) Ability to drive trucks safely. 2) Ability to drive under local conditions. 3) Ability to follow instructions and prepare trip and other reports.

A qualification for postal employment is to be drug-free. This is determined through the use of a urinalysis drug- screen. Applicants who qualify on the examination, and are in the area of consideration for employment, will be scheduled for the drug test.

Applicants must have a vision of at least 30/30 (Snellen) in one eye and 20/50 (Snellen) in the other eye and the ability to read, without strain, printed material the size of typewritten characters, corrective lenses permitted. Operators must also be able to hear the conversational voice, hearing aids permitted.

How to Apply:

Application/Admission Card, (PS Form 2479-A/B), Application for Employment (PS Form 2591), Driving Record (PS Form 2480), and Supplemental Experience Statement (PS Form 5920) are available from and can be submitted to the hiring postal location(s): (Submit only one application)

Applicants will be notified of the date, time, and place of the examination and will be sent material to prepare for the examination.

Selection:

Applicants receive scores based on their examination results and a rating of their qualifications process: listed on the U.S. Postal Service Application for Employment Form, Driving Record, and Supplemental Experience Statement. The application must contain pertinent information detailed enough to establish that the applicant meets all the requirements listed in this announcement. Applicants must provide full details about the types and weight of vehicles they have driven and the companies for which they worked as well as the length of their experience. A score of 70% (exclusive of Veteran Preference) places the applicant's name on a list of eligibles for two years. Names are placed on the hiring list in the order of their scores.

PROCESSING, DISTRIBUTION & DELIVERY POSITIONS

All eligibilities previously established will be canceled upon receipt of the new examination results. Therefore, all applicants must reapply and compete in the new examination to reestablish eligibility.

General Qualifications:

A qualification for postal employment is to be drug-free. This is determined through the use of a urinalysis drug screen. Applicants who qualify on the examination and are in the area of consideration for employment will be scheduled for the drug test. All applicants will be required to take a written examination. The examination and completion of forms will require approximately two hours and fifteen minutes.

At the time of the examination, the applicant may select any or all of the seven different jobs listed below.

Job Choices:

CITY CARRIER	MAIL HANDLER
CLERK	MAILPROCESSOR
DIST. CLERK, MACHINE	MARK UP CLERK
FLAT SORTING MACH. OPER.	

How to Apply:

Application/Admission Card, (PS Form 2479-A/B), is available from and can be submitted to the postal location(s) that are listed in the announcement. (Submit only one application) Applicants will be notified of the date, time, and place of the examination and will be sent material to prepare for the examination.

CITY CARRIER AND CLERK

The Jobs:

Clerks work indoors sorting and distributing mail. They may be required to work with the public selling stamps and weighing parcels, and are responsible for all money and stamps. May include irregular hours.

City Carriers collect and deliver mail in all kinds of weather, and walk and/or drive on their route.

Carrier and clerk positions require prolonged standing, walking, reaching and the ability to lift 70 pounds. Carriers are also required to carry a mail bag weighing as much as 35 pounds.

For positions requiring driving, applicants must have a valid state driver's license and a safe driving record. They must be able to obtain a Government Motor Vehicle Operator's Identification Card.

Applicants must have a vision of 20/40 (Snellen) in one eye and the ability to read without strain, printed material the size of typewritten characters, glasses permitted. Clerks working with the public must be able to hear the conversational voice.

DISTRIBUTION CLERK, MACHINE AND FLAT SORTING MACHINE OPERATORS

The Jobs:

Distribution Clerk, Machine and Flat Sorter Machine Operators are required to operate machinery which sorts and distributes letters or flats (magazines, oversized envelopes etc.). Individuals must read address ZIP Codes and enter codes, using special purpose keyboards. Operators must also load and unload the machines. May include irregular hours.

Distribution Clerk, Machine applicants must pass a vision test and possess the manual dexterity required to operate a two-handed keyboard. Vision requirements are: 20/40 (Snellen) in one eye and at least 20/100 (Snellen) in the other, and the ability to read without strain printed material the size of typewritten characters, corrective lenses permitted.

Flat Sorting Machine Operator applicants must pass a vision test and possess the   manual dexterity required to operate a one-handed keyboard. Vision requirements are: 20/30 (Snellen) in one eye and 20/50 (Snellen) in the other, corrective lenses permitted. The ability to distinguish basic colors and shades is desirable.

MAIL HANDLER

The Job:

Mail Handlers work in an industrial environment. Duties include the loading, unloading and moving of sacks of mail and packages weighing up to 70 pounds. May include irregular hours.

Prior to appointment, applicants will be required to pass a test of physical abilities.   Applicants must demonstrate they can lift and carry up to 70 pounds.

Applicants must have a vision of 20/40 (Snellen) in one eye and the ability to read without strain, printed material the size of typewritten characters, corrective lenses permitted. The ability to distinguish basic colors and shades is desirable.

MAIL PROCESSOR

The Job:

Mail Processors are required to stand for prolonged periods of time loading and unloading mail from a variety of automated mail processing equipment. May include irregular hours.

Applicants must have a vision of 20/40 (Snellen) in one eye and the ability to read without strain, printed material the size of typewritten characters, corrective lenses permitted. The ability to distinguish basic colors and shades is desirable.

AUTOMATED MARK UP CLERK

The Job:

Automated Mark Up Clerks enter change of address data into a computer data base, process mail and perform other clerical functions. May include irregular hours.

Applicants must have six (6) months or equivalent of clerical or office machine operating experience. Typing is required.

Applicants must have a vision of 20/40 (Snellen) in one eye and the ability to read without strain, printed material the size of typewritten characters, corrective lenses permitted. The ability to distinguish basic colors and shades is desirable.

Selection Process:

A minimum score of 70 points (exclusive of Veteran Preference) on the examination places the applicant's name on a list of eligibles for two years. Names are placed on the hiring list according to the score on the examination. An applicant who qualifies on the examination and is in the area of consideration for employment for a certain job will be scheduled for job simulated performance exercises or an additional test. Distribution Clerk, Machine and Flat Sorter Machine Operators will be scheduled for Dexterity Exercises, Mail Handlers for a Strength and Stamina Test and Automated Mark Up Clerks for a Typing Test.

Veteran Preference:

Veteran preference is granted for employment in the Postal Service. Those with a 10-percent or greater compensable service-connected disability are placed at the top of the hiring list in the order of their scores. Other eligibles are listed below this group in rank order.

Age Requirement:

The general minimum age requirement for positions in the Postal Service is 18 at the time of appointment or a high school graduate.

Citizenship:

All applicants must be citizens of or owe allegiance to the United States of America, or have been granted permanent resident alien status in the United States. Verification is required.

Selective Service:

To be eligible for appointment to a position in the Postal Service, males born after December 31, 1959 must (subject to certain exceptions) be registered with the Selective Service System in accordance with Section 3 of the Military Selective Service Act. Males between 18 and 26 years of age (have not reached their 26th birthday) can register with the Selective Service System at any U.S. Post Office or consular officer if outside the United States. Your registration status can be verified with the Selective Service System by calling (708) 688-6888 for information.

OCCUPATIONS LIST
(Partial Listing)

Craft & Wage per hour positions:

Administrative Clerk
Auto Mechanic
Blacksmith-Welder
Building Equipment Mechanic
Carpenter
Carrier
Cleaner, Custodian
Clerk Stenographer
Data Conversion Operator
Distribution Clerk
Electronic Technician
Elevator Mechanic
Engineman
Fireman
Garageman-Driver

General Mechanic
Letter Box Mechanic
Letter Carrier
LSM Operator
Machinist
Mail Handler
Maintenance Mechanic
Mark Up Clerk
Mason
Mechanic Helper
Motor Vehicle Operator
Painter
Plumber
Scale Mechanic
Security Guard

Professional

Accounting Technician
Architect/Engineer
Budget Assistant
Computer Programmer
Computer System Analyst

Electronic Engineer
Transportation Specialist
Industrial Engineer
Technical Writer
Stationery Engineer

Management

Administrative Manager
Foreman of Mail
General Foreman
Labor Relations Representative
Manager Bulk-Mail
Manager-Distribution
Manager-Station/Branch

Postmaster-Branch
Safety Officer
Schemes Routing Officer
Supervisor-Accounting
Supervisor-Customer Service
System Liaison Specialist
Tour Superintendent

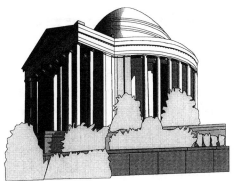

Chapter Four
Customer Service District Offices

In addition to the national headquarters, there are area and district offices supervising approximately 39,000 post offices, branches, stations, and community post offices throughout the United States. The Postal Service has approximately 853,300 employees and handles about 198 billion pieces of mail annually generating more than $60 billion in operating revenues.

If you desire to travel, Postal Service jobs offer abundant opportunities to relocate within the 50 states.

Government jobs offer abundant opportunities to relocate within the 50 states and throughout the world. With more than 39,000 postal facilities in this country individuals have an excellent opportunity to apply for positions in thousands of small towns and in all major metropolitan areas.

CUSTOMER SERVICE AND SALES DISTRICTS

To determine what job vacancies are available and when exams are scheduled, contact the Customer Services and Sales District (CSSD) office nearest you. The Postal Service has established nine Customer Service District areas; Allegheny, Great Lakes, Mid-Atlantic, Midwest, New York Metro, Northeast, Pacific, Southeast, Southwest, and Western. The following list, updated April 1999, provides the District Manager's name, address, phone and fax numbers. Call this number and have them direct you to their Human resource department. Human Resources is responsible for administering exams and hiring. You can also query local CSSD offices to find out what occupations are needed in your area and when they anticipate recruiting if no current vacancies exist or exams aren't scheduled.

Disabled veterans can apply at any time regardless of whether or not exams are scheduled or vacancies exist. This list does not include every Postal Service testing center. Examinations can be given at General Mail Facilities (GMF), Sectional Center Facilities (SCF), Management Sectional Centers (MSC), or Bulk Mail Centers in your area. Call the CSSD nearest you to identify all available testing centers for your location. Also contact local post offices to find out if or when they will be hiring.

CUSTOMER SERVICES DISTRICTS

ALLEGHENY AREA

James A. Johnston
District Manager
Akron District
675 Wolf Ledges Parkway
Akron, OH 44309-9998
(330) 996-9400
(330) 996-9960 (FAX)

Charles Caton
District Manager
Cincinnati District
1591 Dalton Street
Cincinnati, OH 45234-9990
(513) 684-5360
(513) 684-5197 (FAX)

Alexander Lazaroff
District Manager
Cleveland District
2200 Orange Avenue, Room 210
Cleveland, OH 44104-9993
(216) 443-4573
(216) 443-4889 (FAX)

Jeanette M Cooper
District Manager
Columbus District
850 Twin Rivers Drive
Columbus, OH 43216-9993
(614) 469-4515
(614) 469-7605 (FAX)

Nicholas A. Fabozzi
District Manager
Erie District
717 State Street, Suite 300

Erie, PA 16515-9997
(814) 898-0211
(814) 898-0215 (FAX)

Edward B. Burke
District Manager
Harrisburg District
1425 Crooked Hill Road
Harrisburg, PA 17107-0001
(717) 257-2104
(717) 257-2302 (FAX)

Michael W. Benson
District Manager
Lancaster District
1905 Old Philadelphia Pike
Lancaster, PA 17602-9991
(717) 390-7402
(717) 295

DeWitt Harris
District Manager
Philadelphia District
2970 Market Street, Room 306A
Philadelphia, PA 19104-9997
(215) 895-8608
(215) 895-8611

Michael Brose
District Manager
Pittsburgh District
1001 California Avenue
Pittsburgh, PA 15290-9996
(412) 359-7771
(412) 321-3373 (FAX)

Elwood A. Mosley
District Manager
South Jersey District
PO Box 9001
Bellmawr, NJ 08099-9998
(609) 933-4403
(609) 933-4440 (FAX)

GREAT LAKES AREA

Rufus Porter
District Manager
Chicago District
433 West Van Buren street
Chicago, IL 60607-9998
(312) 983-8030
(312) 983-8010 (FAX)

Carl January
District Manager
Detroit District
1401 West Fort Street
Detroit, MI 48233-9992
(313) 226-8605
(313) 226-8005 (FAX)

Charles E. Howe
District Manager
Greater Michigan District
PO Box 999997
Grand Rapids, MI 49599-9997
(616) 336-5300
(616) 336-5399 (FAX)

Thomas Skolak
District Manager
Greater Indiana District
3939 Vincennes Road

PO Box 9850998
Indianapolis, IN 46298-9850
(317) 870-8201
(317) 870-8688 (FAX)

Edward L. Gamache
District Manager
North Illinois District
500 East Fullerton
Carol Stream, IL 60199-9998
(708) 260-5225
(708) 260-5130 (FAX)

Thomas Newman
District Manager
Royal Oak District
200 West Second Street
Royal Oak, MI 48009-9000
(248) 546-1373
(248) 546-0700 (FAX)

James Olden
District Manager
Central Illinois District
6801 West 73rd Street
Bedford Park, IL 60499-9998
(708) 563-7800
(708) 563-2013 (FAX)

MID-ATLANTIC AREA
Anthony J. Vegliante
District Manager
Baltimore District
900 East Fayette Street
Baltimore, MD 21233-9990
(410) 347-4314
(410) 347-4289 (FAX)

Billy H. Smith
District Manager
Appalachian District
PO Box 59992
Charleston, WV 25350-9992
(304) 340-2775
(304) 340-2709 (FAX)

Gordon Jacobs
District Manager

Mid-Carolinas District
2901 Interstate 85 Service Rd
Charlotte, NC 28228-9980
(704) 424-4400 or 4570
(704) 424-4489 (FAX)

Jimmie Manson
District Manager
Greater South Carolina District
PO Box 929998
Columbia, SC 29292-9998
(803) 926-6469
(803) 926-6470 (FAX)

Ronald Campbell
District Manager
Greensboro District
PO Box 27499
Greensboro, NC 27498-9900
(336) 668-1202
(336) 668-1366 (FAX)

J. Buford White, Jr.
District Manager
Kentuckiana District
PO Box 31000
Louisville, KY 40231-1000
(502) 454-1814
(502) 454-1990 (FAX)

Richard J. Strasser, Jr.
District Manager
Northern Virginia District
8409 lee Highway
Merrifield, VA 22081-9996
(703) 698-6464
(703) 698-6609 (FAX)

Joseph J. Rein, III
District manager
Richmond District
1801 Brook Road
Richmond, VA 23232-9990
(804) 775-6365
(804) 775-6058 (FAX)

James P. Cochrane
District Manager
Capital District

900 Brentwood Road, N.E.
Washington, DC 20066-7000
(202) 636-1000
(202) 636-1005 (FAX)

MIDWEST AREA
David C. Fields, Sr.
District Manager
Hawkeye District
PO Box 189800
Des Moines, IA 50318-9800
(515) 251-2100
(515) 251-2050 (FAX)

Ormer Rogers, Jr.
District Manager
Mid-America District
315 West Pershing Road
Kansas City, MO 64108-9000
(816) 374-9104
(816) 374-9487 (FAX)

Dennis Nott
District Manager
Milwaukee District
PO Box 5000
Milwaukee, WI 53201-5000
(414) 287-2240
(414) 287-2296 (FAX)

Michele C. Purton
District Manager
Northland District
100 South lst Street
Minneapolis, MN 55401-9990
(612) 349-3500
(612) 255-3904 (FAX)

Rick Lindsey
District Manager
Central Plains District
PO Box 249500
Omaha, NE 68124-9500
(402) 255-3900
(402) 255-3904 (FAX)

Roger Neinaber
District Manager
Gateway District

1720 Market Street, Rm 3027
St. Louis, MO 63155-9900
(314) 436-4114
(314) 436-4565 (FAX)

Joleen Baxa
District Manager
Dakotas District
PO Box 7500
Sioux Falls, SD 57101-7500
(605) 333-2604
(605) 333-2777 (FAX)

NEW YORK METRO AREA

Thomas Rosati
District Manager
Long Island District
PO Box 7800
Hauptauge, NY 11760-9998
(516) 582-7410
(516) 582-7413 (FAX)

Eugene H. Rear
District Manager
Northern New Jersey District
494 Broad Street, Rm 307
Newark, NJ 07102-9300
(973) 468-7111
(973) 468-7215 (FAX)

Vito J. Cetta
District Manager
Central New Jersey District
21 Kilmer Road
Edison, NJ 08899-9998
(732) 819-3264
(732) 819-3837 (FAX)

Ms. Vinnie E. Malloy
District Manager
New York District
421 5th Avenue, Room 3018
New York, NY 10199-9998
(212) 330-3600
(212) 330-3934 (FAX)

Lily Jung
District Manager

Triboro District
142-02 20th Avenue
Flushing, NY 11351-9998
(718) 321-5144
(718) 321-5999 (FAX)

John Malava
District Manager
Caribbean District
585 F.D. Roosevelt Avenue
San Juan, PR 00936-9998
(787) 767-2159
(787) 250-8065 (FAX)

Rafael Cintron
District Manager
Westchester District
PO Box 9800
White Plains, NY 10610-9800
(914) 997-7104
(914) 697-7128 (FAX)

NORTHEAST AREA

Anderson Hodges, Jr.
District Manager
Albany District
30 Old Karner Road
Albany, NY 12288-9992
(518) 452-2201
(518) 452-2309 (FAX)

William Downers
District Manager
Boston District
25 Dorchester Avenue
Boston, MA 02205-0098
(617) 654-5007
(617) 654-5816 (FAX)

Nicholas Fabozzi
District Manager
Western NY District
1200 William Street
Buffalo, NY 14240-9990
(716) 846-2532
(716) 846-2407 (FAX)

Jo E. Saunders
District Manager
Connecticut District
141 Weston Street
Hartford, CT 06101-9996
(860) 524-6137
(860) 524-6199 (FAX)

Paul G. Guertin
Acting District Manager
New Hampshire District
955 Goffs Falls Road
Manchester, NH 03103-9990
(603) 644-3800
(603) 644-3896 (FAX)

Paul W. Lanzi
District Manager
Middlesex District
74 Main Street
North Reading, MA 01889-9800
(978) 664-7602 or 76036
(978) 664-5998 (FAX)

Barbara A. Patterson
District Manager
Portland District
380 Riverside Street
Portland, ME 04103-7000
(207) 828-8529
(207) 828-8447 (FAX)

Thomas G. Day
District Manager
Providence District
24 Corliss Street
Providence, RI 02904-9998
(401) 276-6950
(401) 276-6967 (FAX)

Philip C. Dennis
District Manager
Springfield District
1883 Main Street
Springfield, MA 01101-9700
(413) 731-0528
(413) 731-0304 (FAX)

PACIFIC AREA

Edward L. Broglio
District Manager
Honolulu District
3600 Aolele Street
Honolulu, HI 96820-3600
(808) 423-3700
(808) 423-3708 (FAX)

Gerald Klein
District Manager
Long Beach District
2300 Redondo Avenue
Long Beach, CA 90809-9798
(310) 301-1100
(310) 301-1104 (FAX)

Al Iniguez
District Manager
Los Angeles District
7001 South Central Avenue
Los Angeles, CA 90052-9998
(323) 586-1200
(323) 586-1248 (FAX)

Katie Hawley
District Manager
Oakland District
1675 7th Street
Oakland, CA 94615-9987
(510) 874-8222
(510) 874-8301 (FAX)

Diane Regan
District Manager
Sacramento District
3775 Industrial Boulevard
West Sacramento, CA 95799-0010
(916) 373-8001
(916) 373-8704 (FAX)

Danny Jackson
District Manager
San Diego District
11251 Rancho Carmel Dr.
San Diego, CA 92199-9990
(619) 674-0301
(619) 674-0405 (FAX)

P. Scott Tucker
District Manager
San Francisco District
PO Box 885050
San Francisco, CA 94188-5050
(415) 550-5591
(415) 550-5327 (FAX)

James H. Aanenson
District Manager
San Jose District
1750 Lundy Avenue
San Jose, CA 95101-7000
(408) 437-6750
(408) 437-6666 (FAX)

David Shapiro
District Manager
Santa Ana District
3101 West Sunflower
Santa Ana, CA 92799-9993
(714) 662-6300
(714) 557-5837 (FAX)

Richard Ordonez
District Manager
Van Nuys District
28201 Franklin Parkway
Santa Clarita, CA 91383-9990
(805) 294-6500
(818) 294-7184 (FAX)

SOUTHEAST AREA

Robert J. Sheehan
District Manager
Atlanta District
PO Box 599300
Duluth, GA 3026-9300
(770) 717-3736
(770) 717-3735 (FAX)

Walter Moon
District Manager
Alabama District
351 24th Street, North
Birmingham, AL 35203-9997
(205) 521-0201
(205) 521-0058 (FAX)

Peter Captain
District Manager
Mississippi District
PO Box 99990
Jackson, MS 39205-9990
(601) 351-7350
(601) 351-7504 (FAX)

Harold L. Swinton
District Manager
North Florida District
PO Box 40005
Jacksonville, FL 32203-0005
(904) 858-6605
(904) 858-6610 (FAX)

Ken Braun
District Manager
South Georgia District
451 College Street
Macon, GA 31213-9900
(912) 752-8530
(912) 752-8600 (FAX)

John P. Barbanti
District Manager
South Florida District
PO Box 829990
Pembroke Pines, FL 33082-9990
(954) 436-4466
(954) 450-3015 (FAX)

Andrew Walker
District Manager
Tennessee District
525 Royal Parkway
Nashville, TN 37229-9998
(615) 885-9252
(615) 885-9317 (FAX)

Viki Brennan
District Manager
Central Florida District
PO Box 999800
Mid Florida, FL 32799-9800
(407) 333-4809
(407) 333-4899 (FAX)

Michael P. Jordan
District Manager
Suncoast District
2203 N. Lois Avenue, Ste. 1001
Tampa, FL 33607-7101
(813) 354-6099
(813) 877-8656 (FAX)

SOUTHWEST AREA

Carlton January
District Manager
Dallas District
951 West Bethel Road
Coppell, TX 75099-9998
(972) 393-6787
(972) 393-6198 (FAX)

Ronnie C. Payne
District Manager
Fort Worth District
4600 Mark IV Parkway
Fort Worth, TX 76161-9100
(817) 317-3301
(817) 317-3320 (FAX)

Ronnie Eley
District Manager
Houston District
PO Box 250001
Houston, TX 77202-0001
(713) 226-3717
(713) 226-3755 (FAX)

Tom Ranft
District Manager
Arkansas District
420 Natural Resources Drive
Little Rock, AR 72205-9800
(501) 228-4100
(501) 228-4105

Anthony J. Ruda
District Manager
Louisiana District
701 Loyola Avenue
New Orleans, LA 70113-9800
(504) 589-1022
(504) 589-1432 (FAX)

Terry Wilson
District Manager
Oklahoma City District
3030 NW Expressway St.
Oklahoma City, OK 73198-9800
(405) 553-6211
(405) 553-6106 (FAX)

R. H. Gonzalez
District Manager
San Antonio District
One Post Office Drive
San Antonio, TX 78284-9997
(210) 368-5548
(210) 368-5511 (FAX)

WESTERN AREA

Charles M. Davis
District Manager
Albuquerque District
500 Marquette Ave., NW Ste. 900
Albuquerque, NM 87101-9999
(505) 346-8501 or 3950
(505) 346-8503 (FAX)

Bill R. Fetterhoff
District Manager
Alaska District
3720 Barrow Street
Anchorage, AK 99599-9998
(907) 261-5418
(907) 261-5409 (FAX)

Robert G. Klein
District Manager
Big Sky District
841 South 26th Street
Billings, MT 59101-8800
(406) 657-5701
(406) 657-5788 (FAX)

George Boettger
District Manager
Colorado/Wyoming District
7500 East 53rd Place, Rm 2204
Denver CO 80266-9998
(303) 853-6160
(303) 853-6099 (FAX)

Michael R. Dornbush
District Manager
Las Vegas District
1001 East Sunset Road
Las Vegas, NV 89119-1000
(702) 361-9280 or 9200
(702) 361-9349 (FAX)

George L. Lopez
District Manager
Arizona District
4949 East Van Buren Street
Phoenix, AZ 85026-9900
(602) 225-5401
(602) 225-3393 (FAX)

William G. Jackson
District Manager
Portland District
715 NW Hoyt Street
Portland, OR 97208-3079
(503) 294-2500
(503) 294-2248 (FAX)

Stephen L. Johnson
District Manager
Salt Lake City District
1760 West 2100 South
Salt Lake City, UT 84199-8800
(801) 974-2947
(801) 974-2975 (FAX)

Dale R. Zinser
District Manager
Seattle District
415 First Avenue North
Seattle, WA 98109-9997
(206) 442-6270
(206) 442-6006 (FAX)

Clair A. Brazington
District Manager
Spokane District
707 W. Maine Avenue, Suite 600
Spokane, WA 99299-1000
(509) 626-6703
(509) 626-6920 (FAX)

Chapter Five
Postal Exams

Clerk, carrier, and other job applicants such as mechanic, electronic technician, motor vehicle operators, machinist, clerical, and trades must pass a written test. The overall rating is based on the test results and your qualifying work experience and education. Certain occupations, including many professionals, don't require a written test. These groups are evaluated under the Postal Service's *Rated-Application Examinations* process. They are rated and hired strictly on their prior work experience, education, and how well they do on the interview.

The **NEW 470 Battery examination** covers seven major entry level positions including:

✔ **Carrier**
✔ **Clerk**
✔ **Distribution Clerk, Machine**
✔ **Flat-Sorting Machine Operator**
✔ **Mail Handler**
✔ **Mail Processor**
✔ **Mark-Up Clerk, Automated**

The *470 Battery Examination* covers the majority of entry level hiring although some offices also maintain custodial registers, which by law, are reserved for veteran preference eligibles. The USPS also maintains *motor vehicle* and *tractor trailer registers* and some highly skilled maintenance positions such as *Building Equipment Mechanic, Engineman, Electronics Technician, and General Mechanic.* All of the skilled maintenance positions require examination 931. A separate announcement, examination number 932, is required for Electronics Technician positions.

Sample exams and test questions are provided in this chapter for most job categories except for the *470 Battery Test.* The 470 Battery Test and completion of forms are covered in Chapter Six with additional practice exams and study tips by Norman Hall. Mr. Hall has scored 100% on the United States Postal Exam four times and he provides in-depth study tips for this exam's four key testing areas.

Norman Hall's *Postal Exam Preparation Book* is an excellent resource for individuals preparing to take the 470 Battery Test. It provides winning test taking strategies and it includes six full-length practice exams, with answer keys and self-scoring tables. A complete description of this valuable reference is included in Chapter Six.

SKILLS TESTS

Ability and skills tests (*performance tests*) are designed to predict future success, both in job training and job performance. The Postal Service uses these tests to obtain an indication of your potential to learn and perform particular job responsibilities. Skills tests can measure specifically what you know about and can perform in a particular job—they test your mastery of tasks. The Postal Service administers skills test when they are interested in filing a position with an applicant who knows the basics of the job and can perform job tasks as soon as he or she starts. Some performance tests are: the road test for operators of postal vehicles, the typing test, and the test of strength and stamina for mail handlers.

ROAD TEST EXAMINATION

The initial road test is a systematic way to measure an individual's ability and skill to drive safely and properly under normal operating conditions. This test is an important part of the overall selection process for positions that require motor vehicle operation, and it is also a practical test to determine whether or not an individual is a skilled and safe driver. The test includes items that have been reported as actual causes of accidents and gives special emphasis to the driving deficiencies identified as major causes of postal motor vehicle accidents.

There is a comprehensive table of disqualifications that apply to the Road Test Examination such as:

1.   Applicant does not have at least two years of documented driving experience.

2.   Applicant has had driving permit suspended once (or more) in the last three years, OR twice (or more) in the last five years.

3.   Applicant has had driving permit revoked once (or more) in last five years.

Specific offenses such as reckless driving, hit-and-run offense, or use of drugs also are disqualifying factors. For the purpose of determining disqualifying violations, consider only offenses followed by a conviction.

STUDY HABITS

It's often helpful to study with a partner, someone to read the question and check your responses. It can be a fellow worker, a spouse, or just a good friend.

Try various study routines until you hit a combination that works. Try studying in 20 to 30 minute sessions with five minute breaks in between, or stretch it out to hour intervals. A good study routine will improve your retention and test scores.

TEST TAKING SECRETS

The following strategies will help you improve your grades. Use these strategies on the practice tests in this book and when you take your actual Postal Service exam. If you practice these techniques now, when you take the postal exam they will become second nature.

- Eliminate the answers in multiple choice questions that make no sense at all. You can often eliminate half of the answers through this method. If you have to guess an answer, you improve your chances through the process of elimination.
- Be skeptical when an answer includes words like, always, never, all, none, generally, or only. These words can be a trap. Only select an answer with these words in it if you are absolutely sure it is the right answer.
- If two answers have opposite meanings, look closer. Many times one of the two is correct.
- Place a mark next to answers that you are unsure about. After completing the remainder of the exam, go back and review these questions and make a final selection. Often, other questions that you've answered will jog your memory.
- One word can dramatically change the meaning of a sentence. Read each question word-for-word before answering.
- Don't let the test get the best of you. Build your confidence by answering the questions you know first. If the first question you read puzzles you, skip it and go on to the next one. When you've completed most of the exam you can go back - if time permits - to the questions that you couldn't answer.
- Get plenty of rest the night before the exam.

SAMPLE EXAMS

Sample practice exams are sent to applicants by the Postal Service when you apply for a test. The Postal Service will only send sample exams and application forms if they are hiring/testing for that specialty. Refer to Chapter Four's Customer Services District Office lists that you can call to obtain job vacancy announcements, test schedules, and applications.

Sample exams are presented in this chapter for the following occupational groups:

EXAM 91 - Motor Vehicle Operator Exam
(Garageman, Motor Vehicle & Tractor Trailer Operators)

EXAM 710 - Clerical Abilities Exam
(Data Conversion Operator, Clerk-Typist, Clerk Stenographer)

EXAM 714 - Data Conversion Operator

EXAM 931 - Maintenance Specialists/Technicians, Engineman, Blacksmith-welder, Custodian, Building Equipment Mechanics, Carpenter, Elevator Mechanic, Fireman, General Mechanic, Machinist, Electrician, Mason, Painter, Oiler, Plumber, Stationary Engineer.

EXAM 932 - Electronic Technician Positions

EXAM 933 - Measures 16 knowledge, skills, and abilities used by a variety of maintenance positions including Maintenance Mechanic and Overhaul Specialist.

SAMPLE EXAM 91

Motor Vehicle Operator Exam
(Garageman, Motor Vehicle & Tractor Trailer Operators)

The sample exam that follows illustrates the types of questions that will be used in Test M/M 91. The samples will also show how the questions in the test are to be answered. Job descriptions for these occupations are included in Chapter Nine.

T0352 000000   SQ 91

SAMPLE QUESTIONS FOR TEST 91

The sample questions in this booklet show the kinds of questions that you will find in the written test. By reading and doing these questions, you will find out how to answer the questions in the test and about how hard the questions will be.

Read the questions carefully. Be sure you know what the questions are about and then answer the questions in the way you are told to do. If you are told the answer to a question, be sure you understand why the answer is right.

Here are the sample questions for you to answer.

Question 1 is about picture 1, below. Look at the picture.

PICTURE 1

1.   How many vehicles are shown in the picture,

(Write your answer for question 1 here.)

Questions 2 and 3 are about picture 2, below. Look at the picture.

PICTURE 2

2.   Who is sitting on the motorcycle ?

_____

(Write your answer for question 2 here.)

3.   What is the policeman probably doing ?

_____

(Write your answer for question 3 here.)

Questions 4 and 5 are about picture 3, below. Look at the picture.

PICTURE 3

4.   What is happening in this picture ?

_____

(Write your answer for question 4 here.)

5.   Show the positions of the truck and the passenger car by drawing boxes like those shown below. (Your boxes will not be the same position as these.)

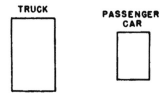

Draw your boxes in the space below.

Questions 6 and 7 are about pictures of oilcans. Each picture has a letter. You are to tell what each picture shows by writing a short description of the picture on the answer line that goes with the question.

Now look at picture X.
6. What does picture X show ?

(Write your answer for question 6 here.)

Picture X shows two oilcans. So, you should have written something like "two oilcans" on the line under question 6.

Now look at picture Y.
7. What does picture Y show?

(Write your answer for question 7 here.)

Question 8 is filling in a chart. You are given the following information to put in the chart. Truck, license number 48-7128, had its oil changed last at speedometer reading 96,005.

Truck, license number 858-232, was greased last at speedometer reading 89,564.

Look at the chart below. The information for the first truck has already been filled in. For question 8, fill in the information for the other truck. You are to show, in the proper columns, the license number of the truck, the kind of service, and the speedometer reading when serviced.

Truck License Number	Kind of Service	Speedometer Reading When Serviced
48-7128	Oil Change	96,005

(For question 8, write the information for the second truck in the proper columns above.)

Questions 9 and 10 are about words that might appear on traffic signs.

In questions like 9, there is one numbered line and then, just below that line, four other lines which are lettered A, B, C, and D. Read the first line. Then read the other four linea. Decide which line—A, B, C, or D—means most nearly the same as the first line in the question. Write the letter of the line that means the same as the numbered line in the answer space.

Here is another example.
9. Speed Limit—20 Miles
A) Do Not Exceed 20 Miles per Hour
B) Railroad Crossing
C) No Turns
D) Dangerous Intersection   _____
                               (Write your answer for question 9 here.)

The first line says "Speed Limit—20 Miles." Line A says "Do Not Exceed 20 Miles per Hour." B says "Railroad Crossing." C says "No Turns." D says "Dangerous Intersection." The line that says almost the same thing as the first line is line A. That is, the one that means most nearly "Speed Limit—20 Miles" is "Do Not Exceed 20 Miles per Hour." The answer to question 9 is A. You should have marked A on the answer line for question 9.

Here is another example.
10. Dead End
A) Merging Traffic
B) No U-Turns
D) Turn on Red
D) No Through Traffic   _____
                           (Write your answer for question 10 here.)

After you answer questions like the ones you have just finished, you will be asked other questions to see how well you understand what you have written. To answer the next questions, you will use the information that you wrote for the first 10 questions. Mark your answers to the next questions on the Sample Answer Sheet on page 6.

The Sample Answer Sheet has spaces that look like these:

If you wanted to mark D for your answer to question 1, you would mark it like this:

If you wanted to mark C for your answer to question 2, you would mark it like this:

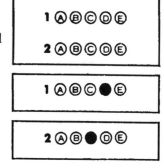

GO ON TO THE NEXT PAGE.

Each of the questions in the next part is about something you should have written on your answer lines.

In answering the next questions in this booklet, you may look back to what you have already written as often as you wish. You may look back while you are marking the Sample Answer Sheet. In the actual test, the pictures and their questions will be taken away from you before you mark the answer sheet, but you will keep what you wrote about the pictures while marking your answer sheet. So, for this practice, try not to look at the pictures but look at what you wrote about them.

Answer each of the following questions by darkening completely space A, B, C, D, or E beside the number that you are told in the question. Mark all your answers on the Sample Answer Sheet.

Question 11 is about question 1. Use what you wrote under question 1 to answer question 11. Mark your answer on the Sample Answer Sheet at the foot of the next page.

11. For number 11 on the Sample Answer Sheet,
     mark space A if only one vehicle is shown in the picture
     mark space B if only two vehicles are shown in the picture
     mark space c if only three vehicles are shown in the picture
     mark space D if only four vehicles are shown in the picture
     mark space E if only five vehicles are shown in the picture

If you look at the answer you gave for question 1, you will see that you wrote that three vehicles were shown in the picture. The question above tells you to mark space C on the Sample Answer Sheet if only three vehicles are shown. So you should have marked space C for number 11 on the Sample Answer Sheet.

Question 12 below is about question 2, and question 13 below is about question 3.
12. For number 12 on the Sample Answer Sheet, mark space
     A if a policeman is sitting on the motorcycle
     B if a man in overall is sitting on the motorcycle
     C if a boy in a sport shirt is sitting on the motorcycle
     D if a nurse is sitting on the motorcycle
     E if a man with a white beard is setting on the motorcycle

Be sure to mark your answer on the Sample Answer Sheet.
13. For number 13 on the Sample Answer Sheet, mark space
     A if the policeman is probably fixing a tire
     B if the policeman is probably using a telephone
     C if the policeman is probably taking off his cap
     D if the policeman is probably blowing a whistle
     E if the policeman is probably writing a "ticket"

Question 14 below is about question 4, and question 15 below is about question 5.
14. For number 14 on the Sample Answer Sheet, mark space
     A if a bus is passing a fire truck
     B if a motorcycle is hitting a fence
     C if a truck is backing up to a platform
     D if a passenger car is getting gas
     E if a passenger car is hitting a truck

GO ON TO THE NEXT PAGE.

15. Look at the boxes you drew for question 5. For number 15 on the Sample Answer Sheet, mark space
>   A if a truck is on a ramp and a passenger car is on the street
>   B if a truck is to the rear of a passenger car
>   C if the front bumpers of a passenger car and a truck are in line
>   D if a passenger car is to the rear of a truck
>   E if a motorcycle is between a truck and a passenger car

Question 16 below is about question 6 under picture X, and question 17 below is about question 7 under picture Y.

16. For number 16 on the Sample Answer Sheet, mark space
>   A if there is only one oilcan in picture X
>   B if there are only two oilcans in picture X
>   C if there are only three oilcans in picture X
>   D if there are only four oilcans in picture X
>   E if there are only five oilcans in picture X

17. For number 17 on the Sample Answer Sheet, mark space
>   A if there is only one oilcan in picture Y
>   B if there are only two oilcans in picture Y
>   C if there are only three oilcans in picture Y
>   D if there are only four oilcans in picture Y
>   E if there are only five oilcans in picture Y

Question 18 below is about the chart you filled in. For this question, mark on the Sample Answer Sheet the letter of the suggested answer—A, B, C, or D—that best answers the question.

18. What is the license number of the truck that was greased? (Look at what you wrote on the chart. Don't answer from memory.)

A) 89,564	C) 858-232
B) 48 - 7128	D) 96,005

For number 19 on the Sample Answer Sheet, mark the space that has the same letter as the letter you wrote on the answer line for question 9.

For number 20 on the Sample Answer Sheet, mark the space that has the same letter as the letter you wrote on the answer line for question 10.

Now see if the answers you have marked on the Sample Answer Sheet are the same as the answers marked in Correct Answers to Sample Questions. If the answers you have picked are the same as the answers in Correct Answers to Sample Questions, you are showing that you can pick right answers. If the answers you have picked are not the same as the answers in Correct Answers to Sample Questions, go back to the questions to see why your answers are wrong.

SAMPLE ANSWER SHEET

11 Ⓐ Ⓑ Ⓒ Ⓓ Ⓔ   16 Ⓐ Ⓑ Ⓒ Ⓓ Ⓔ
12 Ⓐ Ⓑ Ⓒ Ⓓ Ⓔ   17 Ⓐ Ⓑ Ⓒ Ⓓ Ⓔ
13 Ⓐ Ⓑ Ⓒ Ⓓ Ⓔ   18 Ⓐ Ⓑ Ⓒ Ⓓ Ⓔ
14 Ⓐ Ⓑ Ⓒ Ⓓ Ⓔ   19 Ⓐ Ⓑ Ⓒ Ⓓ Ⓔ
15 Ⓐ Ⓑ Ⓒ Ⓓ Ⓔ   20 Ⓐ Ⓑ Ⓒ Ⓓ Ⓔ

CORRECT ANSWERS TO SAMPLE QUESTIONS

11 Ⓐ Ⓑ ● Ⓓ Ⓔ   16 Ⓐ Ⓑ ● Ⓓ Ⓔ
12 ● Ⓑ Ⓒ Ⓓ Ⓔ   17 Ⓐ Ⓑ Ⓒ ● Ⓔ
13 Ⓐ Ⓑ Ⓒ Ⓓ ●   18 Ⓐ Ⓑ ● Ⓓ Ⓔ
14 Ⓐ Ⓑ Ⓒ Ⓓ ●   19 ● Ⓑ Ⓒ Ⓓ Ⓔ
15 Ⓐ Ⓑ Ⓒ ● Ⓔ   20 Ⓐ Ⓑ Ⓒ ● Ⓔ

EXAM 710 - Clerical Abilities Exam
(Data Conversion Operator, Clerk-Typist, Clerk Stenographer)

The sample exam that follows illustrates the types of questions that will be used in Examination 710. The samples will also show how the questions in the test are to be answered. Job descriptions for these occupations are included in Chapter Nine.

SAMPLE QUESTIONS FOR EXAMINATION 710
CLERICAL ABILITIES

The following questions are samples of the types of questions that will be used on Examination 710. Study these questions carefully. Each question has several suggested answers. You are to decide which one is the best answer. Next, on the Sample Answer Sheet below, find the answer space that is numbered the same number as the question, then darken the space that is lettered the same as the answer you have selected. After you have answered all the questions, compare your answers with the ones given in the Correct Answers to Sample Questions below the Sample Answer Sheets

Sample Questions 1 through 14 - Clerical Aptitude

In Sample Questions 1 through 3 below, there is a name or code in a box at the left, and four other names or codes in alphabetical or numerical order at the right. Find the correct space for the boxed name or number so that it will be in alphabetical and/or numerical order with the others and mark the letter of that space as your answer on your Sample Answer Sheet below.

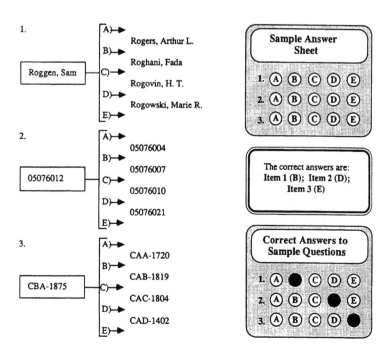

Sample Questions 4 through 8 require you to compare names, addresses, or codes. Ln each line across the page, there are three names, addresses or codes that are much alike. Compare the three and decide which ones are exactly alike. On the Sample Answer Sheet at the bottom, mark the answers:

A if **ALL THREE** names, addresses, or codes are exactly **ALIKE**
B if only the **FIRST** and **SECOND** names, addresses, or codes are exactly **ALIKE**
C if only the **FIRST** and **THIRD** names, addresses, or codes are exactly **ALIKE**
D if only the **SECOND** and **THIRD** names, addresses, or codes are exactly **ALIKE**
E if **ALL THREE** names, addresses, or codes are **DIFFERENT**

4. Helene Bedell	Helene Beddell	Helene Beddell
5. F. T. Wedemeyer	F. T. Wedemeyer	F. T. Wedmeyer
6. 3214 W. Beaumont St.3214	Beaumount St.	3214 Beaumont St.
7. BC 3105T-5	BC 3015T-5	BC 3105T-5
8. 4460327	4460327	4460327

For the next two questions, find the correct spelling of the word and darken the appropriate answer space on your Sample Answer Sheet. If none of the alternatives are correct, darken Space D.

9.   A) accomodate
        B) acommodate
        C) accommadate
        D) none of the above

10.   A) manageble
        B) manageable
        C) manageable
        D) none of the above

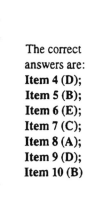

The correct answers are:
Item 4 (D);
Item 5 (B);
Item 6 (E);
Item 7 (C);
Item 8 (A);
Item 9 (D);
Item 10 (B)

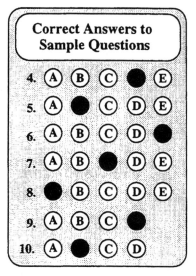

For Questions 11 through 14, perform the computation as indicated in the question and find the answer among the list of alternative responses. Mark your Sample Answer Sheet A, B, C, or D for the correct answer; or, if your answer is not among these, mark E for that question.

11. 32+26 =

A) 69
B) 59
C) 58
D) 54
E) none of the above

Sample Answer Sheet

11. (A) (B) (C) (D) (E)
12. (A) (B) (C) (D) (E)
13. (A) (B) (C) (D) (E)
14. (A) (B) (C) (D) (E)

12. 57- 15=

A) 72
B) 62
C) 54
D) 44
E) none of the above

The correct answers are:
Item 11 (C); Item 12 (E);
Item 13 (B); Item 14 (A)

13. 23 x 7 =

A) 164
B) 161
C) 154
D) 141
E) none of the above

Correct Answers to Sample Questions

11. (A) (B) ● (D) (E)
12. (A) (B) (C) (D) ●
13. (A) ● (C) (D) (E)
14. ● (B) (C) (D) (E)

14. 160 / 5 =

A) 32
B) 30
C) 25
D) 21
E) none of the above

Sample Questions 15 through 22 - Verbal Abilities

Sample items 15 through 17 below test the ability to follow instructions. They direct you to mark a specific number and letter combination on your Sample Answer Sheet. The answers that you are instructed to mark are, for the most part, NOT in numerical sequence (i.e., you would not use Number 1 on your answer sheet to answer Question 1; Number 2 for Question 2, etc.). Instead, you must mark the number and space specifically designated in each test question.

Sample Answer Sheet

15. Ⓐ ⬤Ⓑ Ⓒ Ⓓ Ⓔ
16. Ⓐ Ⓑ Ⓒ Ⓓ Ⓔ
17. Ⓐ Ⓑ Ⓒ Ⓓ Ⓔ

15.   Look at the letters below. Draw a circle around the middle letter. Now, on your Sample Answer Sheet, find Number 16 and darken the space for the letter you just circled.

R   C   H

16.   Draw a line under the number shown below that is more than 10 but less than 20. Find that number on your Sample Answer Sheet, and darken Space A.

5   9   17   22

The correct answers are:
**Item 15 (B); Item 16 (C);
Item 17 (A)**

17.   Add the numbers 11 and 4 and write your answer on the blank line below. Now find this number on your Sample Answer Sheet and darken the space for the second letter in the alphabet.

Correct Answers to Sample Questions

15. Ⓐ ⬤ Ⓒ Ⓓ Ⓔ
16. Ⓐ Ⓑ ⬤ Ⓓ Ⓔ
17. ⬤ Ⓑ Ⓒ Ⓓ Ⓔ

Answer the remaining Sample Test Questions on the Sample Answer Sheet in numerical sequence (i.e., Number 18 on the Sample Answer Sheet for Question 18; Number 19 for Question 19, etc.).

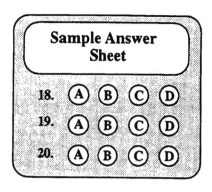

Select the sentence below which is most appropriate with respect to grammar, usage, and punctuation suitable for a formal letter or report.

18. A) He should of responded to the letter by now.
     B) A response to the letter by the end of the week.
     C) The letter required his immediate response.
     D) A response by him to the letter is necessary.

In questions 19 and 20 below, you will be asked to decide what the highlighted word means.

19. The payment was **authorized** yesterday.
     Authorized most nearly means

     A) expected
     B) approved
     C) refunded
     D) received

The correct answers are:
Item 18 (C); Item 19 (B); Item 20 (D)

20. Please **delete** the second paragraph. **Delete** most nearly means

     A) type
     B) read
     C) edit
     D) omit

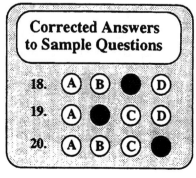

In questions 21 and 22 below, you are asked to read a paragraph, then answer the question that follows it.

Sample Answer Sheet

21. Ⓐ Ⓑ Ⓒ Ⓓ
22. Ⓐ Ⓑ Ⓒ Ⓓ

21.   "Window Clerks working for the Postal Service have direct financial responsibility for the selling of postage. In addition, they are expected to have a thorough knowledge concerning the acceptability of all material offered by customers for mailing. Any information provided to the public by these employees must be completely accurate."

The paragraph best supports the statement that Window Clerks

A) must account for the stamps issued to them for sale
B) have had long training in other Postal Service jobs
C) must help sort mail to be delivered by carriers
D) inspect the contents of all packages offered for mailing

22.   "The most efficient method for performing a task is not always easily determined. That which is economical in terms of time must be carefully distinguished from that which is economical in terms of expended energy. In short, the quickest method may require a degree of physical effort that may be neither essential nor desirable."

The correct answers are:
Item 21 (A); Item 22 (C);

The paragraph best supports the statement that

A) it is more efficient to perform a task slowly than rapidly
B) skill in performing a task should not be acquired at the expense of time
C) the most efficient execution of a task is not always the one done in the shortest time
D) energy and time cannot both be considered in the performance of a single task

Corrected Answers to Sample Questions

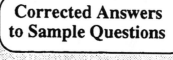

21. ● Ⓑ Ⓒ Ⓓ
22. Ⓐ Ⓑ ● Ⓓ

SAMPLE ITEMS FOR COMPUTER BASED TEST 714

The CB 714 is a computer administered and scored exam. Applicants are assisted with the start-up of the exam and with the exam instructions. You do MI need prior experience on a computer terminal to take this test.

The exam contains a list of alphanumeric postal data entry items just as you see in the sample items below. Applicants must demonstrate that they can type these items on the computer terminal at the following rate(s) based on the requirements of the position. The lower level passing rate is 5 correct lines per minute. The higher level passing rate is 7 correct lines per minute. Credit is given only for correctly typed lines. Practice for the exam by typing the sample provided below.

Type each line as shown in the exercise, beginning with the first column. You may use lower-case or capital letters when typing the sample exercise. When you reach the end of a line, single space and begin typing the next line. If you reach the end of the sample items in the first column, continue with the items in the second column. If you finish both columns, simply begin again with the first column and continue to type until the five minutes have elapsed.

See whether you can copy the entire Sample Test once in a five minute timing. Now count the number of lines you typed correctly and divide this number by five to determine your per minute score. Correctly typing only the items in column 1 is approximately equal to typing 5 correct lines per minute. Correctly typing all of the items in both columns is approximately equal to typing 7 correct lines per minute.

In the exam you will have five minutes in which to type the test material. Keep in mind that in order to pass the test you must type both rapidly and accurately.

SAMPLE TEST COPY

4.90 STEERING DAMPER
16.55 REAR DOOR LATCH
23.80 TIMING CHAIN
8721 8906
2013 2547
5972 6841
HANOVER RD. 600 - 699
ARKANSAS AVE. 4000 - 4199
SO. MAIN ST. 1200 - 1299
CAPITOL DR. 500 - 599
L ON MAPLEWOOD PL.
RETRACE TO 421
R ON MOHICAN TO TOWER
4478267 LSM/LSM
4478271 MPLSM
4478289 EGR SECONDARY
KNIGHT, J.R. 04/17/67
CHARLES, S.M. 11/19/68
JEFFERSON, W.A. 08/20/69
SPRINGFIELD 07215
GREENSBORO 07098
LEXINGTON 07540
FOURTH CLASS 363
INTN. SECTION 27
200 BOX 10

18.25 DOWN SPRING
3.10 VC GASKET
35.45 ROCKER ARM
4973 5261
6057 7352
2783 4195
GREENBRIAR DR. 1100 - 1399
MADISON ST. 3700 - 3799
BRUNSWICK AVE. 8100 - 8199
INDUSTRIAL RD. 2300 - 2499

EXAM 931 - Maintenance Specialists/Technicians, Engineman, Blacksmith-welder, Custodian, Building Equipment Mechanics, Carpenter, Elevator Mechanic, Fireman, General Mechanic, Machinist, Electrician, Mason, Painter, Oiler, Plumber, Stationary Engineer

Test M/N 931 covers the following Knowledge, Skills, and Abilities:

✔ *Knowledge of basic mechanics* refers to the theory of operation, terminology, usage, and characteristics of basic mechanical principles as they apply to such things as gears, pulleys, cams, pawls, power transmissions, linkages, fasteners, chains, sprockets, and belts; and including hoisting, rigging, roping, pneumatics, and hydraulic devices.

✔ *Knowledge of basic electricity* refers to the theory, terminology, usage, and characteristics of basic electrical principles such as ohm's Law, Kirchoff's Law, and magnetism, as they apply to such things as AC-DC circuitry and hardware, relays, switches, and circuit breakers.

✔ *Knowledge of basic electronics* refers to the theory, terminology, usage, and characteristics of basic electronic principles concerning such things as solid state devices, vacuum tubes, coils, capacitors, resistors, and basic logic circuitry.

✔ *Knowledge of safety procedures and equipment* refers to the knowledge of industrial hazards (e.g., mechanical, chemical, electrical, electronic) and procedures and techniques established to avoid injuries to self and others such as lock-out devices, protective clothing, and waste disposal techniques.

✔ *Knowledge of refrigeration* refers to the theory, terminology, usage, and characteristics of refrigeration principles as they apply to such things as the refrigeration cycle, compressors, condensers, receivers, evaporators, metering devices, and refrigerant oils.

✔ *Knowledge of heating, ventilation, and air conditioning (HVAC) equipment operation* refers to the knowledge of equipment operation such as safety considerations, start-up, shut-down, and mechanical and electrical operating characteristics of HVAC equipment (e.g., chillers, direct expansion units, window units, heating equipment). This does not include the knowledge of refrigeration.

✔ *Ability to perform basic mathematical computations* refers to the ability to perform basic calculations such as addition, subtraction, multiplication and division with whole numbers, fractions and decimals.

✔ *Ability to perform more complex mathematics* refers to the ability to perform calculations such as basic geometry, scientific notation, and number conversions, as applied to mechanical, electrical and electronic applications.

✔ *Ability to apply theoretical knowledge to practical applications* refers to mechanical, electrical and electronic maintenance applications such as inspection, troubleshooting equipment repair and modification, preventive maintenance, and installation of electrical equipment.

✔ *Ability to detect patterns* refers to the ability to observe and analyze qualitative factors such as number progressions, spatial relationships, and auditory and visual patterns. This includes combining information and determining how a given set of numbers, objects, or sounds are related to each other.

✔ *Ability to use written reference materials* refers to the ability to locate, read, and comprehend text material such as handbooks, manuals, bulletins, directives, checklists and route sheets.

✔ *Ability to follow instructions* refers to the ability to comprehend and execute written and oral instructions such as work orders, checklists, route sheets, and verbal directions and instructions.

✔ *Ability to use hand tools* refers to knowledge of, and proficiency with, various hand tools. This ability involves the safe and efficient use and maintenance of such tools as screwdrivers, wrenches, hammers, pliers, chisels, punches, taps, dies, rules, gauges, and alignment tools.

✔ *Ability to use technical drawings* refers to the ability to react and comprehend technical materials such as diagrams, schematics, flow charts, and blueprints.

✔ *Ability to use test equipment* refers to the knowledge of, and proficiency with, various mechanical, electrical and electronic test equipment such as VOMS, oscilloscopes, circuit tracers, amprobes, and tachometers.

✔ *Ability to solder* refers to the knowledge of, and the ability to safely and effectively apply, the appropriate soldering techniques.

The sample exam that follows illustrates the types of questions that will be used in Test M/M 931. The samples will also show how the questions in the test are to be answered. Job descriptions for these occupations are included in Chapter Nine.

UNITED STATES POSTAL SERVICE

SAMPLE QUESTIONS - TEST M/N 931

The purpose of this booklet is to illustrate the types of questions that will be used in Test M/M 931. The samples will also show how the questions in the test are to be answered.

Test M/N 931 measures 16 Knowledge, Skills, and Abilities (KSAs) used by a variety of maintenance positions. Exhibit A lists the actual KSAs that are measured, and Exhibit B lists the positions that use this examination. However, not all KSAs that are measured in this test are scored for every position listed. The qualification standard for each position lists the KSAs required for the position. Only those questions that measure KSAs required for the positions) for which you are applying will be scored for the position(s).

The suggested answers to each question are lettered A, B, C, etc. Select the BEST answer and make a heavy pencil mark in the corresponding space on the Sample Answer Sheet. Each mark must be dense black. Each mark must cover more than half the space and must not extend into neighboring spaces. If the answer to Sample 1 is B, you would mark the Sample Answer Sheet like this:

After recording your answers, compare them with those in the Correct Answers to Sample Questions. If they do not agree, carefully re-read the questions that were missed to get a clear understanding of what each question is asking.

During the test, directions for answering questions in Part I will be given orally, either by a cassette tape or by the examiner. You are to listen closely to the directions and follow them. To practice for this part of the test you might have a friend read the direction to you while you mark your answers on the Sample Answer Sheet. Directions for answering questions in Part II will be completely described in the test booklet.

STUDY CAREFULLY BEFORE YOU GO TO THE EXAMINATION ROOM

PART I

In Part I of the test, you will be told to follow directions by writing in a test booklet and then on an answer sheet. The test booklet will have lines of material like the following five samples:

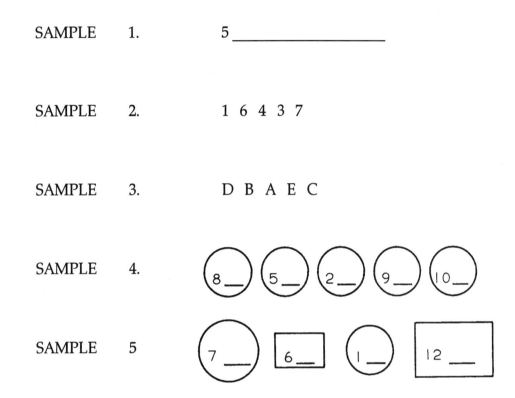

SAMPLE   1.   5 _____

SAMPLE   2.   1 6 4 3 7

SAMPLE   3.   D B A E C

SAMPLE   4.

SAMPLE   5

To practice this test, have someone read the instructions on the **next page** to you and you follow the instructions. When they tell you to darken the space on the Sample Answer Sheet, use the one on this page.

```
                        SAMPLE ANSWER SHEET
  1  Ⓐ Ⓑ Ⓒ Ⓓ Ⓔ     5  Ⓐ Ⓑ Ⓒ Ⓓ Ⓔ     9  Ⓐ Ⓑ Ⓒ Ⓓ Ⓔ
  2  Ⓐ Ⓑ Ⓒ Ⓓ Ⓔ     6  Ⓐ Ⓑ Ⓒ Ⓓ Ⓔ    10  Ⓐ Ⓑ Ⓒ Ⓓ Ⓔ
  3  Ⓐ Ⓑ Ⓒ Ⓓ Ⓔ     7  Ⓐ Ⓑ Ⓒ Ⓓ Ⓔ    11  Ⓐ Ⓑ Ⓒ Ⓓ Ⓔ
  4  Ⓐ Ⓑ Ⓒ Ⓓ Ⓔ     8  Ⓐ Ⓑ Ⓒ Ⓓ Ⓔ    12  Ⓐ Ⓑ Ⓒ Ⓓ Ⓔ
```

Instructions to be read (the words in parentheses should not be read aloud).

You are to follow the instructions that I shall read to you. I cannot repeat them.

Look at the samples. Sample 1 has a number and a line beside it. On the line write an A. (Pause 2 seconds.) Now on the Sample Answer Sheet, find number 5 (pause 2 seconds) and darken the space for the letter you just wrote on the line. (Pause 2 seconds.)

Look at Sample 2. (Pause slightly.) Draw a line under the third number. (Pause 2 seconds.) Now look on the Sample Answer Sheet, find the number under which you just drew a line and darken space B as in baker for that number. (Pause 5 seconds.)

Look at Sample 3. (Pause slightly.) Draw a line under the third letter in the line. (Pause 2 seconds.) Now on your Sample Answer Sheet, find number 9 (pause 2 seconds) and darken the space for the letter under which you drew a line. (Pause 5 seconds.)

Look at the five circles in Sample 4. (Pause slightly.) Each circle has a number and a line in it. write D as in dog on the blank in the last circle. (Pause 2 seconds.) Now on the Sample Answer Sheet, darken the space for the number-letter combination that is in the circle you just wrote in. (Pause 5 seconds.)

Look at Sample 5. (Pause slightly.) There are two circles and two boxes of different sizes with numbers in them. (Pause slightly.) If 4 is more than 2 and if 5 is less than 3, write A in the smaller circle. (Pause slightly.) Otherwise write C in the larger box. (Pause 2 seconds.) Now on the Sample Answer Sheet, darken the space for the number-letter combination in the circle or box in which you just wrote. (Pause 5 seconds.)

Now look at the Sample Answer Sheet. (Pause slightly.) You should have darkened spaces 4B, 5A, 9A, 10D, and 12C on the Sample Answer Sheet. (If the person preparing to take the examination made any mistakes, try to help him or her understand why the mistakes are wrong.)

SAMPLE ANSWER QUESTIONS

1 (A) (B) (C) (D) (E)   18 (A) (B) (C) (D) (E)

2 (A) (B) (C) (D) (E)   19 (A) (B) (C) (D) (E)

3 (A) (B) (C) (D) (E)   20 (A) (B) (C) (D) (E)

4 (A) (B) (C) (D) (E)   21 (A) (B) (C) (D) (E)

5 (A) (B) (C) (D) (E)   22 (A) (B) (C) (D) (E)

6 (A) (B) (C) (D) (E)   23 (A) (B) (C) (D) (E)

7 (A) (B) (C) (D) (E)   24 (A) (B) (C) (D) (E)

8 (A) (B) (C) (D) (E)   25 (A) (B) (C) (D) (E)

9 (A) (B) (C) (D) (E)   26 (A) (B) (C) (D) (E)

10 (A) (B) (C) (D) (E)   27 (A) (B) (C) (D) (E)

11 (A) (B) (C) (D) (E)   28 (A) (B) (C) (D) (E)

12 (A) (B) (C) (D) (E)   29 (A) (B) (C) (D) (E)

13 (A) (B) (C) (D) (E)   30 (A) (B) (C) (D) (E)

14 (A) (B) (C) (D) (E)   31 (A) (B) (C) (D) (E)

15 (A) (B) (C) (D) (E)   32 (A) (B) (C) (D) (E)

16 (A) (B) (C) (D) (E)   33 (A) (B) (C) (D) (E)

17 (A) (B) (C) (D) (E)   34 (A) (B) (C) (D) (E)

PART II

1. Which device is used to transfer power and rotary mechanical motion from one shaft to another?

   A) Bearing
   B) Lever
   C) Idler roller
   D) Gear
   E) Bushing

2. Lead anchors are usually mounted in

   A) steel paneling.
   B) drywall construction.
   C) masonry construction.
   D) wood construction.
   E) gypsum board.

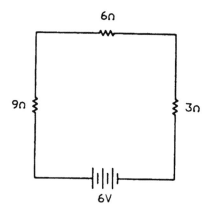

Figure III-A-22

3. Which of the following circuits is shown in Figure III-A-22?

   A) Series circuit
   B) Parallel circuit
   C) Series, parallel circuit
   D) Solid state circuit
   E) None of the above

4. Which component would BEST simulate the actions of the photocell in Figure 24-3-1?

   A) Variable resistor
   B) Variable capacitor
   C) Variable inductor
   D) Auto transformer
   E) Battery

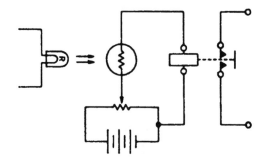

Figure 24-3-1

5. The semi-conductor materials contained in a transistor are designated by the letter(s)

   A) Q
   B) N, P
   C) CR
   D) M, P, M
   E) None of the above

6. Which of the following circuits or devices always has inductance?

   A) Rectifier
   B) Coil
   C) Current limiter
   D) Condenser
   E) Filter

7. Crowbars, light bulbs and vacuumbags are to be stored in the cabinet shown in Figure 75-25-1. Considering the balance of weight, what would be the safest arrangement?

A) Top Drawer - Crowbars
   Middle Drawer - Light Bulbs
   Bottom Drawer - Vacuum bags
B) Top Drawer - Crowbars
   Middle Drawer - Vacuum bags
   Bottom Drawer - Light Bulbs
C) Top Drawer - Vacuum Bags
   Middle Drawer - Crowbars
   Bottom Drawer - Light Bulbs
D) Top Drawer - Vacuum Bags
   Middle Drawer - Light Bulbs
   Bottom Drawer - Crowbars
E) Top Drawer - Light Bulbs
   Middle Drawer - Vacuum Bags
   Bottom Drawer - Crowbars

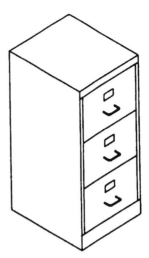

Figure 75-25-1

8. Which is most appropriate for pulling a heavy load?

A) Electric lift
B) Fork lift
C) Tow Conveyor
D) Dolly
E) Pallet truck

9. What measuring device is illustrated in Figure 75-26-1?

A) Screw pitch gage
B) Vernier calipers
C) Inside calipers
D) Outside calipers
E) Outside micrometer

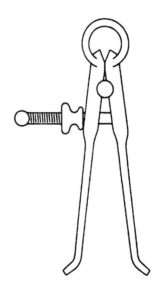

Figure 75-26-1

10. A screw pitch gauge can be used for

A) determining the pitch and number of internal threads.
B) measuring the number of gages available for use.
C) measuring the depth of a screw hole.
D) checking the thread angle.
E) cleaning the external threads.

11. What measuring device is illustrated in Figure 75-20-17?

A) Screw pitch gage
B) Vernier caliper
C) Inside calipers
D) Outside calipers
E) Outside micrometer

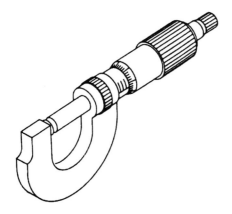

Figure 75-20-17

12. One characteristic of the breast drill is that it

A) is gearless.
B) is hand operated.
C) has a 3 and 1/4 hp motor.
D) has 4 speeds.
E) is steam powered.

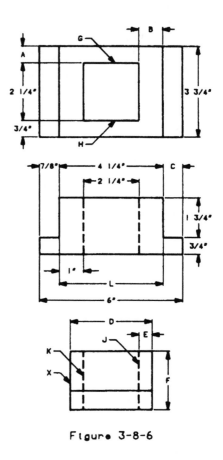

Figure 3-8-6

13. In Figure 3-8-6, what is the measurement of dimension F?

A) 1 3/4 inches
B) 2 1/4 inches
C) 2 ½ inches
D) 3 3/4 inches
E) None of the above

14. The device pictured in Figure 36 is in a rest position. Which position, if any, is the normal closed?

   A) A
   B) B
   C) C
   D) Devices of this sort have no normal closed position
   E) The normal closed is not shown in this diagram

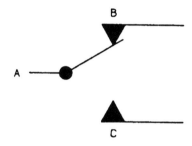

Figure 36

15. Which of the following test equipment would most likely be used in determining amplifier band width?

   A) Clamp-on ammeter
   B) Tube tester
   C) Watt meter
   D) Frequency analyzer
   E) Sweep frequency generator

16. Which instrument is used to test insulation breakdown of a conductor?

   A) Ohmmeter
   B) Ammeter
   C) Megger
   D) Wheatstone bridge
   E) Woltmeter

17. The primary purpose of soldering is to

   A) melt solder to a molten state.
   B) heat metal parts to the right temperature to be joined.
   C) join metal parts by melting the parts.
   D) harden metal.
   E) join metal parts.

18. Which of the following statements is correct of a soldering gun?

   A) Tip is not replaceable
   B) Cannot be used in cramped places
   C) Heats only when trigger is pressed
   D) Not rated by the number of watts they use
   E) Has no light

19. Contaminants have caused bearings to fail prematurely. Which pair of the items listed below should be kept away from bearings?

   A) Dirt and oil
   B) Grease and water
   C) Oil and grease
   D) Dirt and moisture
   E) Water and oil

20. The electrical circuit term "open circuit" refers to a closed loop being opened. When an ohmmeter is connected into this type of circuit, one can expect the meter to

   A) read infinity.
   B) read infinity and slowly return to ZERO.
   C) read ZERO.
   D) read ZERO and slowly return to infinity.
   E) none of the above

21. A change from refrigerant vapor to liquid while the temperature stays constant results in a

    A) latent pressure loss.
    B) sensible heat loss.
    C) sensible pressure loss.
    D) latent heat loss.
    E) super heat loss.

22. The mediums normally used in condensing refrigerants are

    A) air and water.
    B) air and vapor.
    C) water and gas.
    D) liquid and vapor.
    E) vapor and gas.

23. Most condenser problems are caused by

    A) high head pressure.
    B) high suction pressure.
    C) low head pressure.
    D) low suction pressure.
    E) line leaks.

24. Most air conditioners with motors of 1 horsepower, or less, operate on which type of source?

    A) 110-volt, single-phase
    B) 110-volt, three-phase
    C) 220-volt, single-phase
    D) 220-volt, three-phase
    E) 220-440-volt, three-phase

25. 2.6 - .5 =

    A) 2.0
    B) 2.1
    C) 3.1
    D) 3.3
    E) None of the above

26. ½ of 1/4 is

    A) 1/12
    B) 1/8
    C) 1/4
    D) ½
    E) 8

27. A drawing of a certain large building is 10 inches by 15 inches. On this drawing, 1 inch represents 5 feet. If the same drawing had been made 20 inches by 30 inches, 1 inch on the drawing would represent

    A) 2 ½ feet.
    B) 3 1/3 feet.
    C) 5 feet.
    D) 7 ½ feet.
    E) 10 feet.

28. In a shipment of bearings, 51 were defective. This is 30 percent of the total number of bearings ordered. What was the total number of bearings ordered?

    A) 125
    B) 130
    C) 153
    D) 171
    E) None of the above

In sample question 29 below, select the statement which is most nearly correct according to the paragraph.

"Without accurate position descriptions, it is difficult to have proper understanding of who is to do what and when. As the organization obtains newer and different equipment and as more and more data are accumulated to help establish proper preventive maintenance routines, the organization will change. When changes occur, it is important that the organization chart and the position descriptions are updated to reflect them."

29. <u>According to the above paragraph</u>, which of the following statements is most nearly correct?

   A) Job descriptions should be general in nature to encourage job flexibility.

   B) The organizational structure is not dependent upon changes in preventive maintenance routines.

   C) As long as supervisory personnel are aware of organizational changes, there is no need to constantly update the organization chart

   D) Organizational changes can result from procurement of new, advanced equipment.

   E) Formal job descriptions are not needed for an office to function on a day-to-day basis. The supervisor knows who is to do what and when.

30. A small crane was used to <u>raise</u> the heavy part. Raise MOST nearly means

   A) lift
   B) drag
   C) drop
   D) deliver
   E) guide

31. <u>Short</u> MOST nearly means

   A) tall
   B) wide
   C) brief
   D) heavy
   E) dark

In each of the sample questions below, look at the symbols in the first two boxes. Something about the three symbols in the first box makes them alike; something about the two symbols in the other box with the question mark makes them alike. Look for some characteristic that is common to all symbols in the same box, yet makes them different from the symbols in the other box. Among the five answer choices, find the symbol that can best be substituted for the question mark, because it is <u>like</u> the symbols in the second box, and, <u>for the same reason</u>, different from those in the first box.

32.

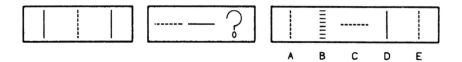

In the sample question above, all the symbols in the first box are vertical lines. The second box has two lines, one broken and one solid. Their <u>likeness</u> to each other consists in their being horizontal; and their being horizontal makes them <u>different</u> from the vertical lines in the other box. The answer must be the only one of the five lettered choices that is a horizontal line, either broken or solid. NOTE: There is not supposed to be a series or progression in these symbol questions. If you look for a progression in the first box and the second box, you will be wasting time. Remember, look for a <u>likeness</u> within each box and a <u>difference</u> between the two boxes. Now do sample question 33.

33.

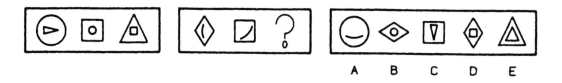

In sample question 34 below, there is at the left a drawing of a flat piece of paper and at the right, four figures labeled A, B, C, and D. When the paper is rolled, it will form one of the figures at its right. Decide which figure can be formed from the flat piece. Then on the Answer Sheet darken the space which has the same letter as your answer.

34.

A   B   C   D

CORRECT ANSWERS TO
SAMPLE QUESTIONS

1.	D		18.	C
2.	C		19.	D
3.	A		20.	A
4.	A		21.	D
5.	B		22.	A
6.	B		23.	A
7.	E		24.	A
8.	E		25.	B
9.	C		26.	B
10.	A		27.	A
11.	E		28.	E
12.	B		29.	D
13.	C		30.	A
14.	B		31.	C
15.	D		32.	A
16.	C		33.	A
17.	E		34.	B

EXHIBIT B

The following positions use Test M/N 931:

Position Title	Register Number
Area Maintenance Specialist	M11
Area Maintenance Technician	M12
Assistant Engineman	M01
Blacksmith-Welder	M36
Building Maintenance Custodian	M13
Building Equipment Mechanic	M02
Carpenter	M14
Elevator Mechanic	M37
Engineman	M03
Fireman	M04
Fireman-Laborer	M05
General Mechanic	M38
Industrial Equipment Mechanic	M39
Letter Box Mechanic (Shop)	M40
Machinist	M41
Maintenance Electrician	M15
Mason	M21
Mechanic Helper	M42
Oiler, MPE	M43
Painter	M22
Painter/Finisher	M23
Plumber	M24
Postal Machines Mechanic	M44
Postal Maintenance Trainee A&B	M45
Scale Mechanic	M46
Stationary Engineer	M06

EXAM 932 - Electronic Technician Positions

Test M/N 932 covers the following Knowledge, Skills, and Abilities:

✔   *Knowledge of basic mechanics* refers to the theory of operation, terminology, usage, and characteristics of basic mechanical principles as they apply to such things as gears, pulleys, cams, pawls, power transmissions, linkages, fasteners, chains, sprockets, and belts; and including hoisting, rigging, roping, pneumatics, and hydraulic devices.

✔   *Knowledge of basic electricity* refers to the theory, terminology, usage, and characteristics of basic electrical principles such as ohm's Law, Kirchoff's Law, and magnetism, as they apply to such things as AC-DC circuitry and hardware, relays, switches, and circuit breakers.

✔   *Knowledge of basic electronics* refers to the theory, terminology, usage, and characteristics of basic electronic principles concerning such things as solid state devices, vacuum tubes, coils, capacitors, resistors, and basic logic circuitry.

✔   *Knowledge of digital electronics* refers to the terminology, characteristics, symbology, and operation of digital components as used in such things as logic gates, registers, adders, counters, memories, encoders and decoders.

✔   *Knowledge of safety procedures and equipment* refers to the knowledge of industrial hazards (e.g., mechanical, chemical, electrical, electronic) and procedures and techniques established to avoid injuries to self and others such as lock-out devices, protective clothing, and waste disposal techniques.

✔   Knowledge of basic computer concepts refers to the terminology, usage, and characteristics of digital memory storage/processing devices such as internal memory, input-output peripherals, and familiarity with programming concepts.

✔   *Ability to perform basic mathematical computations* refers to the ability to perform basic calculations such as addition, subtraction, multiplication and division with whole numbers, fractions and decimals.

✔   *Ability to perform more complex mathematics* refers to the ability to perform calculations such as basic geometry, scientific notation, and number conversions, as applied to mechanical, electrical and electronic applications.

✔   *Ability to apply theoretical knowledge to practical applications* refers to mechanical, electrical and electronic maintenance applications such as inspection, troubleshooting equipment repair and modification, preventive maintenance, and installation of electrical equipment.

✔   *Ability to detect patterns* refers to the ability to observe and analyze qualitative factors such as number progressions, spatial relationships, and auditory and visual patterns. This includes combining information and determining how a given set of numbers, objects, or sounds are related to each other.

✔   *Ability to use written reference materials* refers to the ability to locate, read, and comprehend text material such as handbooks, manuals, bulletins, directives, checklists and route sheets.

✔   *Ability to follow instructions* refers to the ability to comprehend and execute written and oral instructions such as work orders, checklists, route sheets, and verbal directions and instructions.

✔   *Ability to use hand tools* refers to knowledge of, and proficiency with, various hand tools. This ability involves the safe and efficient use and maintenance of such tools as screwdrivers, wrenches, hammers, pliers, chisels, punches, taps, dies, rules, gauges, and alignment tools.

✔   *Ability to use technical drawings* refers to the ability to react and comprehend technical materials such as diagrams, schematics, flow charts, and blueprints.

✔   *Ability to use test equipment* refers to the knowledge of, and proficiency with, various mechanical, electrical and electronic test equipment such as VOMS, oscilloscopes, circuit tracers, amprobes, and tachometers.

✔   *Ability to solder* refers to the knowledge of, and the ability to safely and effectively apply, the appropriate soldering techniques.

The sample exam that follows illustrates the types of questions that will be used in Test M/M 932. The samples will also show how the questions in the test are to be answered. Job descriptions for these occupations are included in Chapter Nine.

UNITED STATES POSTAL SERVICE

SAMPLE QUESTIONS - TEST M/N 932

The purpose of this booklet is to illustrate the types of questions that will be used in Test M/M 932. The samples will also show how the questions in the test are to be answered.

Test M/N 931 measures 16 Knowledge, Skills, and Abilities (KSAs) used by a variety of maintenance positions. Exhibit A lists the actual KSAs that are measured, and Exhibit B lists the positions that use this examination. However, not all KSAs that are measured in this test are scored for every position listed. The qualification standard for each position lists the KSAs required for the position. Only those questions that measure KSAs required for the position(s) for which you are applying will be scored for the position(s).

The suggested answers to each question are lettered A, B, C, etc. Select the BEST answer and make a heavy pencil mark in the corresponding space on the Sample Answer Sheet. Each mark must be dense black. Each mark must cover more than half the space and must not extend into neighboring spaces. If the answer to Sample 1 is B, you would mark the Sample Answer Sheet like this:

After recording your answers, compare them with those in the Correct Answers to Sample Questions. If they do not agree, carefully re-read the questions that were missed to get a clear understanding of what each question is asking.

During the test, directions for answering questions in Part I will be given orally, either by a cassette tape or by the examiner. You are to listen closely to the directions and follow them. To practice for this part of the test you might have a friend read the direction to you while you mark your answers on the Sample Answer Sheet. Directions for answering questions in Part II will be completely described in the test booklet.

STUDY CAREFULLY BEFORE YOU GO TO THE EXAMINATION ROOM

PART I

In Part I of the test, you will be told to follow directions by writing in a test booklet and then on an answer sheet. The test booklet will have lines of material like the following five samples:

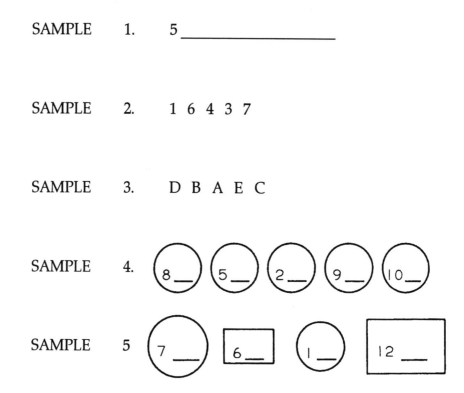

SAMPLE   1.   5 _____

SAMPLE   2.   1 6 4 3 7

SAMPLE   3.   D B A E C

SAMPLE   4.

SAMPLE   5

To practice this test, have someone read the instructions on the **next page** to you and you follow the instructions. When they tell you to darken the space on the Sample Answer Sheet, use the one on this page.

```
                    SAMPLE ANSWER SHEET
  1  Ⓐ Ⓑ Ⓒ Ⓓ Ⓔ      5  Ⓐ Ⓑ Ⓒ Ⓓ Ⓔ      9  Ⓐ Ⓑ Ⓒ Ⓓ Ⓔ
  2  Ⓐ Ⓑ Ⓒ Ⓓ Ⓔ      6  Ⓐ Ⓑ Ⓒ Ⓓ Ⓔ     10  Ⓐ Ⓑ Ⓒ Ⓓ Ⓔ
  3  Ⓐ Ⓑ Ⓒ Ⓓ Ⓔ      7  Ⓐ Ⓑ Ⓒ Ⓓ Ⓔ     11  Ⓐ Ⓑ Ⓒ Ⓓ Ⓔ
  4  Ⓐ Ⓑ Ⓒ Ⓓ Ⓔ      8  Ⓐ Ⓑ Ⓒ Ⓓ Ⓔ     12  Ⓐ Ⓑ Ⓒ Ⓓ Ⓔ
```

Instructions to be read (the words in parentheses should not be read aloud).

You are to follow the instructions that I shall read to you. I cannot repeat them.

Look at the samples. Sample 1 has a number and a line beside it. On the line write an A. (Pause 2 seconds.) Now on the Sample Answer Sheet, find number 5 (pause 2 seconds) and darken the space for the letter you just wrote on the line. (Pause 2 seconds.)

Look at Sample 2. (Pause slightly.) Draw a line under the third number. (Pause 2 seconds.) Now look on the Sample Answer Sheet, find the number under which you just drew a line and darken space B as in baker for that number. (Pause 5 seconds.)

Look at Sample 3. (Pause slightly.) Draw a line under the third letter in the line. (Pause 2 seconds.) Now on your Sample Answer Sheet, find number 9 (pause 2 seconds) and darken the space for the letter under which you drew a line. (Pause 5 seconds.)

Look at the five circles in Sample 4. (Pause slightly.) Each circle has a number and a line in it. write D as in dog on the blank in the last circle. (Pause 2 seconds.) Now on the Sample Answer Sheet, darken the space for the number-letter combination that is in the circle you just wrote in. (Pause 5 seconds.)

Look at Sample 5. (Pause slightly.) There are two circles and two boxes of different sizes with numbers in them. (Pause slightly.) If 4 is more than 2 and if 5 is less than 3, write A in the smaller circle. (Pause slightly.) Otherwise write C in the larger box. (Pause 2 seconds.) Now on the Sample Answer Sheet, darken the space for the number-letter combination in the circle or box in which you just wrote. (Pause 5 seconds.)

Now look at the Sample Answer Sheet. (Pause slightly.) You should have darkened spaces 4B, 5A, 9A, 10D, and 12C on the Sample Answer Sheet. (If the person preparing to take the examination made any mistakes, try to help him or her understand why the mistakes are wrong.)

SAMPLE ANSWER QUESTIONS

1 Ⓐ Ⓑ Ⓒ Ⓓ Ⓔ		18 Ⓐ Ⓑ Ⓒ Ⓓ Ⓔ
2 Ⓐ Ⓑ Ⓒ Ⓓ Ⓔ		19 Ⓐ Ⓑ Ⓒ Ⓓ Ⓔ
3 Ⓐ Ⓑ Ⓒ Ⓓ Ⓔ		20 Ⓐ Ⓑ Ⓒ Ⓓ Ⓔ
4 Ⓐ Ⓑ Ⓒ Ⓓ Ⓔ		21 Ⓐ Ⓑ Ⓒ Ⓓ Ⓔ
5 Ⓐ Ⓑ Ⓒ Ⓓ Ⓔ		22 Ⓐ Ⓑ Ⓒ Ⓓ Ⓔ
6 Ⓐ Ⓑ Ⓒ Ⓓ Ⓔ		23 Ⓐ Ⓑ Ⓒ Ⓓ Ⓔ
7 Ⓐ Ⓑ Ⓒ Ⓓ Ⓔ		24 Ⓐ Ⓑ Ⓒ Ⓓ Ⓔ
8 Ⓐ Ⓑ Ⓒ Ⓓ Ⓔ		25 Ⓐ Ⓑ Ⓒ Ⓓ Ⓔ
9 Ⓐ Ⓑ Ⓒ Ⓓ Ⓔ		26 Ⓐ Ⓑ Ⓒ Ⓓ Ⓔ
10 Ⓐ Ⓑ Ⓒ Ⓓ Ⓔ		27 Ⓐ Ⓑ Ⓒ Ⓓ Ⓔ
11 Ⓐ Ⓑ Ⓒ Ⓓ Ⓔ		28 Ⓐ Ⓑ Ⓒ Ⓓ Ⓔ
12 Ⓐ Ⓑ Ⓒ Ⓓ Ⓔ		29 Ⓐ Ⓑ Ⓒ Ⓓ Ⓔ
13 Ⓐ Ⓑ Ⓒ Ⓓ Ⓔ		30 Ⓐ Ⓑ Ⓒ Ⓓ Ⓔ
14 Ⓐ Ⓑ Ⓒ Ⓓ Ⓔ		31 Ⓐ Ⓑ Ⓒ Ⓓ Ⓔ
15 Ⓐ Ⓑ Ⓒ Ⓓ Ⓔ		32 Ⓐ Ⓑ Ⓒ Ⓓ Ⓔ
16 Ⓐ Ⓑ Ⓒ Ⓓ Ⓔ		33 Ⓐ Ⓑ Ⓒ Ⓓ Ⓔ
17 Ⓐ Ⓑ Ⓒ Ⓓ Ⓔ		34 Ⓐ Ⓑ Ⓒ Ⓓ Ⓔ

PART II

1. The primary function of a take-up pulley in a belt conveyor is to
    A) carry the belt on the return trip.
    B) track the belt.
    C) maintain proper belt tension
    D) change the direction of the belt

2. Which device is used to transfer power and rotary mechanical motion from one shaft to another?

    A) Bearing
    B) Lever
    C) Idler roller
    D) Gear
    E) Bushing

See Figure III-A-22 on Page 66

3. Which of the following circuits is shown in Figure III-A-22?

    A) Series circuit
    B) Parallel circuit
    C) Series, parallel circuit
    D) Solid state circuit
    E) None of the above

4. A circuit has two resistors of equal value in series. The voltage and current in the circuit are 20 volts and 2 amps respectively. What is the value of EACH resistor?

    A) 5 ohms
    B) 10 ohms
    C) 20 ohms

D) Not enough information given

5. What is the total net capacitance of two 60-farad capacitors connected in series?

    A) 30 farads
    B) 60 farads
    C) 90 farads
    D) 120 farads
    E) 360 farads

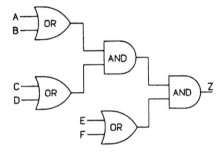

Figure 79-4-17B

6. Select the Boolean equation that matches the circuit diagram in Figure 79-4-17B.

    A) Z = AB+CD+EF
    B) Z z (A+B) (C+D) (E+F)
    C) Z = A+B+C+D+EF
    D) Z = ABCD(E+F)

7. If two 30-mH inductors are connected in series, what is the total net inductance of the combination?

    A) 15 mH
    B) 20 mH
    C) 30 mH
    D) 45 mH
    E) 60 mH

8.   In pure number 6 binary the
      decimal would be expressed as

      A) 001
      B) 011
      C) 110
      D) 111

**File Cabinet Picture
See Figure 75-25-1 on
Page 67**

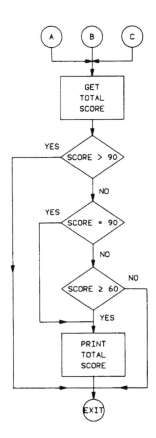

FIGURE 75-8-1 1

10.   Crowbars, light bulbs and vacuum
      bags are to be stored in the cabinet
      shown in Figure 75-25-1. Consid-
      ering the balance of weight, what
      would be the safest arrangement?

      A) Top Drawer - Crowbars
          Middle Drawer - Light Bulbs
          Bottom Drawer - Vacuum bags
      B) Top Drawer - Crowbars
          Middle Drawer - Vacuum bags
          Bottom Drawer - Light Bulbs
      C) Top Drawer - Vacuum Bags
          Middle Drawer - Crowbars
          Bottom Drawer - Light Bulbs
      D) Top Drawer - Vacuum Bags
          Middle Drawer - Light Bulbs
          Bottom Drawer - Crowbars
      E) Top Drawer - Light Bulbs
          Middle Drawer - Vacuum Bags
          Bottom Drawer - Crowbars

9.   In Figure 75-8-11, which of the
      following scores will be printed?

      A) All scores > 90 and < 60
      B) All scores < 90
      C) All scores $\leq$ 90 and $\geq$ 60
      D) All scores < 60

11.   Which is most appropriate for
      pulling a heavy load?

      A) Electric lift
      B) Fork lift
      C) Tow Conveyor
      D) Dolly
      E) Pallet truck

12. The electrical circuit term "open circuit" refers to a closed loop being opened. When an ohmmeter is connected into this type of circuit, one can expect the meter to

A) Read infinity
B) Read infinity and slowly return to ZERO
C) Read ZERO
D) Read ZERO and slowly return to infinity
E) None of the above

13. Contaminants have caused bearings to fail prematurely. Which pair of the items listed below should be kept away from bearings?

A) Dirt and oil
B) Grease and water
C) Oil and grease
D) Dirt and moisture
E) Water and oil

14. In order to operate a breast drill, which direction should you turn it?

A) Clockwise
B) Counterclockwise
C) Up and down
D) Back and forth
E) Right, then left

15. Which is the correct tool for tightening or loosening a water pipe?

A) Slip joint pliers
B) Household pliers
C) Monkey wrench
D) Water pump pliers
E) Pipe wrench

16. What is one purpose of a chuck key?

A) Open doors
B) Remove drill bits
C) Remove screws
D) Remove set screws
E) Unlock chucks

17. When smoke is generated as a result of using a portable electric drill for cutting holes into a piece of angle iron, one should

A) use a fire watch.
B) cease the drilling operation.
C) use an exhaust fan to remove smoke.
D) use a prescribed coolant solution to reduce friction.
E) call the Fire Department.

18. The primary purpose of soldering is to

A) melt solder to a molten state.
B) heat metal parts to the right temperature to be joined.
C) join metal parts by melting the parts.
D) harden metal.
E) join metal parts.

19. Which of the following statements is correct of a soldering gun?

A) Tip is not replaceable
B) Cannot be used in cramped places
C) Heats only when trigger is pressed
D) Not rated by the number of watts they use
E) Has no light

20. What unit of measurement is read on a dial torque wrench?

A) Pounds
B) Inches
C) Centimeters
D) Foot-pounds
E) Degrees

21.   Which instrument is used to test insulation breakdown of a conductor?

A) Ohmmeter
B) Ammeter
C) Megger
D) Wheatstone bridge
E) Voltmeter

22.   ½ of 1/4 =

A) 1/12
B) 1/8
C) 1/4
D) ½
E) 8

23.   2.6 - .5 =

A) 2.0
B) 2.1
C) 3.1
D) 3.3
E) None of the above

24.   Simplify the following expression in terms of amps:

$$563 \times 10^{-6}$$

A) 563,000,000 amps
B) 563,000 amps
C) .563 amps
D) .000563 amps
E) .000000563 amps

25.   Solve the power equation

$$P = I^2 R \text{ for } R$$

A) R = EI
B) R = I²P
C) R = PI
D) R = P/I²
E) R = E/I

26.   The product of 3 kilo ohms times 3 micro ohms is

A) 6×10^{-9} ohms
B) 6×10^{-3} ohms
C) 9×10^{3} ohms
D) 9×10^{-6} ohms
E) 9×10^{-3} ohms

In sample question 25 below, select the statement which is most nearly correct according to the paragraph.

"Prior to 1870, a conveyor that made use of rollers was developed for transporting clay. This construction substituted rolling friction at the idler bearing points for the sliding friction of the slider bed. A primitive type of "roughing belt conveyor was developed about the same time for the handling of grain. This design was improved during the latter part of the century when the "roughing idler was developed."

27.   According to the above paragraph, which of the following statements is most nearly correct?

A) The "roughing belt conveyor was developed about 1870 to handle clay and grain.

B) Rolling friction construction was replaced by sliding friction construction prior to 1870.

C) In the late nineteenth century, conveyors were improved with the development of the "roughing idler.

D) The "roughing idler, a significant design improvement for conveyors, was developed in the early nineteenth century.

E) Conveyor belts were invented and developed in the 1800's.

For sample question 28 below, select from the drawings of objects on the right labeled A, B, C, and D, the one that would have the TOP, FRONT, and RIGHT views shown in the drawing at the left

28.

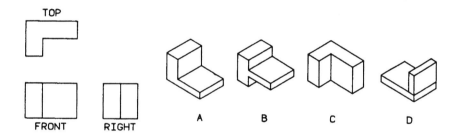

In sample question 29 below, there is, on the left, a drawing of a flat piece of paper and, on the right, four figures labeled A, B, C, and D. When the paper is bent on the dotted lines it will form one of the figures on the right. Decide which alternative can be formed from the flat piece.

29

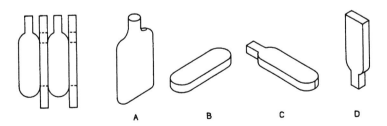

In each of the sample questions below, look at the symbols in the first two boxes. Something about the three symbols in the first box makes them alike; something about the two symbols in the other box with the question mark makes them alike. Look for some characteristic that is common to all symbols in the same box, yet makes them different from the symbols in the other box. Among the five answer choices, find the symbol that can best be substituted for the question mark, because it is <u>like</u> the symbols in the second box, and, for the same reason, different from those in the first box.

30.

USE DIAGRAM ON PAGE 72 QUESTION 32

In sample question 30 above, all the symbols in the first box are vertical lines. The second box has two lines, one broken and one solid. Their <u>likeness</u> to each other consists in their being horizontal; and their being horizontal makes them <u>different</u> from the vertical lines in the other box. The answer must be the only one of the five lettered choices that is a horizontal line, either broken or solid. NOTE: There is not supposed to be a series or progression in these symbol questions. If you look for a progression in the first box and the second box, you will be wasting time. Remember, look for a <u>likeness</u> within each box and a <u>difference</u> between the two boxes.

Now do sample questions 31 and 32.

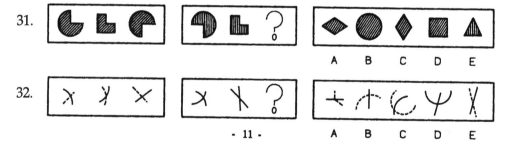

- 11 -

33.   In Figure 3-8-6 below, what is the measurement of Dimension F? Drawing is not actual size.

    A) 1 3/4 inches
    B) 2 1/4 inches
    C) 2 ½ inches
    D) 3 3/4 inches
    E) None of the above

Use Figure 3-8-6 on page 68

34.   In Figure 160-57 below, what is the current flow through R when:

        V = 50 volts
        R1 = 25 ohms
        R2 = 25 ohms
        R3 = 50 ohms
        R4 = 50 ohms
        R5 = 50 ohms

and the current through the entire
circuit totals one amp?

        A   0.5 amp
        B) 5.0 amps
        C) 5.0 milliamps
        D) 50.0 milliamps
        E) None of the above

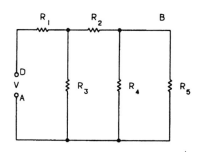

Figure 160-57

EXHIBIT B

The following positions use Test M/N 932:

Position Title	Register
Electronic Technician 8	M26
Electronic Technician 9	M27
Electronic Technician 10	M28

CORRECT ANSWERS TO
SAMPLE QUESTIONS

1.	C		18.	E
2.	D		19.	C
3.	A		20.	D
4.	A		21.	C
5.	A		22.	B
6.	B		23.	B
7.	D		24.	D
8.	C		25.	D
9.	C		26.	E
10.	E		27.	C
11.	E		28.	C
12.	A		29.	C
13.	D		30.	C
14.	A		31.	E
15.	E		32.	D
16.	B		33.	C
17.	D		34.	A

EXAM 933 - Measures 16 knowledge, skills, and abilities used by a variety of maintenance positions including Maintenance Mechanic and Overhaul Specialist.

Test M/N 933 covers the following Knowledge, Skills, and Abilities:

✔ *Knowledge of basic mechanics* refers to the theory of operation, terminology, usage, and characteristics of basic mechanical principles as they apply to such things as gears, pulleys, cams, pawls, power transmissions, linkages, fasteners, chains, sprockets, and belts; and including hoisting, rigging, roping, pneumatics, and hydraulic devices.

✔ *Knowledge of basic electricity* refers to the theory, terminology, usage, and characteristics of basic electrical principles such as ohm's Law, Kirchoff's Law, and magnetism, as they apply to such things as AC-DC circuitry and hardware, relays, switches, and circuit breakers.

✔ *Knowledge of basic electronics* refers to the theory, terminology, usage, and characteristics of basic electronic principles concerning such things as solid state devices, vacuum tubes, coils, capacitors, resistors, and basic logic circuitry.

✔ *Knowledge of safety procedures and equipment* refers to the knowledge of industrial hazards (e.g., mechanical, chemical, electrical, electronic) and procedures and techniques established to avoid injuries to self and others such as lock-out devices, protective clothing, and waste disposal techniques.

✔ *Knowledge of lubrication materials and procedures* refers to the terminology, characteristics, storage, preparation, disposal, and usage techniques involved with lubrication materials such as oils, greases, and other types of lubricants.

✔ *Ability to perform basic mathematical computations* refers to the ability to perform basic calculations such as addition, subtraction, multiplication and division with whole numbers, fractions and decimals.

✔ *Ability to perform more complex mathematics* refers to the ability to perform calculations such as basic geometry, scientific notation, and number conversions, as applied to mechanical, electrical and electronic applications.

✔ *Ability to apply theoretical knowledge to practical applications* refers to mechanical, electrical and electronic maintenance applications such as inspection, troubleshooting equipment repair and modification, preventive maintenance, and installation of electrical equipment.

✔ *Ability to detect patterns* refers to the ability to observe and analyze qualitative factors such as number progressions, spatial relationships, and auditory and visual patterns. This includes combining information and determining how a given set of numbers, objects, or sounds are related to each other.

✔   *Ability to use written reference materials* refers to the ability to locate, read, and comprehend text material such as handbooks, manuals, bulletins, directives, checklists and route sheets.

✔   *Ability to follow instructions* refers to the ability to comprehend and execute written and oral instructions such as work orders, checklists, route sheets, and verbal directions and instructions.

✔   *Ability to use hand tools* refers to knowledge of, and proficiency with, various hand tools. This ability involves the safe and efficient use and maintenance of such tools as screwdrivers, wrenches, hammers, pliers, chisels, punches, taps, dies, rules, gauges, and alignment tools.

✔   *Ability to use technical drawings* refers to the ability to react and comprehend technical materials such as diagrams, schematics, flow charts, and blueprints.

✔   *Ability to use test equipment* refers to the knowledge of, and proficiency with, various mechanical, electrical and electronic test equipment such as VOMS, oscilloscopes, circuit tracers, amprobes, and tachometers.

✔   *Ability to solder* refers to the knowledge of, and the ability to safely and effectively apply, the appropriate soldering techniques.

The sample exam that follows illustrates the types of questions that will be used in Test M/N 933. The samples will also show how the questions in the test are to be answered. Job descriptions for these occupations are included in Chapter Nine.

UNITED STATES POSTAL SERVICE

SAMPLE QUESTIONS - TEST M/N 933

The purpose of this booklet is to illustrate the types of questions that will be used in Test M/M 933. The samples will also show how the questions in the test are to be answered.

Test M/N 933 measures 16 Knowledge, Skills, and Abilities (KSAs) used by a variety of maintenance positions. Exhibit A lists the actual KSAs that are measured, and Exhibit B lists the positions that use this examination. However, not all KSAs that are measured in this test are scored for every position listed. The qualification standard for each position lists the KSAs required for the position. Only those questions that measure KSAs required for the position(s) for which you are applying will be scored for the position(s).

The suggested answers to each question are lettered A, B, C, etc. Select the BEST answer and make a heavy pencil mark in the corresponding space on the Sample Answer Sheet. Each mark must be dense black. Each mark must cover more than half the space and must not extend into neighboring spaces. If the answer to Sample 1 is B, you would mark the Sample Answer Sheet like this:

After recording your answers, compare them with those in the Correct Answers to Sample Questions. If they do not agree, carefully re-read the questions that were missed to get a clear understanding of what each question is asking.

During the test, directions for answering questions in Part I will be given orally, either by a cassette tape or by the examiner. You are to listen closely to the directions and follow them. To practice for this part of the test you might have a friend read the direction to you while you mark your answers on the Sample Answer Sheet. Directions for answering questions in Part II will be completely described in the test booklet.

STUDY CAREFULLY BEFORE YOU GO TO THE EXAMINATION ROOM

PART I

In Part I of the test, you will be told to follow directions by writing in a test booklet and then on an answer sheet. The test booklet will have lines of material like the following five samples:

SAMPLE   1.   5 _____

SAMPLE   2.   1 6 4 3 7

SAMPLE   3.   D B A E C

SAMPLE   4.

    8 ___   5 ___   2 ___   9 ___   10 ___

SAMPLE   5

    7 ___   6 ___   1 ___   12 ___

To practice this test, have someone read the instructions on the **next page** to you and you follow the instructions. When they tell you to darken the space on the Sample Answer Sheet, use the one on this page.

SAMPLE ANSWER SHEET

1 Ⓐ Ⓑ Ⓒ Ⓓ Ⓔ	5 Ⓐ Ⓑ Ⓒ Ⓓ Ⓔ	9 Ⓐ Ⓑ Ⓒ Ⓓ Ⓔ
2 Ⓐ Ⓑ Ⓒ Ⓓ Ⓔ	6 Ⓐ Ⓑ Ⓒ Ⓓ Ⓔ	10 Ⓐ Ⓑ Ⓒ Ⓓ Ⓔ
3 Ⓐ Ⓑ Ⓒ Ⓓ Ⓔ	7 Ⓐ Ⓑ Ⓒ Ⓓ Ⓔ	11 Ⓐ Ⓑ Ⓒ Ⓓ Ⓔ
4 Ⓐ Ⓑ Ⓒ Ⓓ Ⓔ	8 Ⓐ Ⓑ Ⓒ Ⓓ Ⓔ	12 Ⓐ Ⓑ Ⓒ Ⓓ Ⓔ

<u>Instructions to be read</u> (the words in parentheses should not be read aloud).

You are to follow the instructions that I shall read to you. I cannot repeat them.

Look at the samples. Sample 1 has a number and a line beside it. On the line write an A. (Pause 2 seconds.) Now on the Sample Answer Sheet, find number 5 (pause 2 seconds) and darken the space for the letter you just wrote on the line. (Pause 2 seconds.)

Look at Sample 2. (Pause slightly.) Draw a line under the third number. (Pause 2 seconds.) Now look on the Sample Answer Sheet, find the number under which you just drew a line and darken space B as in baker for that number. (Pause 5 seconds.)

Look at Sample 3. (Pause slightly.) Draw a line under the third letter in the line. (Pause 2 seconds.) Now on your Sample Answer Sheet, find number 9 (pause 2 seconds) and darken the space for the letter under which you drew a line. (Pause 5 seconds.)

Look at the five circles in Sample 4. (Pause slightly.) Each circle has a number and a line in it. write D as in dog on the blank in the last circle. (Pause 2 seconds.) Now on the Sample Answer Sheet, darken the space for the number-letter combination that is in the circle you just wrote in. (Pause 5 seconds.)

Look at Sample 5. (Pause slightly.) There are two circles and two boxes of different sizes with numbers in them. (Pause slightly.) If 4 is more than 2 and if 5 is less than 3, write A in the smaller circle. (Pause slightly.) Otherwise write C in the larger box. (Pause 2 seconds.) Now on the Sample Answer Sheet, darken the space for the number-letter combination in the circle or box in which you just wrote. (Pause 5 seconds.)

Now look at the Sample Answer Sheet. (Pause slightly.) You should have darkened spaces 4B, 5A, 9A, 10D, and 12C on the Sample Answer Sheet. (If the person preparing to take the examination made any mistakes, try to help him or her understand why the mistakes are wrong.)

SAMPLE ANSWER QUESTIONS

1 Ⓐ Ⓑ Ⓒ Ⓓ Ⓔ   18 Ⓐ Ⓑ Ⓒ Ⓓ Ⓔ
2 Ⓐ Ⓑ Ⓒ Ⓓ Ⓔ   19 Ⓐ Ⓑ Ⓒ Ⓓ Ⓔ
3 Ⓐ Ⓑ Ⓒ Ⓓ Ⓔ   20 Ⓐ Ⓑ Ⓒ Ⓓ Ⓔ
4 Ⓐ Ⓑ Ⓒ Ⓓ Ⓔ   21 Ⓐ Ⓑ Ⓒ Ⓓ Ⓔ
5 Ⓐ Ⓑ Ⓒ Ⓓ Ⓔ   22 Ⓐ Ⓑ Ⓒ Ⓓ Ⓔ
6 Ⓐ Ⓑ Ⓒ Ⓓ Ⓔ   23 Ⓐ Ⓑ Ⓒ Ⓓ Ⓔ
7 Ⓐ Ⓑ Ⓒ Ⓓ Ⓔ   24 Ⓐ Ⓑ Ⓒ Ⓓ Ⓔ
8 Ⓐ Ⓑ Ⓒ Ⓓ Ⓔ   25 Ⓐ Ⓑ Ⓒ Ⓓ Ⓔ
9 Ⓐ Ⓑ Ⓒ Ⓓ Ⓔ   26 Ⓐ Ⓑ Ⓒ Ⓓ Ⓔ
10 Ⓐ Ⓑ Ⓒ Ⓓ Ⓔ   27 Ⓐ Ⓑ Ⓒ Ⓓ Ⓔ
11 Ⓐ Ⓑ Ⓒ Ⓓ Ⓔ   28 Ⓐ Ⓑ Ⓒ Ⓓ Ⓔ
12 Ⓐ Ⓑ Ⓒ Ⓓ Ⓔ   29 Ⓐ Ⓑ Ⓒ Ⓓ Ⓔ
13 Ⓐ Ⓑ Ⓒ Ⓓ Ⓔ   30 Ⓐ Ⓑ Ⓒ Ⓓ Ⓔ
14 Ⓐ Ⓑ Ⓒ Ⓓ Ⓔ   31 Ⓐ Ⓑ Ⓒ Ⓓ Ⓔ
15 Ⓐ Ⓑ Ⓒ Ⓓ Ⓔ   32 Ⓐ Ⓑ Ⓒ Ⓓ Ⓔ
16 Ⓐ Ⓑ Ⓒ Ⓓ Ⓔ   33 Ⓐ Ⓑ Ⓒ Ⓓ Ⓔ
17 Ⓐ Ⓑ Ⓒ Ⓓ Ⓔ   34 Ⓐ Ⓑ Ⓒ Ⓓ Ⓔ

PART II

1. The primary function of a take-up pulley in a belt conveyor is to

   A) carry the belt on the return trip.
   B) track the belt.
   C) maintain proper belt tension.
   D) change the direction of the belt.
   E) regulate the speed of the belt.

2. Which device is used to transfer power and rotary mechanical motion from one shaft to another?

   A) Bearing
   B) Lever
   C) Idler roller
   D) Gear
   E) Bushing

3. What special care is required in the storage of hard steel roller bearings? They should be

   A) cleaned and spun dry with compressed air.
   B) oiled once a month.
   C) stored in a humid place.
   D) wrapped in oiled paper.
   E) stored at temperatures below 90 degrees Fahrenheit.

4. Which is the correct method to lubricate a roller chain?

   A) Use brush to apply lubricant while chain is in motion
   B) Use squirt can to apply lubricant while chain is in motion
   C) Use brush to apply lubricant while chain is not in motion
   D) Soak chain in pan of lubricant and hang to allow excess to drain
   E) Chains do not need lubrication

5. A circuit has two resistors of equal value in series. The voltage and current in the circuit are 20 volts and 2 amps respectively. What is the value of EACH resistor?

   A) 5 ohms
   B) 10 ohms
   C) 15 ohms
   D) 20 ohms
   E) Not enough given

See Figure III-A-22 on Page 66

6. Which of the following circuits is shown in Figure III-A-22?

   A) Series circuit
   B) Parallel circuit
   C) Series, parallel circuit
   D) Solid state circuit
   E) None of the above

7. What is the total net capacitance of two 60 farad capacitors connected in series?

   A) 30 F
   B) 60 F
   C) 90 F
   D) 120 F
   E) 360 F

8. If two 30 mH inductors are connected in series, what is the total net inductance of the combination?

   A) 15 mH
   B) 20 mH
   C) 30 mH
   D) 45 mH
   E) 60 mH

**File Cabinet Picture
See Figure 75-25-1 on
Page 67**

9. Crowbars, light bulbs and vacuum bags are to be stored in the cabinet shown in Figure 75-25-1. Considering the balance of weight, what would be the safest arrangement?

   A) Top Drawer - Crowbars
      Middle Drawer - Light Bulbs
      Bottom Drawer - Vacuum bags
   B) Top Drawer - Crowbars
      Middle Drawer - Vacuum bags
      Bottom Drawer - Light Bulbs
   C) Top Drawer - Vacuum Bags
      Middle Drawer - Crowbars
      Bottom Drawer - Light Bulbs
   D) Top Drawer - Vacuum Bags
      Middle Drawer - Light Bulbs
      Bottom Drawer - Crowbars
   E) Top Drawer - Light Bulbs
      Middle Drawer - Vacuum Bags
      Bottom Drawer - Crowbars

10. Contaminants have caused bearings to fail prematurely. Which pair of the items listed below should be kept away from bearings?

   A) Dirt and oil
   B) Grease and water
   C) Oil and grease
   D) Dirt and moisture
   E) Water and oil

11. The electrical circuit term "open circuit" refers to a closed loop being opened. When an ohmmeter is connected into this type of circuit, one can expect the meter to

   A) read infinity.
   B) read infinity and slowly return to ZERO.
   C) read ZERO.
   D) read ZERO and slowly return to infinity.
   E) None of the above

12. Which is most appropriate for pulling a heavy load?

   A) Electric lift
   B) Fork lift
   C) Tow conveyor
   D) Dolly
   E) Pallet truck

13. In order to operate a breast drill, which direction should you turn it?

   A) Clockwise
   B) Counterclockwise
   C) Up and down
   D) Back and forth
   E) Right, then left

14. Which is the correct tool for tightening or loosening a water pipe?

   A) Slip joint pliers
   B) Household pliers
   C) Monkey wrench
   D) water pump pliers
   E) Pipe wrench

15. What is one purpose of a chuck key?

   A) Open doors
   B) Remove drill bits
   C) Remove screws
   D) Remove set screws
   E) Unlock chucks

16. When smoke is generated as a result of using a portable electric drill for cutting holes into a piece of angle iron. One should

    A) use a fire watch.
    B) cease the drilling operation.
    C) use an exhaust fan to remove smoke.
    D) use a prescribed coolant solution to reduce friction.
    E) call the Fire Department.

17. The primary purpose of soldering is to

    A) melt solder to a molten state.
    B) heat metal parts to the right temperature be joined.
    C) join metal parts by melting the parts.
    D) harden metal.
    E) join metal carts.

18. Which of the following statements is correct concerning a soldering gun?

    A) Tip is not replaceable
    B) Cannot be used in cramped places
    C) Heats only when trigger is pressed
    D) Not rated by the number of watts it uses
    E) Has no light

19. What unit of measurement is read on a dial torque wrench?

    A) Pounds
    B) Inches
    C) Centimeters
    D) Foot-pounds
    E) Degrees

20. Which instrument is used to test insulation breakdown of a conductor?

    A) Ohmmeter
    B) Ammeter
    C) Megger
    D) Wheatstone bridge
    E) Voltmeter

21. ½ of 1/4 =

    A) 1/12
    B) 1/8
    C) 1/4
    D) ½
    E) 8

22. 2.6 - .5 =

    A) 2.0
    B) 2.1
    C) 3.1
    D) 3.3
    E) None of the above

23. Solve the power equation

    $P = I^2R$ for R

    A) $R = EI$
    B) $R = I^2P$
    C) $R = PI$
    D) $R = P/I^2$
    E) $R = E/I$

24. The product of 3 kilo ohms times 3 micro ohms is

    A) 6×10^{-9} ohms
    B) 6×10^{-3} ohms
    C) 9×10^{3} ohms
    D) 9×10^{-6} ohms
    E) 9×10^{-3} ohms

In sample question 25 below, select the statement which is most nearly correct according to the paragraph.

"Prior to 1870, a conveyor that made use of rollers was developed for transporting clay. This construction substituted rolling friction at the idler bearing points for the sliding friction of the slider bed. A primitive type of roughing belt conveyor was developed about the same time for the handling of grain. This design was improved during the latter part of the century when the roughing idler was developed."

25. According to the above paragraph, which of the following statements is most nearly correct?

A) The troughing belt conveyor was developed about 1870 to handle clay and grain.

B) Rolling friction construction was replaced by sliding friction construction prior to 1870.

C) In the late nineteenth century, conveyors were improved with the development of the roughing idler.

D) The roughing idler, a significant design improvement for conveyors, was developed in the early nineteenth century.

E) Conveyor belts were invented and developed in the 1800's.

26. A small crane was used to raise the heavy part. Raise MOST nearly means

A) lift
B) drag
C) drop
D) deliver
E) guide

27. Short MOST nearly means

A) tall
B) wide
C) brief
D) heavy
E) dark

For sample question 28 below, select from the drawings of objects on the right labeled A, B, C, and D, the one that would have the TOP, FRONT, and RIGHT views shown in the drawing at the left

28.

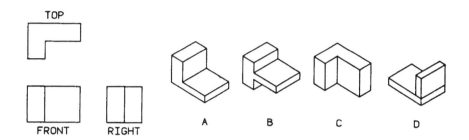

In sample question 29 below, there is, on the left, a drawing of a flat piece of paper and, on the right, four figures labeled A, B, C, and D. When the paper is bent on the dotted lines it will form one of the figures on the right. Decide which alternative can be formed from the flat piece.

29

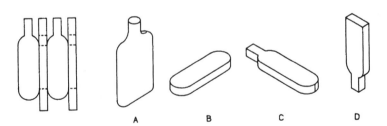

In each of the sample questions below, look at the symbols in the first two boxes. Something about the three symbols in the first box makes them alike; something about the two symbols in the other box with the question mark makes them alike. Look for some characteristic that is common to all symbols in the same box, yet makes them different from the symbols in the other box. Among the five answer choices, find the symbol that can best be substituted for the question mark, because it is like the symbols in the second box, and, for the same reason, different from those in the first box.

30.

USE DIAGRAM ON PAGE 72 QUESTION 32

In sample question 30 above, all the symbols in the first box are vertical lines. The second box has two lines, one broken and one solid. Their <u>likeness </u>to each other consists in their being horizontal; and their being horizontal makes them <u>different </u>from the vertical lines in the other box. The answer must be the only one of the five lettered choices that is a horizontal line, either broken or solid. NOTE: There is not supposed to be a series or progression in these symbol questions. If you look for a progression in the first box and the second box, you will be wasting time. Remember, look for a <u>likeness </u>within each box and a <u>difference </u>between the two bo xes.

Now do sample questions 31 and 32.

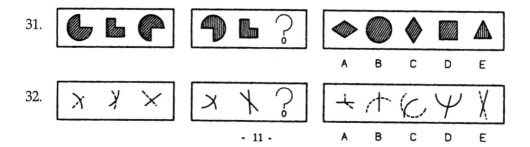

33. In Figure 3-8-6 below, what is the measurement of Dimension F? Drawing is not actual size.

A) 1 3/4 inches
B) 2 1/4 inches
C) 2 ½ inches
D) 3 3/4 inches
E) None of the above

Use Figure 3-8-6 on page 68

---

34. In Figure 160-57 below, what is the current flow through R when:

V = 50 volts
R1 = 25 ohms
R2 = 25 ohms

R3 = 50 ohms
R4 = 50 ohms
R5 = 50 ohms

and the current through the entire circuit totals one amp?

A 0.5 amp
B) 5.0 amps
C) 5.0 milliamps
D) 50.0 milliamps
E) None of the above

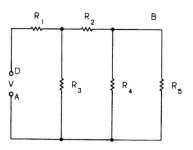

Figure 160-57

EXHIBIT B

The following positions use test M/N 933:

Position Title	Register Number
Maintenance Mechanic, MPE/06	M32
Maintenance Mechanic, MPE/07	M33
Overhaul Specialist	M34

CORRECT ANSWERS TO
SAMPLE QUESTIONS

1. C
2. D
3. D
4. D
5. A
6. A
7. A
8. E
9. E
10. D
11. A
12. E
13. A
14. E
15. B
16. D
17. E

18. C
19. D
20. C
21. B
22. B
23. D
24. E
25. C
26. A
27. C
28. C
29. C
30. C
31. E
32. D
33. C
34. A

Chapter Six
The 470 Battery Test

This chapter presents sample test questions for the 470 Battery Test including test taking tips and strategies that you can practice prior to taking the official exam. The 470 exam covers seven of the major entry level positions – over half of all Postal service jobs, including:

- ✔ **Carrier**
- ✔ **Clerk**
- ✔ **Distribution Clerk, Machine**
- ✔ **Flat-Sorting Machine Operator**
- ✔ **Mail handler**
- ✔ **Mail Processor**
- ✔ **Mark-Up Clerk, Automated**

Review this entire chapter to improve your test scores and to become familiar with the test taking process and strategies, application forms, answer sheets, and sample questions. The 470 examination and completion of forms will require approximately two hours and fifteen minutes.

The first section of this chapter presents the Postal Service's practice exam, including a sample answer sheet, that is sent out to applicants prior to taking a scheduled exam. The second section provides additional practice exams with study tips by Norman Hall for the 470 Battery Test's four key testing areas. Mr. Hall has scored 100% on the United States Postal Exam four times and he provides in-depth study tips for this exam's key testing areas.

★★   TEST 470
APPLICANT INSTRUCTIONS

YOU MUST BRING THE FOLLOWING TO BE ADMITTED:

Completed Sample Answer Sheet,
Admission Card/Notice,
Photo ID and
2 Sharpened No. 2 Pencils

LATECOMERS WILL NOT BE ADMITTED.

These instructions will prepare you for the exam. Please take time to carefully read ALL of the instructions. THIS IS YOUR RESPON-SIBILITY. You should read all of the instructions and complete the required items even if you have taken a Postal exam before. We are providing you with

1. A SAMPLE ANSWER SHEET TO FILL OUT AT HOME. This will enable you to complete the Answer Sheet in the exam room.

2. WHAT YOU CAN EXPECT DURING THE ACTUAL TEST PART OF THE EXAM SESSION.

3. SAMPLE QUESTIONS FOR PRACTICE. So that you will be familiar with the type of questions on the test, sample questions are included for practice.

4. HOW THE FOUR PARTS OF THE TEST WILL BE SCORED.

To fill out the Sample Answer Sheet, you'll need:

This booklet,

Sample Answer Sheet,

Your Admission Card/Notice,

No. 2 pencil,

Social Security card,

ZIP Code for current address and

zip+4 Code for current address.

In the exam room, you will be given 15 minutes to copy your work from the Sample Answer Sheet to the Answer Sheet. The test will be~n soon thereafter. You will not have time in the exam room to become familiar with these instructions.

The Answer Sheet will be given to you in the exam room. It is processed by a high-speed scanner. It is important that you precisely complete the grids on the Sample Answer Sheet. This is so you will know **exactly how** to fill out the Answer Sheet in the exam room.

You are responsible for correctly completing the Sample Answer Sheet. When you report to take the test, you must bring it with you.

Your Sample Answer Sheet will be checked for accurate and total completion. You may not have **time** to fix any errors or complete items not filled out before the session starts. Only those who have a properly completed Sample Answer Sheet will be admitted. Those who still have an incomplete Sample Answer Sheet by the time the exam starts will NOT be admitted.

EFFECTIVE SEPTEMBER 1994

THE FOLLOWING INSTRUCTIONS EXPLAIN HOW TO FILL OUT EACH GRID ON THE SAMPLE ANSWER SHEET. Examples of correct and incorrect marks are:

CORRECT MARKS   **INCORRECT MARKS**

1 NAME. Use your full, legal name when completing this grid. Use the same name every time you take a postal exam. Use of a nickname could result in a delay in processing the result.

GRID 1 is divided into three parts: Last Name, First Name and MI (Middle Initial). Each part is surrounded by a border. Each **part of your name must be entered ONLY in the place for that part.**

Last Name. Enter your last name one letter to a box. You must start with the first square box to the left.

If you are a JR, SR, III or IV this should be included as a part of your last name. After entering your last name, skip a box and enter the correct letters.

To help you complete the grids correctly, you will use the EDGE of the Admission Card/Notice or the envelope as a guide. Place the Admission Card/Notice or envelope on top of GRID 1 so that the edge is to the LEFT of the first column. For example, when the last name is "HALL III":

EDGE

(If you are left handed, place the edge to the RIGHT of the first column.)

For the letter in the box, find the matching circle in the column below and darken that circle.

Next, move the edge with one hand so that it is against the next column. Darken the circle with the ether hand for that letter.

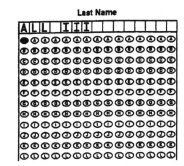

EDGE

Then proceed until you have darkened the circle for each letter you have entered in a box.

If your name has the letter "O" in it, make sure to darken the circle that comes after "N". Do not mistake the letter "Q" for the letter "O".

When you come to a blank box, do nothing.

The following is an example of a completed grid when the last name is "HALL III":

First Name. Enter your first name one letter to a box. You must start with the first box after the border line.

As you did for Last Name, take the edge and place it on top of this grid against the first column.

Find the matching circle below and darken that circle. Next, move the edge so it is against the next column. Darken the circle for that letter. Then proceed until you have darkened the circle for each letter you have entered in a box.

Do not mistake the letter "Q" for the letter "O".

When you come to a blank box, do nothing.

MI (Middle Initial). Enter your middle initial and darken the circle for the letter. If you do not have a middle initial, do not enter anything in the box or darken a circle

2 SOCIAL SECURITY NUMBER. Look at your Social Security card. Compare the number with the one on the Admission Card/Notice. If the number on the Admission Card/Notice is not correct, draw a line through it and make the correction.

Enter your correct Social Security Number in GRID 2 on the Sample Answer Sheet.

Using the edge, darken the matching numerical circles.

3 BIRTH DATE. For GRID 3, in the box labeled "MM", enter the two numbers for your birth month, one number to a box. If you were born in January through September, you would enter a "0" in the first box and the number for the month in the second box. Using the edge, darken the matching circles.

In the box labeled "DD", enter the two numbers for your day of birth, one number to a box. If your day of birth is from one to nine, enter a "0" in the first box and the number for the day in the second box. Using the edge, darken the matching circles.

In the box labeled "YY", enter the last two numbers of the year in which you were born, one number to a box. Do not use the current year. Using the edge, darken the matching circles.

WHEN YOU FINISH GRID 3, YOU SHOULD HAVE I ENTERED AND GRIDDED SIX NUMBERS.

4 LEAD OFFICE/INSTALLATION FINANCE NUMBER. Look at the Admission Card/Notice. On it there **is a six digit number end** the name of the office for **which you have applied. With your pencil, enter** this number in GRID 4, one

number to a box. Using the edge, darken the matching numerical circles.

5 JOB CHOICE. Refer to the Choice Sheet for instructions.

6 TEST SERIES. Do nothing with GRID 6.

7 EXAM DATE. Look at the Admission Card/Notice for the date you are scheduled to take this exam. For GRID 7, in the box labeled "MM", enter the two numbers for the exam month, one number to a box. If the exam is in January through September, you would enter a "0" in the first box and the number for the month in the second box. Using the edge, darken the matching circles.

In the box labeled "DD", enter the two numbers for your day of exam, one number to a box. If your day of exam is from one to nine, enter a "0" in the first box and the number for the day in the second box. Using the edge, darken the matching circles.

In the box labeled "YY", enter the last two numbers of the year of the exam, one number to a box" Using the edge, darken the matching circles.

WHEN YOU FINISH GRID 7, YOU SHOULD HAVE ENTERED AND GRIDDED SIX NUMBERS.

IMPORTANT NOTE. If you are a current career Postal employee OR your Admission Card/Notice is stamped "INSERVICE", DO NOT COMPLETE GRIDS 8, 9,17,18 AND 19.

8 YOUR CHOICE OF INSTALLATIONS. Refer to the Choice Sheet for instructions.

9 VETERAN PREFERENCE. If you are not eligible to claim Veteran Preference, do nothing with GRID 9. The following is an explanation of the different types of Veteran Preference

5 Points (tentative). This preference is usually given to honorably separated veterans who served on active duty in the Armed Forces of the United States under one of the following conditions:

a. During a declared war (the last one was World War II): or

b. During the period April 28,1952 to July 1,1955; or

c. During the period February 1, 1955 through October 14, 1976 for which any part of more than 180 consecutive days was served. (An initial period of active duty for training under the 6-month Reserve or National Guard Program does not count.)

d. In any campaign or expedition for which a campaign badge was authorized.

Veterans who served in Southwest Asia or in the surrounding contiguous waters or air space on or after August 2, 1990 AND who were awarded the Southwest Asia Service Medal can claim five points.

10 Points - Compensable (Less than 30%). This preference is given to honorably separated veterans who served on active duty in the Armed Forces at any time and have a service-connected disability for which compensation is provided **at 10% or more, but** less than 30%.

10 Points - Compensable (30% or more). This preference is given to honorably separated veterans who served on active duty in the Armed Forces at any time and have a service-connected disability for which compensation is provided at 30% or more.

10 Points (other). This preference is claimed by a variety of people:

a. Veterans who were awarded the Purple Heart; or

b. Veterans who have a recognized service connected disability for which no compensation is received; or

c. Until remarried, the widow or widower of an honorably separated veteran, provided the deceased veteran served in active duty during a war, or the veteran died while in the Armed Forces; or

d. Spouses of certain veterans with a service connected disability; or

e. Mothers of certain deceased or disabled veterans.

Darken only one circle in GRID 9 if you wish to claim Veteran Preference. Do not darken more than one circle. **Points claimed will** be **added to your score** ONLY if you pass the exam with a score of 70 or better.

10 EXAM TYPE. In GRID 10, for:

Entrance, darken this circle if you applied for this exam in response to a public announcement or are taking **the test for other reasons** (see 11 below). **Current career Postal employees do NOT darken this** circle.

Inservice, darken this circle if you are a current career Postal employee. Also, darken this circle if you are taking this exam on a noncompetitive basis -- **your Admission Card/Notice will be stamped** "INSERVICE."

11 SPECIAL INSTRUCTIONS. **If you do not have** "DELAYED" or "REOPENED" **stamped on your Admission Card/Notice, do nothing with** GRID 11. This grid is only for people who are taking this exam because they either:

a. missed an opportunity to take the exam when last opened to the public because they were on active military duty, "DELAYED" status OR

b. entitled to 10 point Veteran Preference, "REOPENED" status.

Grid the circle labeled "3" for "DELAYED", or the circle labeled "4" for "REOPENED."

12 LEAD OFFICE (Name). **Look at the right side of the Admission Card/Notice for the name of the installation for which you are applying. Print the** name in the block labeled: "Lead Office/Installation (Please Print)". Print the two-letter abbreviation for the state in the block labeled "State."

Sign your name in the block labeled "Signature."

13 PRINT YOUR CITY AND STATE. Turn to Page 2 of the Sample Answer Sheet. **Print the city and state of your current mailing address.**

14 STREET ADDRESS. This is for the one line address that will be used to deliver your test result. If you pass and later your score is reached for consideration, the address you grid will be used to notify you. The address you grid must meet Postal standards. Study the following examples:

1234 MAIN ST APT 999

45678 MADISON BLVD S

331/2 IVY DR SW

4329-02 MONTGOMERY PL

2342 NW SMITH RD

RR 2 BOX 50

PO BOX 4502

You must use the correct shortened format for your one line address. Also, such an address will be easier and quicker to grid.

This grid is different from the other ones because it contains numbers, special symbols and letters. Enter your one line address in the boxes. You must start with the first box to the left. Skip a blank box where there needs to be a space. By using the edge and starting with the first column to the left, darken the circles.

Do not mistake the letter "Q" for the letter "O".

When you come to a blank box, do nothing.

15 ZIP (Code). You must have your correct ZIP Code to complete this grid. An incorrect ZIP Code will result in a delay in sending your rating to you. Your ZIP Code is found on magazines, utility bills and other business mail you receive at home. Enter your correct five digit ZIP Code in the boxes. Then use the edge to darken the matching numerical circles.

16 +4 (Code). You must have your correct ZIP+4 Code to complete this gad. Your ZIP +4 is usually found on mail you receive at home. This four digit number appears after the five digit ZIP Code. Enter this number in GRID 16. Use the edge and darken the numerical circles.

FOR GRIDS 17, 18 AND 19, read the General Instructions for the RESEARCH QUESTION-NAIRE on Page 2 of the Sample Answer Sheet.

17 SEX. Darken the appropriate circle in GRID 17.

18 DISABILITY CODE. If you do not have a disability, enter 0 in the first box and 5 in the second box in GRID 18. Code "05" indicates "No Disability." Using the edge, darken the numerical circles.

A disability refers to a physical or mental disability or history of such disability which is likely to cause difficulty in obtaining, maintaining, or advancing in employment. On Page 4, you will find a list of various disabilities. Each of the disabilities has a number. If you have a disability, read the list carefully and select the code that best describes your disability. If you have multiple disabilities, choose the code for the one that is most disabling. Enter the two numbers of the disability code in the boxes at the top of GRID 18. If your disability is not listed, enter zero in the first column and six in the second column. Using the edge, darken the numerical circles.

19 RACIAL AND NATIONAL ORIGIN. This grid is for the collection of your racial and national origin. Darken the circle for the category that applies to you. If you are of mixed racial and/or national origin, you should identify yourself by the one category for which you most closely associate yourself by darkening the appropriate circle in GRID 19.

Checking your work. After you have finished, go back and check your work. For a letter or number in a box, you should have only one circle darkened in the column found directly below. Make sure that you have completed all items as requested.

After checking your work, go back to Page 1 of the Sample Answer Sheet. In the upper left corner is the United States Postal Service eagle. Draw a circle around the eagle.

Get someone else to check your work. Since the scanner that reads the Answer Sheet only picks up what is gridded, you should have someone else check your work. Let them tell you if you made a mistake so that you can correct it. This will help make sure that you do the best job you possibly can on the Answer Sheet in the exam room.

TEST INSTRUCTIONS

During the test session, it will be your responsibility to pay close attention to what the examiner has to say and to follow all instructions. One of the purposes of the test is to see how quickly and accurately you can work. Therefore, each part of the test will be carefully timed. You will not START until being told to do so. Also, when you are told to STOP, you must immediately STOP answering the questions. When you are told to work on a particular part of the examination, regardless of which part, you are to work on that part ONLY. **If you finish a part before time is called, you may review your answers for that** part, but **you will not go on or back to any other** part. **Failure to follow** ANY directions given to you by the examiner may be grounds for disqualification. Instructions read by the examiner are intended to ensure that each applicant has the same fair and objective opportunity to compete in the examination.

SAMPLE QUESTIONS

Study carefully before the examination.

The following questions are like the ones that will be on the test. Study these carefully. This will give you practice with the different kinds of questions and show you how to mark your answers.

Part A: Address Checking

In this part of the test, you will have to decide whether two addresses are alike or different. If the two addresses are exactly *Alike* in every way, darken circle A for the question. If the two addresses are *Different* in any way, darken circle D for the question.

★

SAMPLE ANSWER SHEET
for
TEST 470

UNITED STATES POSTAL SERVICE.

USE NO. 2 PENCIL ONLY

USE NO. 2 PENCIL ONLY

1 In the boxes below, print your last name, first name and middle initial in the proper sections as indicated, one letter per box. Below each box, blacken the oval which is lettered the same as the letter in the box. For each blank letter box, do not blacken any of the ovals.

Last Name | **First Name** | **MI**

(A through Z ovals for each column)

2 Social Security Number

3 Birth Date
| MM | DD | YY |

A false or dishonest answer in blocks 1, 2 or 3 may be grounds for not employing you or for dismissing you after you begin work.

4 Lead Office/Installation Finance Number

5 Job Choice
- City Carrier
- Clerk
- Dist. Clerk, Machine
- Flat Sorter Machine
- Mail Handler
- Mail Processor
- Mark Up Clerk
- Other

6 Test Series

DO NOT COMPLETE

7 Exam Date
| MM | DD | YY |

8 Your choice of installations where you want to be considered (not more than 3)
1 2 3 4 5 6 7 8 9 10
11 12 13 14 15 16 17 18 19 20
21 22 23 24 25 26 27 28 29 30
31 32 33 34 35 36 37 38 39 40
41 42 43 44 45 46 47 48 49 50
51 52 53 54 55 56 57 58 59 60
61 62 63 64 65 66 67 68 69 70
71 72 73 74 75 76 77 78 79 80
81 82 83 84 85 86 87 88 89 90
91 92 93 94 95 96 97 98 99

9 Veteran Preference
- 5 points (tentative)
- 10 points-Compensable (Less than 30%)
- 10 points-Compensable (30% or more)
- 10 points (other)

10 Exam Type
- Entrance
- In Service

11 Special Instructions
1 2 3 4 5 6 7 8 9 10 11 12
13 14 15 16 17 18 19 20 21 22 23 24

12 Lead Office/Installation (Please Print) | State | Signature (Required To Process Test)

PS Form **8155-S**, July 1994

Page 1

13 Print your city and state ⟶

14 In the boxes below, print your street address or post office box (one letter, number, or symbol per box).

15 ZIP

16 +4

RESEARCH QUESTIONNAIRE

General Instructions

The U.S. Postal Service wants to make sure that its part in the recruitment and hiring of postal employees is fair for everyone. To do this we need your answers to the three questions below. Your responses are voluntary. Please answer each of the questions to the best of your ability. Your answers will be used for research purposes only and to help assure equal employment opportunity. Please provide accurate information. Your cooperation is important. Completely darken the oval corresponding to your response choice.

17 Indicate Sex

○ Male

○ Female

18 Disability Code
see page 4

19 The categories below are designed to identify your basic racial and national origin category. If you are of mixed racial and/or national origin, indicate the category with which you most closely identify yourself.

Name of Category	Definition of Category
○ American Indian or Alaskan Native	A person having origins in any of the original peoples of North America, and who maintains cultural identification through community recognition or tribal affiliation.
○ Asian or Pacific Islander	A person having origins in any of the original peoples of the Far East, Southeast Asia, the Indian subcontinent, or the Pacific Islands. This area includes, for example China, India, Japan, Korea, the Philippine Islands, Samoa, and Vietnam.
○ Black, not of Hispanic Origin	A person having origins in any of the black racial groups of Africa. Does not include persons of Mexican, Puerto Rican, Cuban, Central or South American, or other Spanish cultures or origins (see Hispanic).
○ Hispanic	A person of Mexican, Puerto Rican, Cuban, Central or South American, or other Spanish cultures or origins. Does not include persons of Portuguese culture or origin.
○ White, not of Hispanic Origin	A person having origins in any of the original peoples of Europe, North Africa, or the Middle East. Does not include persons of Mexican, Puerto Rican, Cuban, Central or South American, or other Spanish cultures or origins (see Hispanic). Also includes persons not included in other categories.

Page 2

DID YOU READ ALL OF THE
INSTRUCTIONS

THANK YOU FOR FOLLOWING THE
DIRECTIONS AND COMPLETING
THE SAMPLE ANSWER SHEET

THE UNITED STATES POSTAL SERVICE IS
AN EQUAL OPPORTUNITY EMPLOYER

Disability Code Listing

CODE	GENERAL	CODE	PARTIAL PARALYSIS (continued)
01	Disability Not Reported	66	Both arms, any part
05	No Disability	67	One side of body, including one arm and one leg
06	Disability Not Listed on This Form	68	Three or more major parts of the body (arms and legs)

CODE	SPEECH IMPAIRMENTS		COMPLETE PARALYSIS
13	Severe speech malfunction or inability to speak, hearing is normal. Example: defects of articulation (unclear language sounds); stuttering; aphasia; laryngectomy (removal of the voice box).		(Because of a brain, nerve, or muscle problem, including palsy and cerebral palsy, there is complete loss of ability to move or use a part of the body, including legs, arms, and/or trunk.)
		70	One hand

CODE	HEARING IMPAIRMENTS		
		71	Both hands
15	Hard of hearing; correctable by hearing aid	72	One arm
16	Total deafness with understandable speech	73	Both arms
17	Total deafness with inability to speak clearly	74	One leg

CODE	VISION IMPAIRMENTS		
		75	Both legs
22	Can read ordinary size print with glasses, but with loss of peripheral (side) vision	76	Lower half of body, including legs
		77	One side of body, including one arm and one leg
23	Cannot read ordinary size print; not correctable by glasses	78	Three or more major parts of the body (arms and legs)
24	Blind in one eye		OTHER IMPAIRMENTS
25	Blind in both eyes	80	Heart disease with no restriction or limitation of activity (history of heart problem with complete recovery)

CODE	MISSING EXTREMITIES		
27	One hand	81	Heart disease with restriction or limitation of activity
28	One arm		
29	One foot	82	Convulsive disorder (e.g., epilepsy)
32	One leg		
33	Both hands or arms	83	Blood disease (e.g., sickle cell disease, leukemia, hemophilia)
34	Both feet or legs		
35	One hand or arm and one foot or leg	84	Diabetes
36	One hand or arm and both feet or legs		
37	Both hands or arms and one foot or leg	86	Pulmonary or respiratory (e.g., tuberculosis, emphysema, asthma)
38	Both hands or arms and both feet or legs		
		87	Kidney dysfunctioning (e.g., use of an artificial kidney machine)

CODE	NONPARALYTIC ORTHOPEDIC IMPAIRMENTS (Because of chronic pain, stiffness, or weakness in bones or joints, there is some loss of ability to move or use a part of the body.)		
		88	Cancer (history of cancer with complete recovery)
44	One or both hands		
45	One or both feet	89	Cancer (undergoing surgical and/or medical treatment)
46	One or both arms		
47	One or both legs	92	Severe distortion of limbs and/or spine (e.g., dwarfism, kyphosis – severe distortion of back, etc.)
48	Hip or pelvis		
49	Back	93	Disfigurement of face, hands, or feet (e.g., distortion of features on skin, such as those caused by burns, gunshot injuries, and birth defects, gross facial birth marks, club feet, etc.)
57	Any combination of two or more parts of the body		

CODE	PARTIAL PARALYSIS (Because of a brain, nerve, or muscle problem, including palsy and cerebral palsy, there is some loss of ability to move or use a part of the body, including legs, arms, and/or trunk.)		MENTAL RETARDATION/EMOTIONAL PROBLEMS
61	One hand	90	A chronic and lifelong condition involving a limited ability to learn, to be educated and to be trained for useful productive employment as certified by a State Vocational Rehabilitation Agency.
62	One arm, any part		
63	One leg, any part	91	Mental or emotional illness (history of treatment for mental or emotional problems)
64	Both hands		
65	Both legs, any part	94	Learning Disability

Mark your answers to these sample questions on the Sample Answer Grid at the right.

1...2134 S 20th St   2134 S 20th St

Since the two addresses are exactly alike, mark A for question 1 on the Sample Answer Grid.

2...4608 N Warnock St   4806 N Warnock St

3...1202 W Girard Dr   1202 W Girard Rd

4...Chappaqua NY 10514   Chappaqua NY 10514

5...2207 Markland Ave   2207 Markham Ave

Sample Answer Grid		
1	Ⓐ	Ⓓ
2	Ⓐ	Ⓓ
3	Ⓐ	Ⓓ
4	Ⓐ	Ⓓ
5	Ⓐ	Ⓓ

The correct answers to questions 2 to 5 are: 2D, 3D, 4A, and 5D.

Your score on Part A of the actual test will be based on the number of wrong answers as well as on the number of right answers. Part A is scored right answers minus wrong answers. Random guessing should not help your score. For the Part A test, you will have six minutes to answer as many of the 95 questions as you can. It will be to your advantage to work as quickly and as accurately as possible. You will not be expected to be able to answer all the questions in the time allowed.

Part B: Memory for Addresses

In this part of the test, you will have to memorize the locations (A, B, C, D, or E) of 25 addresses shown in five boxes, like those below. For example, "Sardis" is in Box C, "6800-6999 Table" is in Box B, etc. (The addresses in the actual test will be different.)

4700-5599 Table Lismore 5600-6499 West Hesper 4400-4699 Blake	6800-6999 Table Kelford 6500-6799 West Musella 5600-6499 Blake	5600-6499 Table Joel 6800-6999 West Sardis 6500-6799 Blake	6500-6799 Table Tatum 4400-4699 West Porter 4700-5599 Blake	4400-4699 Table Ruskin 4700-5599 West Nathan 6800-6999 Blake

Study the locations of the addresses for five minutes. As you study, silently repeat these to yourself. Then cover the boxes and try to answer the questions below. Mark your answers for each question by darkening the circle as was done for questions 1 and 2.

1. Musella
2. 4700-5599 Blake
3. 4700-5599 Table
4. Tatum

5. 4400-4699 Blake
6. Hesper
7. Kelford
8. Nathan

9. 6500-6799 Blake
10. Joel
11. 4400-4699 Blake
12. 6500-6799 West

13. Porter
14. 6800-6999 Blake

Sample Answer Grid				
1 Ⓐ ● Ⓒ Ⓓ Ⓔ	5 Ⓐ Ⓑ Ⓒ Ⓓ Ⓔ	9 Ⓐ Ⓑ Ⓒ Ⓓ Ⓔ	13 Ⓐ Ⓑ Ⓒ Ⓓ Ⓔ	
2 Ⓐ Ⓑ Ⓒ ● Ⓔ	6 Ⓐ Ⓑ Ⓒ Ⓓ Ⓔ	10 Ⓐ Ⓑ Ⓒ Ⓓ Ⓔ	14 Ⓐ Ⓑ Ⓒ Ⓓ Ⓔ	
3 Ⓐ Ⓑ Ⓒ Ⓓ Ⓔ	7 Ⓐ Ⓑ Ⓒ Ⓓ Ⓔ	11 Ⓐ Ⓑ Ⓒ Ⓓ Ⓔ		
4 Ⓐ Ⓑ Ⓒ Ⓓ Ⓔ	8 Ⓐ Ⓑ Ⓒ Ⓓ Ⓔ	12 Ⓐ Ⓑ Ⓒ Ⓓ Ⓔ		

The correct answers for questions 3 to 14 are: 3A, 4D, 5A, 6A, 7B, 8E, 9C, 10C, 11A, 12B, 13D, and 14E.

During the examination, you will have three practice exercises to help you memorize the location of addresses shown in five boxes. After the practice exercises, the actual test will be given. Part B is scored right answers minus one-fourth of the wrong answers. Random guessing should not help your score. But, if you can eliminate one or more alternatives, it is to your advantage to guess. For the Part B test, you will have five minutes to answer as many of the 88 questions as you can. It will be to your advantage to work as quickly and as accurately as you can. You will not be expected to be able to answer all the questions in the time allowed.

Part C: Number Series

For each *Number Series* question there is at the left a series of numbers which follow some definite order and at the right five sets of two numbers each. You are to look at the numbers in the series at the left and find out what order they follow. Then decide what the next two numbers in that series would be if the same order were continued.

1. 1 2 3 4 5 6 7................. A) 1 2   B) 5 6   C) 8 9   D) 4 5   E) 7 8

The numbers in this series are increasing by 1. If the series were continued for two more numbers, it would read: 1 2 3 4 5 6 7 8 9. Therefore the correct answer is 8 and 9.

2. 15 14 13 12 11 10 9...... A) 2 1   B) 17 16   C) 8 9   D) 8 7   E) 9 8

The numbers in this series are decreasing by 1. If the series were continued for two more numbers, it would read: 15 14 13 12 11 10 9 8 7. Therefore the correct answer is 8 and 7.

3. 20 20 21 21 22 22 23.... A) 23 23   B) 23 24   C) 19 19   D) 22 23   E) 21 22

Each number in this series is repeated and then increased by 1. If the series were continued for two more numbers, it would read: 20 20 21 21 22 22 23 23 24 Therefore the correct answer is 23 and 24.

4. 17 3 17 4 17 5 17.......... A) 6 17   B) 6 7   C) 17 6   D) 5 6   E) 17 7

This series is the number 17 separated by numbers increasing by 1, beginning with the number 3. If the series were continued for two more numbers, it would read: 17 3 17 4 17 5 17 6 17. Therefore the correct answer is 6 and 17.

5. 1 2 4 5 7 8 10................. A) 11 12   B) 12 14   C) 10 13   D) 12 13   E) 11 13

The numbers in this series are increasing first by 1 (plus 1) and then by 2 (plus 2). If the series were continued for two more numbers, it would read: 1 2 4 5 7 8 10 (plus 1) *11* and (plus 2) 13. Therefore the correct answer is 11 and 13.

Now read and work sample questions 6 through 10 and mark your answers on the Sample Answer Grid.

	A)	B)	C)	D)	E)
6. 21 21 20 20 19 19 18.....	A) 18 18	B) 18 17	C) 17 18	D) 17 17	E) 18 19
7. 1 22 1 23 1 24 1............	A) 26 1	B) 25 26	C) 25 1	D) 1 26	E) 1 25
8. 1 20 3 19 5 18 7............	A) 8 9	B) 8 17	C) 17 10	D) 17 9	E) 9 18
9. 4 7 10 13 16 19 22........	A) 23 26	B) 25 27	C) 25 26	D) 25 28	E) 24 27
10. 30 2 28 4 26 6 24........	A) 23 9	B) 26 8	C) 8 9	D) 26 22	E) 8 22

```
                           Sample Answer Grid
6  Ⓐ Ⓑ Ⓒ Ⓓ Ⓔ    8  Ⓐ Ⓑ Ⓒ Ⓓ Ⓔ    9  Ⓐ Ⓑ Ⓒ Ⓓ Ⓔ    10  Ⓐ Ⓑ Ⓒ Ⓓ Ⓔ
7  Ⓐ Ⓑ Ⓒ Ⓓ Ⓔ
```

The correct answers to sample questions 6 to 10 are: 6B, 7C, 8D, 9D and 10E. Explanations follow.

6. Each number in the series repeats itself and then decreases by 1 or minus 1; *21* (repeat) *21* (minus 1) *20* (repeat) *20* (minus 1) 19 (repeat) 19 (minus 1) 18 (repeat) ? (minus 1) ?

7. The number 1 is separated by numbers which begin with 22 and increased by 1; 1 22 1 (increase 22 by 1) *23 1* (increase 23 by 1) *24 1* (*increase* 24 by 1) ?

8. This is best explained by two alternating series -- one series starts with 1 and increases by 2 or plus 2; the other series starts with 20 and decreases by 1 or minus 1.

$$1 \quad \stackrel{\wedge}{20} \quad 3 \quad \stackrel{\wedge}{19} \quad 5 \quad \stackrel{\wedge}{18} \quad 7 \quad \stackrel{\wedge}{?} \quad ?$$

9. This series of numbers increases by 3 (plus 3) beginning with the first number—*4 7 10 13 16 19 22 ? ?*

10. Look for two alternating series -- one series starts with 30 and decreases by 2 (minus 2); the other series starts with 2 and increases by 2 (plus 2).

Now try questions 11 to 15.

11. 5 6 20 7 8 19 9..........   A) 10 18   B) 18 17   C) 10 17   D) 18 19   E) 10 11

12. 4 6 9 11 14 16 19......   A) 21 24   B) 22 25   C) 20 22   D) 21 23   E) 22 24

13. 8 8 1 10 10 3 12.......   A) 13 13   B) 12 5   C) 12 4   D) 13 5   E) 4 12

14. 10 12 50 15 17 50 20.   A) 50 21   B) 21 50   C) 50 22   D) 22 50   E) 22 24

15. 20 21 23 24 27 28 32 33 38 39.   A) 45 46   B) 45 52   C) 44 45   D) 44 49   E) 40 46

```
                           Sample Answer Grid
11  Ⓐ Ⓑ Ⓒ Ⓓ Ⓔ    13  Ⓐ Ⓑ Ⓒ Ⓓ Ⓔ    14  Ⓐ Ⓑ Ⓒ Ⓓ Ⓔ    15  Ⓐ Ⓑ Ⓒ Ⓓ Ⓔ
12  Ⓐ Ⓑ Ⓒ Ⓓ Ⓔ
```

The correct answers to the sample questions above are: 11A, 12A, 13B, 14D and 15A.

It will be to your advantage to answer every question in Part C that you can, since your score on this part of the test will be based on the number of questions that you answer correctly. Answer first those questions which are easiest for you. For the Part C test, you will have 20 minutes to answer as many of the 24 questions as you can.

Part D: Following Oral Instructions

In this part of the test, you will be told to follow directions by writing in a test booklet and then on an answer sheet. The test booklet will have lines of material like the following five samples:

SAMPLE   1.   5 _____

SAMPLE   2.   1 6 4 3 7

SAMPLE   3.   D B A E C

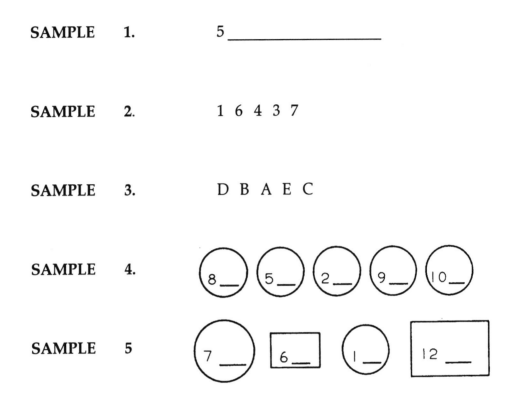

SAMPLE   4.

SAMPLE   5

To practice this test, have someone read the instructions on the **next page** to you and you follow the instructions. When they tell you to darken the space on the Sample Answer Sheet, use the one on this page.

Sample Answer Grid			
1 Ⓐ Ⓑ Ⓒ Ⓓ Ⓔ	4 Ⓐ Ⓑ Ⓒ Ⓓ Ⓔ	7 Ⓐ Ⓑ Ⓒ Ⓓ Ⓔ	10 Ⓐ Ⓑ Ⓒ Ⓓ Ⓔ
2 Ⓐ Ⓑ Ⓒ Ⓓ Ⓔ	5 Ⓐ Ⓑ Ⓒ Ⓓ Ⓔ	8 Ⓐ Ⓑ Ⓒ Ⓓ Ⓔ	11 Ⓐ Ⓑ Ⓒ Ⓓ Ⓔ
3 Ⓐ Ⓑ Ⓒ Ⓓ Ⓔ	6 Ⓐ Ⓑ Ⓒ Ⓓ Ⓔ	9 Ⓐ Ⓑ Ⓒ Ⓓ Ⓔ	12 Ⓐ Ⓑ Ⓒ Ⓓ Ⓔ

Your score for part D will be based on the number of questions that you answer correctly. Therefore, if you are not sure of an answer, it will be to your advantage to guess. Part D will take about 25 minutes.

<u>Instructions to be read</u> (the words in parentheses should not be read aloud).

You are to follow the instructions that I shall read to you. I cannot repeat them.

Look at the samples. Sample 1 has a number and a line beside it. On the line write an A. (Pause 2 seconds.) Now on the Sample Answer Sheet, find number 5 (pause 2 seconds) and darken the space for the letter you just wrote on the line. (Pause 2 seconds.)

Look at Sample 2. (Pause slightly.) Draw a line under the third number. (Pause 2 seconds.) Now look on the Sample Answer Sheet, find the number under which you just drew a line and darken space B as in baker for that number. (Pause 5 seconds.)

Look at Sample 3. (Pause slightly.) Draw a line under the third letter in the line. (Pause 2 seconds.) Now on your Sample Answer Sheet, find number 9 (pause 2 seconds) and darken the space for the letter under which you drew a line. (Pause 5 seconds.)

Look at the five circles in Sample 4. (Pause slightly.) Each circle has a number and a line in it. write D as in dog on the blank in the last circle. (Pause 2 seconds.) Now on the Sample Answer Sheet, darken the space for the number-letter combination that is in the circle you just wrote in. (Pause 5 seconds.)

Look at Sample 5. (Pause slightly.) There are two circles and two boxes of different sizes with numbers in them. (Pause slightly.) If 4 is more than 2 and if 5 is less than 3, write A in the smaller circle. (Pause slightly.) Otherwise write C in the larger box. (Pause 2 seconds.) Now on the Sample Answer Sheet, darken the space for the number-letter combination in the circle or box in which you just wrote. (Pause 5 seconds.)

Now look at the Sample Answer Sheet. (Pause slightly.) You should have darkened spaces 4B, 5A, 9A, 10D, and 12C on the Sample Answer Sheet.

KEEP THESE INSTRUCTIONS FOR FUTURE REFERENCE. YOUR PARTICIPATION AND COOPERATION IN THIS POSTAL EXAM IS APPRECIATED.

The following sections offer successful test taking strategies and study tips by Norman Hall plus additional practice exams for the 470 Battery Test's four key testing areas. Mr. Hall has scored 100% on the United States Postal Exam four times and he provides in-depth study tips for this exam's key testing areas.

ADDRESS CROSS COMPARISON

Every stage of the mail sorting process must be done accurately and efficiently. If either a Postal Clerk or Carrier misreads an address, mail is misdirected or delayed. Therefore, Postal personnel must be able to tell whether two addresses are the same or if they represent two entirely different destinations. Sometimes, differences between addresses are subtle—small differences in spelling, for example, or transposed numerals. An applicant must be able to quickly scan the address lists in this section and make an accurate determination to this effect.

At first glance, most people view this exercise as perhaps the easiest section in the exam. However, there is only a limited amount of time allowed (6 minutes) to complete the ninety-five questions given. Therefore, it is important to spend as little time as possible on each question, and yet, be thorough enough to select the correct answer without guessing. In fact, because of the time constraints, examiners will point out at the beginning of this test that you are not expected to finish.

This section of the test provides ninety-five pairs of addresses. You need to determine if each pair of addresses is different or exactly alike. The answer sheet to this test will have two choices from which you may select. Darken answer **(A)** if the pair of addresses shown are exactly alike. Darken answer **(D)** if the addresses are different. The ten pairs of sample addresses that follow will lend a general understanding of how this test is constructed. Take no more than 30 seconds to complete the samples.

1.	40407 Hayworth Ave.	44007 Hayworth Ave.	Ⓐ	Ⓓ
2.	Chatowaga Blvd.	Chatowega Blvd S	Ⓐ	Ⓓ
3.	Phoenix, Arizona 80553	Phoenix, Arizona 80553	Ⓐ	Ⓓ
4.	New York, NY 05130	New Haven, CT 05130	Ⓐ	Ⓓ
5.	Newport, KY	Newport, KY	Ⓐ	Ⓓ
6.	498 W.12th Ave.	498 12th Ave. W.	Ⓐ	Ⓓ
7.	1156 Beaumont Cr.	1156 Beaumont Cr.	Ⓐ	Ⓓ
8.	Roanoke, VA 32075	Roanoke, VA 32075	Ⓐ	Ⓓ
9.	4200 3rd St. Apt 2400	2400 3rd ST. Apt 4200	Ⓐ	Ⓓ
10.	Reno, NV	Reno, NV	Ⓐ	Ⓓ

Only pairs number 3, 5, 7, 8, and 10 are exactly alike and should have the answer **(A)** darkened. Answer **(D)** would be darkened for the remaining pairs (1, 2, 4, 6, and 9). If you missed any of these samples, review the pairs and determine what was overlooked.

As you can see, subtle differences in either the numbers or the spelling can be unrecognizable at first glance. Most people, for one reason or another, can spot transposed numbers in either the Zip Code or the street address. However, applicants frequently overlook differences in addresses that sound the same. Pay particularly close attention to addresses of this nature before marking your answer sheet. Caution exercised here will pay off in terms of a higher test score.

You may have noticed too, that while working on the sample exercises a straightedge or ruler could have helped reduce confusion. Unfortunately, such aids are not allowed in the examination room. However, you are allowed two pencils, one of which can serve as a crude straightedge, if necessary.

One other helpful trick to reduce confusion while comparing a set of addresses is to place your index finger on one column of addresses and your little finger on the other column. As you proceed with each pair, move your fingers in unison down the page. This does essentially the same thing as a straight edge. Using this method makes it substantially easier to focus your attention on just the two addresses you are comparing. You also save precious time by not having to search for where you left off in order to mark your answer sheet.

One practice exercise is provided in this section. Additional practice exercises are included in *Norman Hall's Postal Exam Preparation Book* available toll free at 1-800/872-5627. Complete information about this book is included at the end of this chapter. To help you get an idea of how the actual exam is conducted, you should use a kitchen timer or have someone time you for the allotted six minutes as you work each exercise. This will protect you from the unnecessary distraction of timing yourself. When time is called, do not work any further on the exercise. If you continue, you will lose the true sense of what will be required of you on the actual exam.

A scale is provided at the end of each exercise to allow you to determine your standings. Simply count the number of correct answers you have made and then subtract those that were missed. As mentioned earlier, this is the one exercise in which applicants are penalized for wrong answers. Guessing answers for this part of the exam is not recommended.

ADDRESS CROSS COMPARISON/EXERCISE 1   **TIME: 6 MINUTES**

1.	Burien Ave.	Burein Avenue
2.	12137 Hartford Dr.	12317 Hartford Dr.
3.	Marguriete Pl.	Margurete Pl.
4.	4731 E. 19th St.	4731 E. 19th St.
5.	Truman W.	Trueman W.
6.	45-D Levenworth Ave.	45-D Levenworth Ave.
7.	Cottage Blvd.	Hut Blvd.
8.	753 Pinecone	753 Pinecone
9.	Ft. Worth, TX	Ft. Apache, AR
10.	Oakland, CA 94371	Oakland, CA 94371
11.	Deception Pass	Deseption Pass
12.	20-L Hogan Ln.	20-L Hogan Ln.
13.	4536 SW 103rd St.	4536 NW 103rd St.
14.	Hutchinson Blvd.	Hutchenson Blvd.
15.	30785 Elliot Bay Rd.	30785 Elliot Bay Rd.
16.	Sparks, NV	Sparks, NY
17.	Springfield, MO 97132	Springfield, MO 97132
18.	Coos Lane	Coos Ln.
19.	Evergreen, ND	Evergrein, MD
20.	Butt, MT 05317	Butte, MT 03517
21.	41-RT 3 Colo, IA	41-RT 3 Colo, IA
22.	Highland Pl.	Highland Place
23.	478 Beach Dr.	478 Beach Dr.
24.	22 Falcon W.	33 Falcon W.

25.	Anderson Heights	Andersin Heights
26.	Falcon Hills Rd.	Eagle Hills Rd.
27.	3249 Brice Pl.	3249 Brice Pl.
28.	42-A Savon DR.	42-D Savon Dr.
29.	Jamestown, NJ	Jameston, NJ
30.	Victoria, BC 090	Victoria, BC 090
31.	359119 Galloway Ln.	359119 Galloway Ln.
32.	Rome, Georgia 31152	Rome, Georgia 31152
33.	Phinney Place	Phiney Place
34.	Constantine Rd.	Constantine Rd.
35.	44-AB Wilkes Dr.	44-AB Wilikes Dr.
36.	Ft. Collins, Colo.	Ft. Collins, CO
37.	2780 ST. John Rd.	2780 ST. Johns Rd.
38.	Livingston Blvd.	Livingston Blvd.
39.	Bloomington, Ill 61653	Bloomington, Ill 61563
40.	4802-E Blaine	4802-W Blaine
41.	Dallas, TX 25109	Dallas, TX 25108
42.	3103 Porter Way	3103 Porter Way
43.	Snohomish, WA	Snohamish, VA
44.	2516 Johnson Pl.	2516 Johnston Pl.
45.	32-D Jensen Way	354 Jensen Way
46.	4012 Rolling Oaks Rd.	4012 Rolling Oaks Rd.
47.	3710 Harsten Blvd.	3710 Harsten Blvd.
48.	Ankorage, AL	Anchorage, AK
49.	Petersville, KY 45108	Petersville, KY 45108

50.	3845 Reid Dr.	3844 Reid Dr.
51.	401-A Westin Pl.	401-A Westin Pl.
52.	20121 Dakota Point	20211 Dakota Point
53.	Faunterloy Center	Founterloy Center
54.	4013 Brussels Dr.	4013 Brussels Dr.
55.	Stovington, Conn.	Stovers, CO 43212
56.	12 Ash Place	12 Ash Pl.
57.	9040 Country Ln.	9040 Country Ln.
58.	Marguriette Ave.	Marguriete Ave.
59.	7140 Constitution Dr.	140 Constitution Pl.
60.	30-R Bloomfield Apts.	30-R Bloomfield Apts.
61.	4099 Harbel Rd.	4099 Harbel Rd.
62.	W. Palm Beach, CA	Palm Beach, CA
63.	Phoenix, Ariz	Phoenix, AR 85021
64.	4037 Nipsic Pl.	4037 Nipsic Pl.
65.	1109 Tangerine Dr.	1109 Tangerine Dr.
66.	20A Abernathy Ct.	20A Abernathy Ct.
67.	Newberry, W. VA	Newberry, W. VA
68.	3401 E. 19th St.	3401 E. 20th St.
69.	1280 12th Ave.	1280 13th Ave.
70.	7800 Forest Ridge	7800 Forest Ridge
71.	Montgomery Pl.	Montgomery Pl.
72.	10 Pierce Grahm Cr.	10 Pierce Grahm Cr.
73.	New York, NY 11940	New York, NY 19140
74.	7780 Proxmire Rd.	8077 Proxmire Rd.

75.	1341 Ivy Terrace	1341 Ivy Terrace
76.	257 Rampert Dr.	275 Ramport Dr.
77.	Newport, WA 99510	Newport, PA 99510
78.	1144 60th St. SW	4411 60th St. NW
79.	117 Chespeke Ct.	117 Chesepeak Ct.
80.	Willow Way E.	Willow Way E.
81.	3030 Prairie Pl.	3030 Prairie Pl.
82.	1212 Seneca Point	2121 Seneca Court
83.	7999 Mercury Blvd.	7999 Mercury Blvd.
84.	Waterloo, IA 50578	Waterloo, IA 50758
85.	14818 1st Ave.	14818 2nd Ave.
86.	S. 120th Pl.	S. 120th Pl.
87.	South Port, KY 98451	South Port, WY 98950
88.	Twelve Oaks, MI	Twelve Oaks, MI
89.	4045 S. Duff St.	4045 N. Duff St.
90.	1391 Fremont Pkwy	1931 Preemont Pksy
91.	Terrington Park	Terrington Park
92.	Essex, MD	Essex, MD
93.	Covings, NM 53845	Sante Fe, NM
94.	Bessert Dr.	Bessert Dr.
95.	30921 W. Hamilton	93021 W. Hamilton

END OF TEST

ANSWER SHEET TO ADDRESS CROSS COMPARISON/EXERCISE 1

1. (A) (D)	33. (A) (D)	65. (A) (D)
2. (A) (D)	34. (A) (D)	66. (A) (D)
3. (A) (D)	35. (A) (D)	67. (A) (D)
4. (A) (D)	36. (A) (D)	68. (A) (D)
5. (A) (D)	37. (A) (D)	69. (A) (D)
6. (A) (D)	38. (A) (D)	70. (A) (D)
7. (A) (D)	39. (A) (D)	71. (A) (D)
8. (A) (D)	40. (A) (D)	72. (A) (D)
9. (A) (D)	41. (A) (D)	73. (A) (D)
10. (A) (D)	42. (A) (D)	74. (A) (D)
11. (A) (D)	43. (A) (D)	75. (A) (D)
12. (A) (D)	44. (A) (D)	76. (A) (D)
13. (A) (D)	45. (A) (D)	77. (A) (D)
14. (A) (D)	46. (A) (D)	78. (A) (D)
15. (A) (D)	47. (A) (D)	79. (A) (D)
16. (A) (D)	48. (A) (D)	80. (A) (D)
17. (A) (D)	49. (A) (D)	81. (A) (D)
18. (A) (D)	50. (A) (D)	82. (A) (D)
19. (A) (D)	51. (A) (D)	83. (A) (D)
20. (A) (D)	52. (A) (D)	84. (A) (D)
21. (A) (D)	53. (A) (D)	85. (A) (D)
22. (A) (D)	54. (A) (D)	86. (A) (D)
23. (A) (D)	55. (A) (D)	87. (A) (D)
24. (A) (D)	56. (A) (D)	88. (A) (D)
25. (A) (D)	57. (A) (D)	89. (A) (D)
26. (A) (D)	58. (A) (D)	90. (A) (D)
27. (A) (D)	59. (A) (D)	91. (A) (D)
28. (A) (D)	60. (A) (D)	92. (A) (D)
29. (A) (D)	61. (A) (D)	93. (A) (D)
30. (A) (D)	62. (A) (D)	94. (A) (D)
31. (A) (D)	63. (A) (D)	95. (A) (D)
32. (A) (D)	64. (A) (D)	

ADDRESS CROSS COMPARISON/EXERCISE 1 ANSWERS

1.	D	33.	D	65.	A
2.	D	34.	A	66.	A
3.	D	35.	D	67.	A
4.	A	36.	D	68.	D
5.	D	37.	D	69.	D
6.	A	38.	A	70.	A
7.	D	39.	D	71.	A
8.	A	40.	D	72.	A
9.	D	41.	D	73.	D
10.	A	42.	A	74.	D
11.	D	43.	D	75.	A
12.	A	44.	D	76.	D
13.	D	45.	D	77.	D
14.	D	46.	A	78.	D
15.	A	47.	A	79.	D
16.	D	48.	D	80.	A
17.	A	49.	A	81.	A
18.	D	50.	D	82.	D
19.	D	51.	A	83.	A
20.	D	52.	D	84.	D
21.	A	53.	D	85.	D
22.	D	54.	A	86.	A
23.	A	55.	D	87.	D
24.	D	56.	D	88.	A
25.	D	57.	A	89.	D
26.	D	58.	D	90.	D
27.	A	59.	D	91.	A
28.	D	60.	A	92.	A
29.	D	61.	A	93.	D
30.	A	62.	D	94.	A
31.	A	63.	D	95.	D
32.	A	64.	A		

If you scored:

90 or more correct, you have an excellent score.
85-89 correct, you have a good score.
84 or fewer correct, you should practice more.

MEMORY

The second portion of this test involves memorization. Most postal employees are required to memorize city-wide route schematics in order to become proficient at sorting mail. Depending on the size of city in question, those schemes can become quite involved. If an employee cannot memorize what is required, he or she will have little chance of retaining a job beyond probation. This is no doubt a test section that many people struggle with. Doing well on this section should make the difference between excelling and settling for average. This is not meant to minimize the importance of doing well on the rest of the test. However, the other three sections of this test are fairly straight forward and most people will do fairly well on them, even if their preparation for this exam is minimal. Assuming that you do not possess a photographic memory, the memory system described in this book is designed to help you. This system of memory is easy to learn. Over 100,000 people who have purchased *Norman Hall's Postal Exam Preparation Book* have successfully employed this technique on their exams.

On the exam you will be given a key such as the one provided below that will contain twenty-five addresses in five categories (A through E). Ten addresses are plain street names while the remainder are numerical street addresses.

A	B	C	D	E
1200-1299 Brewster	6700-6799 Brewster	6900-6999 Brewster	2100-2199 Brewster	1300-1399 Brewster
Hoover Ct.	Highland St.	Beaver Ave.	Lamplight Ct.	Bellvue St.
1400-1499 Lakemont	2700-2799 Lakemont	3100-3199 Lakemont	4200-4299 Lakemont	0900-0999 Lakemont
Sycamore St.	Aspen Dr.	Johnson Ave.	Time Square	Harbor View
9200-9299 Terrace	5800-5899 Terrace	1800-1899 Terrace	8700-8799 Terrace	4300-4399 Terrace

You will be given 11 minutes to study this key at which point further reference is not permitted. You then have five minutes to answer as many of the eighty-eight questions pertaining to the key as possible.

Even if you have marginal memory skills, the techniques discussed here (imagery and association) will help you improve in this area. The technique requires you to form images in your mind related to the items to be memorized. Each of these images is then linked together in a specific order by means of association. It may sound complicated, but learning to stretch the boundaries of your imagination can be enjoyable.

A. NAMES

Street names will be among the items that need to be committed to memory for the exam. Use the following street names as examples:

Jorganson Street
Phillips Avenue
Tremont
Tricia
Edgewater Boulevard
Bloomington

Many people approach this exercise by rote memorization, or in other words, drilling the street names into their head by sheer repetition. Not only is this a boring way to memorize, but this method of recall lasts only a short time. On the other hand, imagery and association techniques can be fun and your ability to recall can be substantially extended.

Now, look at those same street names again and see what key word derivatives have been used and what images we can associate with them.
For example:

> Jorganson Street—Jogger
> Phillips Avenue—Phillips screwdriver
> Tremont—Tree
> Tricia—Tricycle
> Edgewater—Edge
> Bloomington—Blossoms

Carry the process one step further and place those key word derivatives in a bizarre context, story or situation. Using this process, we have developed the following story:

> A JOGGER with his pockets completely stuffed with PHILLIPS SCREWDRIVERS wasn't paying attention and ran into a giant TREE. After dusting himself off, he jumped on a child's TRICYCLE and pedaled it to the EDGE of a pool filled with flower BLOSSOMS.

Sounds ridiculous, doesn't it? However, because of its strong images, you will not easily forget this kind of story.

Another advantage of the imagery technique is that you can remember items in their respective order by simply reviewing where they fit in relation to the other items in the story.

Look at each of the street names below and develop a story using imagery. There are no right or wrong key word derivatives. What is important is that the images conjure up a clear picture in your mind and then interlink.

Work on each of these columns separately:

Bedford Ave.	Apple Dr.	Anderson Blvd.	Bayberry Rd.
Wellington	Constantine Way	Cannon Ave.	Hickory Ridge
Walker St.	Bristol	Foxtail Run	Ebony Ln.
Penny Ln.	Echo Ave.	Arsenal Way	Ester Ct.
Ridgemont Dr	Darrington	Jacobson St.	Steinbald Ln.
Bowmont	Smalley St.	Prince Williams	Georgia St.

Once you have finished this exercise, cover the street names and see if you can remember all 24 items. If your four stories are bizarre enough, you can have this entire list committed to long-term memory in a short time.

B. NUMBERS

Numbers are another problem in memory recall. For most people, numbers are difficult to memorize because they are intangible. To rectify this problem, numbers can be transposed into letters so that words can be formed and associated accordingly. Below is the format for transposition. Remember this format as if it were your Social Security number because on the exam you will draw from it regularly.

0	1	2	3	4	5	6	7	8	9
G or V	B or D	C or K	F or P	M	N	R	S	T	L

All other letters can be incorporated into words without any significance. For instance, let's say you are given the number 10603328157. Memorizing this number so well that you can recall it after any length of time could be very difficult. However, by using this memory system, you could use the number to spell out a variety of memorable things. Here is your chance to use your creativity!

After you have had the chance to figure out what words can code such a number, one problem becomes apparent: The more numbers you try to cram into one word, the harder it is to find a compatible word in the English vocabulary. To simplify matters, there are two alternative ways to form words. The first method is to take two numbers at a time, form a word and associate it with the next word. Dealing with the same number (10603328157) DOG could be derived from the number 10, RUG from 60, PIPE from 33, CAT from 28, BONE from 15, and S from 7. There are many ways you could imagine and link these words. One possibility would be a DOG lying on a RUG and smoking a PIPE while a CAT prances by carrying a BONE shaped like an S. This is just one way to memorize this long number. Other words and stories could work just as well.

The second alternative, which offers greater flexibility, is using words of any length but making only the first two significant letters of the word applicable to your story. For example, the word DIG/GING could represent 10 in the number 10603328157.

RAV/EN = RUG/BY = REV/OLVER = 60
POP/ULATION = PUP/PY = PEP/PER = 33
CAT/ERPILLAR = CAT/TLE = COT/TON = 28
BIN/OCULAR = BEAN/S = DIN/NER = 15

By doing this, you have a larger number of words at your disposal to put into stories. With a little originality, it can be fun to see what you can imagine for any number given.

Below are exercises to help you apply this system. The first group of numbers is meant to be used as a transposition exercise. See how many different words you can use to represent each number. The second series is for practice with transposition and story fabrication. This technique may seem difficult at first, but with practice, you will enhance your memory capabilities.

I.			
44	63	86	40
53	97	93	32
61	10	48	26
13	3	60	91
12	57	35	99
8	52	27	16
41	11	21	68

II.   1 7 5 4 7 3 2 1 1 5 8 1 0   6 3 2 1 1 3 4 7 8 9 0
       6 9 8 0 4 2 1 5 6 9 4 9 7   1 4 5 3 2 2 1 7 5 3 2 8
       1 4 7 2 9 9 4 4 7 1 0   9 1 7 4 0 3 2 1 8 9 7 7
       8 3 2 1 3 5 5 5 7 2 1 1 9   6 3 8 1 4 6 1 1 9 9 0 0
       4 8 8 7 7 0 5 0 9 4 5 3   4 3 3 3 5 1 8 9 6 4 8 7
       1 5 3 0 1 9 7 8 6 5 3 2 1   7 6 5 3 2 1 0 4 6 9 9 1

Now that you have a basic grasp of how to remember street names and numbers more easily, let's take a typical test sample and break it down into the order in which the material should be memorized.

A	B	C	D	E
1200-1299 Brewster	6700-6799 Brewster	6900-6999 Brewster	2100-2199 Brewster	1300-1399 Brewster
Hoover Ct.	Highland St.	Beaver Ave.	Lamplight Ct.	Bellvue St.
1400-1499 Lakemont	2700-2799 Lakemont	3100-3199 Lakemont	4200-4299 Lakemont	0900-0999 Lakemont
Sycamore St.	Aspen Dr.	Johnson Ave.	Time Square	Harbor View
9200-9299 Terrace	5800-5899 Terrace	1800-1899 Terrace	8700-8799 Terrace	4300-4399 Terrace

What should become immediately apparent by looking at the key is the fact that all numerical addresses are redundant with respect to street name and all but the first two numbers in each address shown are redundant as well. A lot of time and effort can be saved by looking at the key in the manner shown below.

A	B	C	D	E
BREWSTER - 12	67	69	21	13
Hoover Ct.	Highland St.	Beaver Ave.	Lamplight Ct.	Bellvue St.
LAKEMONT - 14	27	31	42	09
Sycamore St.	Aspen Dr.	Johnson Ave.	Time Square	Harbor View
TERRACE - 92	58	18	87	43

Now, each line of information needs to be set up in story format so that recall references can be easily made. As an example, let's use the sequence of numbers that represents Brewster on the exam.

A	B	C	D	E
12	67	69	21	13

There are virtually thousands of different words that can be transposed from these numbers, but for this particular illustration, we'll use the words BUCKET, ROSES, ROLLING, KID and DIP. Imagine, if you will, a BUC/KET (fashioned from a huge beer can) full of ROS/ES ROL/LING down a hillside knocks over a KID trying to balance a 30-DIP ice cream cone. This is a strange story, but the underlying principle is quite effective. Not only can you reference the street name (i.e., beer represents BREW or BREWSTER) but, as long as the story's chronological order remains intact, you can easily determine the category (i.e., A through E) that each number belongs under.

For example, let's say on the test you were asked what category 1300-1399 Brewster belongs to? (Look at it as the number 13.) Referring back to the BREW-BUCKET story, the number 13 represents the word DIP. Since DIP was the last image in the story, we would know that it belongs in category E and the answer E should be marked accordingly on our answer sheet.

As another example, let's say you were asked in what category 6700-6799 Brewster belongs. Since 67 was transposed into the word ROS/ES in the BEER-BUCKET story, and it was the second image in our story, answer B would be the correct choice.

Now let's examine the next line of street names and see what kind of bizarre story can be concocted.

A	B	C	D	E
Hoover Ct.	Highland St.	Beaver Ave.	Lamplight Ct.	Bellvue St.

How about a HOOVER vacuum cleaner that has arms, both of which are waving to say HI to a BEAVER standing beneath a street LAMP with a huge BELL for a tail? Quiz yourself. At what point in the story did the beaver stand beneath the street lamp (i.e., Lamplight Ct.)? It was the fourth image in the story. Had this been an actual exam question, category D would have been marked as the answer.

As a final example to this system of memory, let's look at the third line of information in the key and work up another story format.

A	B	C	D	E
14	27	31	42	09

How about the Lakemont DAM which instead of retaining water, retains Hershey KIS/SES. At the base of the DAM was a PUD/DLE of melted chocolate that had oozed forth from a crack in the DAM. Standing in the middle of the PUDDLE was a MEC/HANIC frantically attempting to stop the leak by stuffing his GL/OVES into the crack.

At this point, you should be getting a pretty good idea of how this concept works. Transposition of numbers to letters and then back again may seem a little difficult at first. However, the more you practice at using this system, the easier it will become.

During the actual exam, you will be given a 3 minute pretest with a *sample* key and a short sample answer sheet. Examiners almost always fail to tell you that the sample key is the same key used on the rest of the exam. In other words, you will actually be provided an extra 3 minutes to study the key.
Don't bother marking the sample answer sheets in the pretest: Focus all of your attention on making up your five story lines. If you have a solid feel for your stories, you will be able to answer questions accurately and without hesitation. At the close of the first 3 minutes, the examiner will instruct you to turn the page, where the answer key is provided by itself. You are then given 3 minutes to work on your stories. After this time period is up, you will again be instructed to flip another page where the same key and a full length practice question and answer sheet will be provided. You are allotted three more minutes to either study the key or work practice exercises. Again, it is suggested that you completely ignore the practice exercises and continue working on your stories. If you feel compelled to check yourself, limit answering questions to only a few.

After the 3 minutes are up, you will be instructed to turn to the next page in your booklet, which has practice questions and an answer sheet minus the key. You have 3 minutes to work as many practice questions as you feel comfortable doing. Here again, it is strongly recommended that you simply ignore this section and continue working the stories in your mind. Close your eyes if you want to alleviate any visual distractions. If you still feel it necessary to work the practice questions, keep it to an absolute minimum. When time is up, you will be instructed to turn to the next page in the booklet which has only the key. You will be given 5 more minutes to study. At this point, you should know your five stories forward and backward. By the time the actual exam has begun, you should be able to answer all eighty-eight questions in well under 5 minutes.

A couple of words of caution are needed here. If, by chance, you somehow have a mental block to an occasional question, waste no time and skip over it. Be absolutely certain that you also skip over the corresponding answer blank. You can come back to the question later and make an educated guess, if necessary.

The second point is that the new postal exams will intentionally try to confuse you by utilizing duplicate numbers. In other words, there may be three or four 2400-2499 street addresses. Rest assured that if you keep all of your various stories in their respective orders, duplicate numbers on an exam will matter very little. The practice exams toward the back of this study guide are all comparable to what will be seen on the actual test. The practice exams in this chapter are somewhat easier due to a minimum of duplicate numbers. This will allow you to work up to proficiency before attempting the more challenging exercises.

Before you begin any of these exercises, get yourself a timer with an alarm. Set it for the allotted time for each part of the exercise. This will spare you from losing time watching the clock. If you finish before the exam is finished, you can always check your answers once over for accuracy as well as neatness. Erase any miscellaneous marks on the answer sheet because as mentioned earlier, it can impact your test score at the time of grading. A scale is provided at the end of each exercise to allow you to determine your standings.

MEMORIZATION/EXERCISE 1   STEP 2 TIME: 3 MINUTES
                                    STEP 3 TIME: 3 MINUTES (cover key)

A	B	C	D	E
7700-7799 Rose Cactus Ln. 6100-6199 Clem Beechnut Dr. 2300-2399 King	6200-6299 Rose Maleroy Rd. 4900-4999 Clem Carver Blvd. 2700-2799 King	7100-7199 Rose Phillips Dr. 8500-8599 Clem Washington Ave. 1900-1999 King	5400-5499 Rose Falcon Ridge 6000-6099 Clem Scotts Bluff 3000-3099 King	6600-6699 Rose Franklin 5900-5999 Clem Keyport St. 2000-2099 King

1. Maleroy Rd.
2. Phillips Dr.
3. 7700-7799 Rose
4. 4900-4999 Clem
5. Falcon Ridge
6. 1900-1999 King
7. Cactus Ln.
8. 6200-6299 Rose
9. Washington Ave.
10. 2300-2399 King
11. Beechnut Dr.
12. 8500-8599 Clem
13. 5400-5499 Rose
14. Franklin
15. 2000-2099 King
16. 6000-6099 Clem
17. Carver Blvd.
18. Keyport St.
19. 6600-6699 Rose
20. Scotts Bluff
21. 5400-5499 Rose
22. 6100-6199 Clem
23. Cactus Ln.
24. Washington Ave.
25. Franklin
26. 7700-7799 Rose
27. Maleroy Rd.
28. 5900-5999 Clem
29. Falcon Ridge
30. 1900-1999 King

31. Beechnut Dr.
32. 6000-6099 Clem
33. 2000-2099 King
34. 7100-7199 Rose
35. Phillips Dr.
36. 7700-7799 Rose
37. Scotts Bluff
38. 8500-8599 Clem
39. 2000-2099 King
40. Carver Blvd.
41. Falcon Ridge
42. Keyport St.
43. 1900-1999 King
44. Beechnut Dr.
45. 6000-6099 Clem
46. 2000-2099 King
47. Franklin
48. 6100-6199 Clem
49. 2700-2799 King
50. Cactus Ln.
51. Maleroy Rd.
52. 7100-7199 Rose
53. 3000-3099 King
54. Carver Blvd.
55. 6200-6299 Rose
56. 5900-5999 Clem
57. Scotts Bluff
58. 2300-2399 King
59. 6600-6699 Rose
60. Washington Ave.

61. 4900-4999 Clem
62. Keyport St.
63. 3000-3099 King
64. 7700-7799 Rose
65. Cactus Ln.
66. Phillips Dr.
67. 2700-2799 King
68. 6100-6199 Clem
69. 7100-7199 Rose
70. 6000-6099 Clem
71. Maleroy Rd.
72. 3000-3099 King
73. 8500-8599 Clem
74. Scotts Bluff
75. 5400-5499 Rose
76. 5900-5999 Clem
77. Keyport St.
78. Franklin
79. 6600-6699 Rose
80. Scotts Bluff
81. Phillips Dr.
82. 2300-2399 King
83. Falcon Ridge
84. 4900-4999 Clem
85. 6200-6299 Rose
86. Beechnut Dr.
87. Washington Ave.
88. Carver Blvd.

PRACTICE ANSWER SHEET TO MEMORIZATION/EXERCISE 1

1. Ⓐ Ⓑ Ⓒ Ⓓ Ⓔ	31. Ⓐ Ⓑ Ⓒ Ⓓ Ⓔ	61. Ⓐ Ⓑ Ⓒ Ⓓ Ⓔ
2. Ⓐ Ⓑ Ⓒ Ⓓ Ⓔ	32. Ⓐ Ⓑ Ⓒ Ⓓ Ⓔ	62. Ⓐ Ⓑ Ⓒ Ⓓ Ⓔ
3. Ⓐ Ⓑ Ⓒ Ⓓ Ⓔ	33. Ⓐ Ⓑ Ⓒ Ⓓ Ⓔ	63. Ⓐ Ⓑ Ⓒ Ⓓ Ⓔ
4. Ⓐ Ⓑ Ⓒ Ⓓ Ⓔ	34. Ⓐ Ⓑ Ⓒ Ⓓ Ⓔ	64. Ⓐ Ⓑ Ⓒ Ⓓ Ⓔ
5. Ⓐ Ⓑ Ⓒ Ⓓ Ⓔ	35. Ⓐ Ⓑ Ⓒ Ⓓ Ⓔ	65. Ⓐ Ⓑ Ⓒ Ⓓ Ⓔ
6. Ⓐ Ⓑ Ⓒ Ⓓ Ⓔ	36. Ⓐ Ⓑ Ⓒ Ⓓ Ⓔ	66. Ⓐ Ⓑ Ⓒ Ⓓ Ⓔ
7. Ⓐ Ⓑ Ⓒ Ⓓ Ⓔ	37. Ⓐ Ⓑ Ⓒ Ⓓ Ⓔ	67. Ⓐ Ⓑ Ⓒ Ⓓ Ⓔ
8. Ⓐ Ⓑ Ⓒ Ⓓ Ⓔ	38. Ⓐ Ⓑ Ⓒ Ⓓ Ⓔ	68. Ⓐ Ⓑ Ⓒ Ⓓ Ⓔ
9. Ⓐ Ⓑ Ⓒ Ⓓ Ⓔ	39. Ⓐ Ⓑ Ⓒ Ⓓ Ⓔ	69. Ⓐ Ⓑ Ⓒ Ⓓ Ⓔ
10. Ⓐ Ⓑ Ⓒ Ⓓ Ⓔ	40. Ⓐ Ⓑ Ⓒ Ⓓ Ⓔ	70. Ⓐ Ⓑ Ⓒ Ⓓ Ⓔ
11. Ⓐ Ⓑ Ⓒ Ⓓ Ⓔ	41. Ⓐ Ⓑ Ⓒ Ⓓ Ⓔ	71. Ⓐ Ⓑ Ⓒ Ⓓ Ⓔ
12. Ⓐ Ⓑ Ⓒ Ⓓ Ⓔ	42. Ⓐ Ⓑ Ⓒ Ⓓ Ⓔ	72. Ⓐ Ⓑ Ⓒ Ⓓ Ⓔ
13. Ⓐ Ⓑ Ⓒ Ⓓ Ⓔ	43. Ⓐ Ⓑ Ⓒ Ⓓ Ⓔ	73. Ⓐ Ⓑ Ⓒ Ⓓ Ⓔ
14. Ⓐ Ⓑ Ⓒ Ⓓ Ⓔ	44. Ⓐ Ⓑ Ⓒ Ⓓ Ⓔ	74. Ⓐ Ⓑ Ⓒ Ⓓ Ⓔ
15. Ⓐ Ⓑ Ⓒ Ⓓ Ⓔ	45. Ⓐ Ⓑ Ⓒ Ⓓ Ⓔ	75. Ⓐ Ⓑ Ⓒ Ⓓ Ⓔ
16. Ⓐ Ⓑ Ⓒ Ⓓ Ⓔ	46. Ⓐ Ⓑ Ⓒ Ⓓ Ⓔ	76. Ⓐ Ⓑ Ⓒ Ⓓ Ⓔ
17. Ⓐ Ⓑ Ⓒ Ⓓ Ⓔ	47. Ⓐ Ⓑ Ⓒ Ⓓ Ⓔ	77. Ⓐ Ⓑ Ⓒ Ⓓ Ⓔ
18. Ⓐ Ⓑ Ⓒ Ⓓ Ⓔ	48. Ⓐ Ⓑ Ⓒ Ⓓ Ⓔ	78. Ⓐ Ⓑ Ⓒ Ⓓ Ⓔ
19. Ⓐ Ⓑ Ⓒ Ⓓ Ⓔ	49. Ⓐ Ⓑ Ⓒ Ⓓ Ⓔ	79. Ⓐ Ⓑ Ⓒ Ⓓ Ⓔ
20. Ⓐ Ⓑ Ⓒ Ⓓ Ⓔ	50. Ⓐ Ⓑ Ⓒ Ⓓ Ⓔ	80. Ⓐ Ⓑ Ⓒ Ⓓ Ⓔ
21. Ⓐ Ⓑ Ⓒ Ⓓ Ⓔ	51. Ⓐ Ⓑ Ⓒ Ⓓ Ⓔ	81. Ⓐ Ⓑ Ⓒ Ⓓ Ⓔ
22. Ⓐ Ⓑ Ⓒ Ⓓ Ⓔ	52. Ⓐ Ⓑ Ⓒ Ⓓ Ⓔ	82. Ⓐ Ⓑ Ⓒ Ⓓ Ⓔ
23. Ⓐ Ⓑ Ⓒ Ⓓ Ⓔ	53. Ⓐ Ⓑ Ⓒ Ⓓ Ⓔ	83. Ⓐ Ⓑ Ⓒ Ⓓ Ⓔ
24. Ⓐ Ⓑ Ⓒ Ⓓ Ⓔ	54. Ⓐ Ⓑ Ⓒ Ⓓ Ⓔ	84. Ⓐ Ⓑ Ⓒ Ⓓ Ⓔ
25. Ⓐ Ⓑ Ⓒ Ⓓ Ⓔ	55. Ⓐ Ⓑ Ⓒ Ⓓ Ⓔ	85. Ⓐ Ⓑ Ⓒ Ⓓ Ⓔ
26. Ⓐ Ⓑ Ⓒ Ⓓ Ⓔ	56. Ⓐ Ⓑ Ⓒ Ⓓ Ⓔ	86. Ⓐ Ⓑ Ⓒ Ⓓ Ⓔ
27. Ⓐ Ⓑ Ⓒ Ⓓ Ⓔ	57. Ⓐ Ⓑ Ⓒ Ⓓ Ⓔ	87. Ⓐ Ⓑ Ⓒ Ⓓ Ⓔ
28. Ⓐ Ⓑ Ⓒ Ⓓ Ⓔ	58. Ⓐ Ⓑ Ⓒ Ⓓ Ⓔ	88. Ⓐ Ⓑ Ⓒ Ⓓ Ⓔ
29. Ⓐ Ⓑ Ⓒ Ⓓ Ⓔ	59. Ⓐ Ⓑ Ⓒ Ⓓ Ⓔ	
30. Ⓐ Ⓑ Ⓒ Ⓓ Ⓔ	60. Ⓐ Ⓑ Ⓒ Ⓓ Ⓔ	

ANSWERS TO PRACTICE MEMORIZATION/EXERCISE 2

1.	B	31.	A	61.	B
2.	C	32.	D	62.	E
3.	B	33.	E	63.	D
4.	B	34.	C	64.	A
5.	D	35.	C	65.	A
6.	C	36.	A	66.	C
7.	A	37.	D	67.	B
8.	B	38.	C	68.	A
9.	C	39.	E	69.	C
10.	A	40.	B	70.	D
11.	A	41.	D	71.	B
12.	C	42.	E	72.	D
13.	D	43.	C	73.	C
14.	E	44.	A	74.	D
15.	E	45.	D	75.	D
16.	D	46.	E	76.	E
17.	B	47.	E	77.	E
18.	E	48.	A	78.	E
19.	E	49.	B	79.	E
20.	D	50.	A	80.	D
21.	D	51.	B	81.	C
22.	A	52.	C	82.	A
23.	A	53.	D	83.	D
24.	C	54.	B	84.	B
25.	E	55.	B	85.	B
26.	A	56.	E	86.	A
27.	B	57.	D	87.	C
28.	E	58.	A	88.	B
29.	D	59.	E		
30.	C	60.	C		

If you scored:

84 or more correct, you have an excellent score.

78-83 correct, you have a good score.

77 or fewer correct, you should practice more.

NUMBER SERIES

Number series tests are used to determine your skill at discerning number patterns. For clerks, this has direct relevance to code recognition as information is typed into a special purpose keyboard to sort either letters or flats.

Number series tests are not difficult if you can quickly establish the pattern in the numbers listed. For example, look at the question below:

2	4	6	8	10	12	?	?

As you can see, there is an addition constant of +2 between each number. Therefore, the next two numbers in the sequence should be 14 and 16.

2   4   6   8   10   12   <u>14</u>   <u>16</u>
  +2   +2   +2   +2   +2   +2   +2

Subtraction and multiplication number series are much the same as the prior example. An example of each is given below. Try to determine what the last two numbers are in each of the number sequences.

23	20	17	14	11	8	?	?
1	3	9	27	81	?	?	

The first example shown is a subtraction number series. If you determined that there was a subtraction constant of -3 between numbers, you were correct. So the last two numbers in the first sequence should be 5 and 2.

23   20   17   14   11   8   <u>5</u>   <u>2</u>
  -3   -3   -3   -3   -3   -3   -3

The second example represents a multiplication number series. If you determined that there was a multiplication constant of 3 between the numbers in the sequence, you were right again. Therefore, the last two numbers in this series are 243 and 729.

1   3   9   27   81   <u>243</u>   <u>729</u>
  x3   x3   x3   x3   x3   x3

The last kind of number series that will appear on the exam is an alternating number series. This kind of number sequence is a little more involved and consequently takes extra time to solve. The series involves alternating uses of addition and/or subtraction to create a pattern. A pattern may not be immediately evident but with a little diligence, it should become apparent. Two examples are given below. Try to determine what the last two numbers are in each sequence.

0	12	10	3	6	8	6	9	?	?
0	16	17	4	18	19	8	20	?	?

If you guessed 12 and 4, and 21 and 12, respectively, you are right. You can see how these patterns can become a bit more complicated.

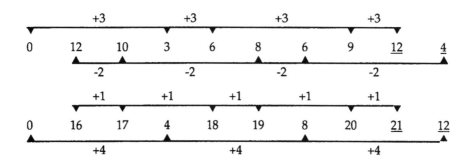

If a pattern in an alternating number series is not discernable, there is a method you can use to help. The first step involves determining the differences between each successive number in sequence. For example:

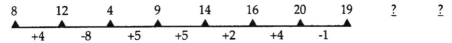

Note that there are two +4 and two +5 constants. The next step is to check these differences to see if, indeed, some kind of pattern can be established. Let's start with the +4 constant. The numbers involved are 8, 12, 16, and 20. What should become evident is that this series of four numbers represents an addition number series pattern. To better clarify the pattern, if you diagram it as shown below, it should alleviate some confusion

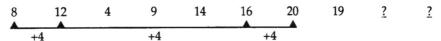

If there were one more answer blank, the number 24 would be the right answer. However, the addition number series pattern already established does not encompass the two answer blanks. Now, look at the remaining numbers: 4, 9, 14, and 19. Do you see a pattern emerge there? If you determined the series is another addition number series with +5 as a constant, you are correct.

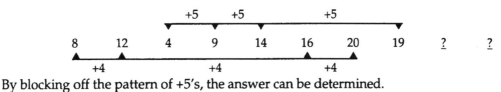

By blocking off the pattern of +5's, the answer can be determined.

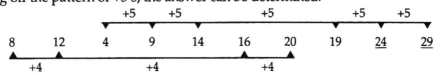

Since you are allotted only 20 minutes on the actual exam to complete twenty-four number series questions, time is of the essence. If an answer to an alternating number series question is not apparent within the scope of 30 seconds, skip the question and go on to the next one. If you have any time remaining after you have completed the test questions that you know, return to those questions you skipped, and try to solve them. If you still have trouble determining the answer, systematically plug in each of the options provided and by the process of elimination you can determine the correct answer. This is somewhat time consuming, but it is better than just guessing. Whatever the case, don't leave any answers blank. Guess only as a last resort.

For your convenience, the first number series exercise questions have been segregated into the four number series groups (i.e., addition, subtraction, multiplication, and alternating). This should clue you in as to what kind of pattern to be searching for. However, you will not be given the same convenience on number series exercises 2 and 3. On those exams, the series will be relatively well mixed for variety. The answers will provide the correct number combinations and establish the set pattern involved. Thus, you can see how the answer to the question was determined. A scale has been provided for determination of your performance on each exam.

NUMBER SERIES/EXERCISE 1

Addition Number Series

1.   7   10   13   16   19   22   ___   ___

    A.   25, 28   C.   23, 27   E.   27, 30
    B.   23, 24   D.   25, 26

2.   24   30   36   42   48   54   ___   ___

    A.   56, 66   C.   60, 56   E.   60, 66
    B.   58, 64   D.   58, 66

3.   18   27   36   45   54   63   ___   ___

    A.   70, 81   C.   72, 81   E.   72, 83
    B.   71, 81   D.   71, 82

4.   4   20   36   52   68   84   ___   ___

    A.   96, 114   C.   100, 110   E.   110, 116
    B.   98, 110   D.   100, 116

5.   13   15   17   19   21   23   ___   ___

    A.   24, 25   C.   25, 28   E.   26, 28
    B.   27, 28   D.   25, 27

6.   1   18   35   52   69   86   ___   ___

    A.   105, 122   C.   101, 119   E.   105, 120
    B.   103, 120   D.   103, 102

Subtraction Number Series

7.   14   12   10   8   6   4   ___   ___

    A.   2, 0   C.   2, 2   E.   0, 0
    B.   4, 2   D.   0, 2

8.   174   150   126   102   78   54   ___   ___

    A.   40, 6   C.   30, 6   E.   28, 2
    B.   30, 4   D.   28, 4

9.   45   40   35   30   25   20   ___   ___

    A.   10, 5   C.   10, 15   E.   15, 10
    B.   15, 5   D.   5, 10

10.   81   72   63   54   45   36   ___   ___

    A.   18, 27   C.   17, 28   E.   27, 18
    B.   28, 17   D.   26, 18

11.   163   149   135   121   107   93   ___   ___

    A.   65, 79   C.   81, 67   E.   67, 81
    B.   79, 65   D.   79, 59

12.   1205   1088   971   854   737   620   ___   ___

    A.   386, 503   C.   503, 286   E.   500, 286
    B.   403, 386   D.   503, 386

Multiplication Number Series

13. 2   4   8   16   32   ___   ___

    A. 32, 64   C. 64, 128   E. 60, 128
    B. 64, 32   D. 60, 120

14. 4   20   100   500   2500   ___   ___

    A. 5000, 12,500   C. 62,500, 12,500   E. 12,000, 60,000
    B. 12,500, 62,500   D 18,500, 25,500

15. 3   9   27   81   243   ___   ___

    A. 729, 2187   C. 739, 2187   E. 723, 2187
    B. 715, 2180   D. 715, 2387

16. 1   7   49   343   ___   ___

    A. 2401, 16,807   C. 2401, 16,907   E. 4085, 17,250
    B. 2400, 16,000   D. 2400, 16,807

17. 6   12   24   48   96   ___   ___

    A. 182, 384   C. 192, 375   E. 192, 384
    B. 190, 380   D. 195, 380

18. 2   8   32   128   512   ___   ___

    A. 2408, 8192   C. 2348, 8792   E. 2040, 8029
    B. 2580, 8092   D. 2048, 8192

Alternating Number Series

19. 12   10   16   17   8   6   18   ___   ___

    A. 19, 2   C. 2, 20   E. 20, 3
    B. 4, 19   D. 19, 4

20. 7   11   3   8   13   15   19   18   ___   ___

    A. 25, 28   C. 23, 24   E. 22, 28
    B. 23, 28   D. 21, 23

21. 20   3   6   9   17   14   12   15   18   ___   ___

    A. 5, 8   C. 11, 8   E. 8, 11
    B. 7, 11   D. 12, 8

22. 30   20   25   28   30   35   26   40   ___   ___

    A. 45, 24   C. 47, 24   E. 41, 22
    B. 46, 25   D. 43, 25

23. 18   14   13   16   12   11   14   10   ___   ___

    A. 8, 10   C. 10, 9   E. 10, 8
    B. 9, 12   D. 12, 9

24. 36   42   35   28   45   21   14   7   ___   ___

    A. 54, 0   C. 43, 14   E. 48, 7
    B. 36, 7   D. 48, 0

ANSWER SHEET TO NUMBER SERIES/EXERCISE 1

1. Ⓐ Ⓑ Ⓒ Ⓓ Ⓔ
2. Ⓐ Ⓑ Ⓒ Ⓓ Ⓔ
3. Ⓐ Ⓑ Ⓒ Ⓓ Ⓔ
4. Ⓐ Ⓑ Ⓒ Ⓓ Ⓔ
5. Ⓐ Ⓑ Ⓒ Ⓓ Ⓔ
6. Ⓐ Ⓑ Ⓒ Ⓓ Ⓔ
7. Ⓐ Ⓑ Ⓒ Ⓓ Ⓔ
8. Ⓐ Ⓑ Ⓒ Ⓓ Ⓔ

9. Ⓐ Ⓑ Ⓒ Ⓓ Ⓔ
10. Ⓐ Ⓑ Ⓒ Ⓓ Ⓔ
11. Ⓐ Ⓑ Ⓒ Ⓓ Ⓔ
12. Ⓐ Ⓑ Ⓒ Ⓓ Ⓔ
13. Ⓐ Ⓑ Ⓒ Ⓓ Ⓔ
14. Ⓐ Ⓑ Ⓒ Ⓓ Ⓔ
15. Ⓐ Ⓑ Ⓒ Ⓓ Ⓔ
16. Ⓐ Ⓑ Ⓒ Ⓓ Ⓔ

17. Ⓐ Ⓑ Ⓒ Ⓓ Ⓔ
18. Ⓐ Ⓑ Ⓒ Ⓓ Ⓔ
19. Ⓐ Ⓑ Ⓒ Ⓓ Ⓔ
20. Ⓐ Ⓑ Ⓒ Ⓓ Ⓔ
21. Ⓐ Ⓑ Ⓒ Ⓓ Ⓔ
22. Ⓐ Ⓑ Ⓒ Ⓓ Ⓔ
23. Ⓐ Ⓑ Ⓒ Ⓓ Ⓔ
24. Ⓐ Ⓑ Ⓒ Ⓓ Ⓔ

ANSWER TO NUMBER SERIES/EXERCISE 1

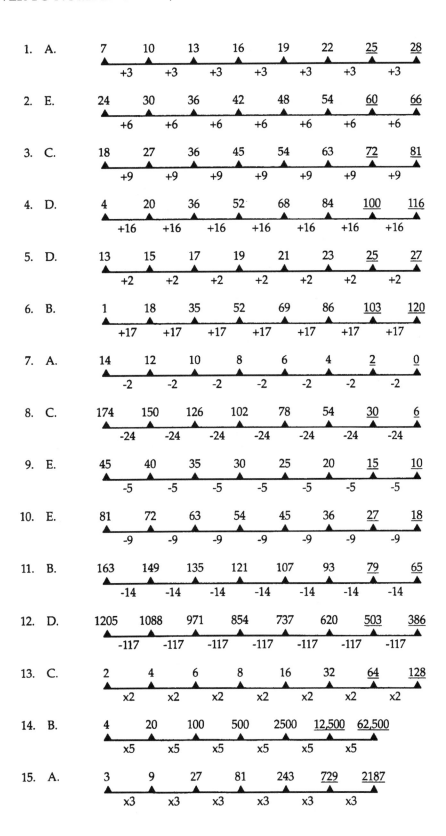

1. A.   7   10   13   16   19   22   25   28
         +3   +3   +3   +3   +3   +3   +3

2. E.   24   30   36   42   48   54   60   66
         +6   +6   +6   +6   +6   +6   +6

3. C.   18   27   36   45   54   63   72   81
         +9   +9   +9   +9   +9   +9   +9

4. D.   4   20   36   52   68   84   100   116
        +16   +16   +16   +16   +16   +16   +16

5. D.   13   15   17   19   21   23   25   27
         +2   +2   +2   +2   +2   +2   +2

6. B.   1   18   35   52   69   86   103   120
        +17   +17   +17   +17   +17   +17   +17

7. A.   14   12   10   8   6   4   2   0
         -2   -2   -2   -2   -2   -2   -2

8. C.   174   150   126   102   78   54   30   6
         -24   -24   -24   -24   -24   -24   -24

9. E.   45   40   35   30   25   20   15   10
         -5   -5   -5   -5   -5   -5   -5

10. E.   81   72   63   54   45   36   27   18
          -9   -9   -9   -9   -9   -9   -9

11. B.   163   149   135   121   107   93   79   65
          -14   -14   -14   -14   -14   -14   -14

12. D.   1205   1088   971   854   737   620   503   386
          -117   -117   -117   -117   -117   -117   -117

13. C.   2   4   6   8   16   32   64   128
          x2   x2   x2   x2   x2   x2   x2

14. B.   4   20   100   500   2500   12,500   62,500
          x5   x5   x5   x5   x5   x5

15. A.   3   9   27   81   243   729   2187
          x3   x3   x3   x3   x3   x3

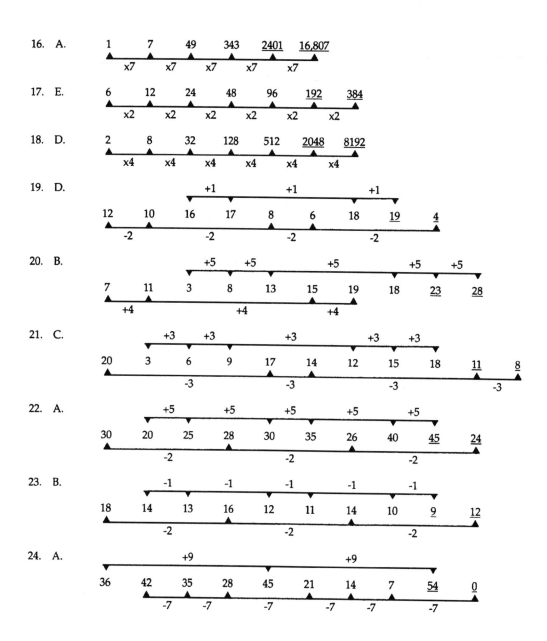

FOLLOWING DIRECTIONS

This exam determines how well you follow directions. How you perform here has a bearing on the amount of time and effort required by Postal supervisory staff to train you for a specific job. Obviously, a person who needs to be told only once how to do something stands a better chance of being hired than someone who needs directions repeated. This is not a difficult test, particularly if you pay full attention to the examiner's every direction. You will be given ample time between directions to respond on your answer sheet. This is not a time-oriented section. One note of caution here: Be alert for words such as IF, OR, BUT, AND, ONLY, EXCEPT, OTHERWISE, or any other conditional terms, because they alter the instructions. Ignoring such terms will cause you to mark incorrect choices.

In the practice session that follows, a friend or relative will be needed to play the part of the test examiner. He or she will be responsible for reading the directions orally to you at a rate of 75–80 words per minute, pausing where indicated in the test. As a suggestion, have whoever you choose to help you read with a timer until they can judge what the rate of 75–80 words per minute is like. Pauses between directions should be timed also.

.When you are ready to do the exercise in this chapter, you should be left with only the samples and answer sheets on which to mark your responses. Once a direction has been read by the examiner, it cannot be repeated. If you happen to miss part of a direction or do not understand the direction completely, you can attempt a guess at the correct answer. Place a greater emphasis on listening more closely to the next set of directions given. Most importantly, do not panic if a question has to be skipped. Overlooking one or two questions will not substantially affect your test score. Additional practice exercises are included in *Norman Hall's Postal Exam Preparation Book.* Ordering information is included at the end of this chapter

There are more answer blanks provided than there are directions on the exam, so a great deal of your answer sheet will remain blank after you have completed the test. **NOTE:** Unlike any other test section, the answer sheet in this exercise may not be filled out in numerical order. In other sections, question number 1 corresponds with answer blank number 1, question number 2 with answer blank number 2, etc. On this particular test, however, question number 1 may direct you to darken a particular letter in answer blank number 82; question number 2 many concern answer blank number 25, etc.

Following Directions/exercise 1

Note To Person Assisting In This Exercise:

Remove from this test guide the pages of this exercise that comprise the directions. The test applicant should be left with only the samples and the answer sheet.

Read the following directions out loud at the suggested rate of 75-80 words per minute, pausing only where indicated in parentheses. Speak as clearly as possible: Once a statement has been read, it cannot be repeated.

Examine Sample 1. (Pause 2-3 seconds.) If any of the months listed in Sample 1 can be categorized as winter months, find number 12 on your answer sheet and darken the letter E, as in "elephant." Otherwise, find number 14 on your answer sheet and darken the letter A, as in "apple." (Pause 7 seconds.)

Examine Sample 1 again. (Pause 2-3 seconds.) If more than two months begin with the letter J, as in "jack," go to number 15 on your answer sheet and darken the letter B, as in "boy." (Pause 7 seconds.) Otherwise, darken the letter C, as in "cat" on number 5 on your answer sheet. (Pause 7 seconds.)

Examine Sample 2. (Pause 2-3 seconds.) Write the number 17 in the smallest circle shown. Darken the resulting number-letter combination on your answer sheet only if there are two larger circles shown in the sample. (Pause 10 seconds.) Otherwise, write the number 16 in square D, as in "dog," and darken that number-letter combination on your answer sheet. (Pause 10 seconds.)

Examine Sample 3. (Pause 2-3 seconds.) This sample illustrates the respective number of routes originating from each of three Postal substations in a metropolitan area. Select the largest substation, designated by the highest number of routes, and write the letter C, as in "cat," beside it. (Pause 7 seconds.) Darken the resulting number-letter combination on your answer sheet. (Pause 7 seconds.)

Examine Sample 3 again. (Pause 2-3 seconds.) If the Chaney Street station has more routes than the Myers Boulevard station, write the letter B, as in "boy," beside the Clifford Avenue station. (Pause 5 seconds.) If not, write the letter A, as in "apple," beside the Myers Boulevard station (Pause 5 seconds.) Darken the number-letter combination you have selected on your answer sheet. (Pause 7 seconds.)

Examine Sample 4. (Pause 2-3 seconds.) If the third number is greater than the second number, but less than the fifth number, write the letter A, as in "apple," beside 42. (Pause 5 seconds.) Otherwise, write the letter D, as in "dog," beside the fourth number. (Pause 5 seconds.) Darken the number-letter combination that you have selected on your answer sheet. (Pause 7 seconds.)

Examine Sample 3 again. (Pause 2-3 seconds.) Darken the letter D, as in "dog," on number 9 of your answer sheet if the Chaney Street substation has the smallest number of routes. (Pause 7 seconds.) Otherwise, go to number 82 on your answer sheet and darken the letter D, as in "dog." (Pause 7 seconds.)

Examine Sample 4 again. (Pause 2-3 seconds.) If there are any numbers greater than 53, but less than 70, write the letter B, as in "boy," beside that number and darken the resulting number-letter combination on your answer sheet. (Pause 7 seconds.) Otherwise, write the letter E, as in "elephant," beside the second number of the sample and darken that number-letter combination on your answer sheet. (Pause 10 seconds.)

Examine Sample 5. (Pause 2-3 seconds.) This sample shows four numbers, each representing a combined Zip Code and route direct number. The first five digits of each number identify the Zip Code and the last two digits represent intercity route numbers. If all of the Zip Codes in Sample 5 are the same and there is not a route number higher than 50, darken the letter A, as in "apple," on number 50 of your answer sheet. (Pause 10 seconds.) Otherwise, darken the letter C, as in "cat," on number 49 of your answer sheet. (Pause 7 seconds.)

Examine Sample 6. (Pause 2-3 seconds.) Write the letter A, as in "apple," beside the lowest number if the first number in the sample is less than the last number in the sample, and if there is a number greater than 91. (Pause 7 seconds.) Otherwise, write the letter E, as in "elephant," beside the number 30. (Pause 5 seconds.) Darken the number-letter combination you have selected on your answer sheet. (Pause 7 seconds.)

Examine Sample 6 again. (Pause 2-3 seconds.) Write the letter B, as in "boy," beside the number 84 if the preceding number is less than 84. (Pause 5 seconds.) Otherwise, write the letter C, as in "cat," beside 84. (Pause 5 seconds.) Darken the number-letter combination you have chosen on your answer sheet. (Pause 7 seconds.)

Examine Sample 6 one more time. (Pause 2-3 seconds.) If there is a number which is greater than 43, yet less than 53, write the letter D, as in "dog," beside it. Darken that number-letter combination on your answer sheet. (Pause 10 seconds.) If not, go to number 14 on your answer sheet and darken the letter B, as in "boy." (Pause 7 seconds.)

Examine Sample 7. (Pause 2-3 seconds.) If Los Angeles is located in Florida, and Washington, D.C. is in California, write the number 16 on the line beside the letter E, as in "elephant." (Pause 5 seconds.) If the preceding statement is false, write the number 16 beside the letter E, as in "elephant," anyway, and darken the resulting number-letter combinations on your answer sheet. (Pause 10 seconds.)

Examine Sample 8. (Pause 2-3 seconds.) Each of the five boxes show the starting and finishing times of five rural routes on a particular day. The time at the top is the rural carriers' starting time and the time listed below shows when they finished for the day. Find the carrier who spends the longest time on his or her route and write the number 10 beside the letter representing that carrier. (Pause 10 seconds.) Darken your answer sheet with this number-letter combination. (Pause 7 seconds.)

Examine Sample 8 again. (Pause 2-3 seconds.) If Carrier A, as in "apple," finished for the day before Carrier B, as in "boy," write the number 2 beside the letter A, as in "apple." (Pause 5 seconds.) Otherwise, find which of the carriers had the latest starting time and write the number 7 beside the letter representing that carrier. (Pause 7 seconds.) Darken the number-letter combination you have chosen on your answer sheet. (Pause 7 seconds.)

Examine Sample 8 one more time. (Pause 2-3 seconds.) Write the number 11 beside the letter representing the carrier with the second latest finishing time. (Pause 7 seconds.) Darken that number-letter combination on your answer sheet. (Pause 7 seconds.)

Examine Sample 9. (Pause 2-3 seconds.) Write the letter E, as in "elephant," beside the number that is in the circle and darken your answer with the resulting number-letter combination. (Pause 5 seconds.) If there is no circle in the sample, write the number 47 beside the letter within the rectangle and darken that number-letter combination on your answer sheet. (Pause 10 seconds.)

Examine Sample 10. (Pause 2-3 seconds.) If any one of the states shown in the sample is not located in the western part of the United States, go to number 36 on your answer sheet and darken the letter E, as in "elephant." (Pause 7 seconds.) Otherwise, go to number 3 on your answer sheet and darken the letter B, as in "boy." (Pause 7 seconds.)

Examine Sample 10 again. (Pause 2-3 seconds.) If any of the states listed begin with the letter C, as in "cat," go to number 49 on your answer sheet, and darken the letter C, as in "cat." (Pause 7 seconds.)

Examine Sample 11. (Pause 2-3 seconds.) If 9 is greater than 7, and 20 is less than 21, write the number 60 on the line provided and darken that number-letter combination on your answer sheet. (Pause 10 seconds.) Otherwise, go to number 23 on your answer sheet and darken the letter B, as in "boy."

Examine Sample 12. (Pause 2-3 seconds.) Find the number that is greater than 13 and less than 64, and go to that number on your answer sheet and darken the letter C, as in "cat." (Pause 10 seconds.)

Examine Sample 13. (Pause 2-3 seconds.) Choose the number that is shown in identically sized shapes and go to that number on your answer sheet and darken in the letter E, as in "elephant." (Pause 10 seconds.)

Examine Sample 14. (Pause 2-3 seconds.) If 40 is less than 69 and greater than 15, go to 40 on your answer sheet and darken the letter A, as in "apple." (Pause 7 seconds.) If not, write the letter C, as in "cat," beside the number 15 in the sample. (Pause 5 seconds.) Darken that number-letter combination on your answer sheet. (Pause 7 seconds.)

FOLLOWING DIRECTIONS/EXERCISE 1 SAMPLES

1. March   :   December   :   November   :   July   :   January

2. (A)   (C)   [D]   [E]   (B)

3. Myers Blvd.   Clifford Ave.   Chaney St.
    32___routes   45___routes   9___routes

4. 42_____   1_____   50_____   73_____   79_____

5. 9837841   9837810   9837814   9837813

6. 43_____   27_____   84_____   91_____   30_____   52_____

7. _____B   _____E

8. 7:30 AM   7:00 AM   6:00 AM   6:45 AM   7:00 AM
    2:45 PM   2:15 PM   4:00 PM   3:30 PM   3:00 PM
    __A   __B   __C   __D   __E

9. B_____   12_____   A_____   47_____

10. California   :   Oregon   :   Alaska   :   Florida   :   Washington

11. _____D

12. 13   51   64   65   80

13. [20]   (6)   [20]   (6)

14. _____A   15_____   69_____   40_____   _____C

ANSWER SHEET TO FOLLOWING DIRECTIONS/EXERCISE 1

1. A B C D E
2. A B C D E
3. A B C D E
4. A B C D E
5. A B C D E
6. A B C D E
7. A B C D E
8. A B C D E
9. A B C D E
10. A B C D E
11. A B C D E
12. A B C D E
13. A B C D E
14. A B C D E
15. A B C D E
16. A B C D E
17. A B C D E
18. A B C D E
19. A B C D E
20. A B C D E
21. A B C D E
22. A B C D E
23. A B C D E
24. A B C D E
25. A B C D E
26. A B C D E
27. A B C D E
28. A B C D E
29. A B C D E
30. A B C D E
31. A B C D E
32. A B C D E

33. A B C D E
34. A B C D E
35. A B C D E
36. A B C D E
37. A B C D E
38. A B C D E
39. A B C D E
40. A B C D E
41. A B C D E
42. A B C D E
43. A B C D E
44. A B C D E
45. A B C D E
46. A B C D E
47. A B C D E
48. A B C D E
49. A B C D E
50. A B C D E
51. A B C D E
52. A B C D E
53. A B C D E
54. A B C D E
55. A B C D E
56. A B C D E
57. A B C D E
58. A B C D E
59. A B C D E
60. A B C D E
61. A B C D E
62. A B C D E
63. A B C D E
64. A B C D E

65. A B C D E
66. A B C D E
67. A B C D E
68. A B C D E
69. A B C D E
70. A B C D E
71. A B C D E
72. A B C D E
73. A B C D E
74. A B C D E
75. A B C D E
76. A B C D E
77. A B C D E
78. A B C D E
79. A B C D E
80. A B C D E
81. A B C D E
82. A B C D E
83. A B C D E
84. A B C D E
85. A B C D E
86. A B C D E
87. A B C D E
88. A B C D E
89. A B C D E
90. A B C D E
91. A B C D E
92. A B C D E
93. A B C D E
94. A B C D E
95. A B C D E

ANSWERS TO FOLLOWING DIRECTIONS/EXERCISE 1

1.	12 E	9.	50 A	17.	47 B
2.	5 C	10.	30 E	18.	36 E
3.	17 B	11.	84 B	19.	49 C
4.	45 C	12.	52 D	20.	60 D
5.	32 A	13.	16 E	21.	51 C
6.	42 A	14.	10 C	22.	20 E
7.	9 D	15.	7 A	23.	40 A
8.	1 E	16.	11 D		

If you scored:

22 or more correct, you have an excellent score.

20 or 21 correct, you have a good score.

19 or fewer correct, you need more practice.

ADDITIONAL REFERENCE MATERIAL

Norman Hall's Postal Exam Preparation Book is an excellent resource for those actively seeking employment with the USPS. Mr. Hall has scored 100% on the United States Postal Exam four times and he provides in-depth study tips for the new 470 Battery Test's four key testing areas. A small part of Mr. Hall's comprehensive 296 page book was excerpted by permission for this chapter. Many additional sample tests and exam strategies are included in his *Postal Exam Preparation Book*. He also guarantees that anyone who purchases his book will score between 90 to 100%. If you don't, your purchase price will be refunded.

Norman hall knows the techniques, winning strategies, and preparation necessary for the Postal Exam... and it's all here and guaranteed to work for you! His *Postal Exam Preparation Book* includes six full-length practice postal exams, with answer keys and self-scoring tables.

Everything you need to know to come out on top!

Complete Coverage of:

✳ Address Cross Comparison
✳ Memory (Names and Numbers)
✳ Number Series
✳ Following Directions
✳ Test-taking Strategies and Study Suggestions

You can order *Norman Hall's Postal Exam Preparation Book* direct from Adams Publishing for $10.95 plus $4.50 shipping and handling. BY PHONE: Call 1-800-872-5627 (In Massachusetts: 617-767-8100). They accept Visa, MasterCard, and American Express. BY MAIL: Write out the full title of the book and send payment of $10.95 per book, including $4.50 for shipping and handling to: Adams Publishing, 260 Center Street, Holbrook, MA 02343. 30-day money-back guarantee.

Adams Publishing also offers three additional references for job seekers including:

The Adams Job Almanac, $15.95, 915 pages, provides an unprecedented amount of information on career opportunities. The book includes names and addresses of over 7,000 leading employers; information on which jobs each company commonly fill and much more.

The Adams Cover Letter Almanac and *The Adams Resume Almanac* , $10.95 each, contains over 600 cover letters and 600 resumes used by real people to win jobs. It features complete information on all types of letters and resumes.

Chapter Seven
The Interview Process

There are several types of interviews which you may encounter. The most common interview is the called a *Structured Interview*. Most traditional interviews are based on this format. Below are some descriptions of the different types of interviews and what you can expect in each of them.[1]

How you do in the interview can often determine whether you get the job.

Types of Interviews

■ *Screening Interview*. A preliminary interview either in person or by phone, in which an agency or company representative determines whether you have the basic qualifications to warrant a subsequent interview.

■ **Structured Interview.** In a structured interview, the interviewer explores certain predetermined areas using questions which have been written in advance. The interviewer has a written description of the experience, skills and personality traits of an "ideal" candidate. Your experience and skills are compared to specific job tasks. This type of interview is very common and most traditional interviews are based on this format.

■ *Unstructured Interview*. Although the interviewer is given a written description of the "ideal" candidate, in the unstructured interview the interviewer is not given instructions on what specific areas to cover.

---

[1] The Job Search Guide, U.S. Department of Labor 1993.

- *Multiple Interviews.* Multiple interviews are commonly used with professional jobs. This approach involves a series of interviews in which you meet individually with various representatives of the organization.

- *Stress Interview.* The interviewer intentionally attempts to upset you to see how you react under pressure. You may be asked questions that make you uncomfortable or you may be interrupted when you are speaking. Although it is uncommon for an entire interview to be conducted under stress conditions, it is common for the interviewer to incorporate stress questions as a part of a traditional interview. Examples of common stress questions are given later in this chapter.

- *Targeted Interview.* Although similar to the structured interview, the areas covered are much more limited. Key qualifications for success on the job are identified and relevant questions are prepared in advance.

- *Situational Interview.* Situations are set up which simulate common problems you may encounter on the job. Your responses to these situations are measured against pre-determined standards. This approach is often used as one part of a traditional interview rather than as an entire interview format.

- *Group Interview.* You may be interviewed by two or more agency or company representatives simultaneously. Sometimes, one of the interviewers is designated to ask "stress" questions to see how you respond under pressure.

  NOTE: Many government agencies including the Postal Service have initiated quality of worklife and employee involvement groups to build viable labor/management teams and partnerships. In this environment agencies may require applicants to be interviewed by several groups that often include peers and subordinates.

The interview strategies discussed below can be used effectively in any type of interview you may encounter.

BEFORE THE INTERVIEW

Prepare in advance. The better prepared you are, the less anxious you will be and the greater your chances for success.

- *Role Play.* Find someone to role play the interview with you. This person should be someone with whom you feel comfortable and with whom you can discuss your weaknesses freely. The person should be objective and knowledgeable, perhaps a business associate.

- Use a mirror or video camera when you role play to see what kind of image you project.

Assess your interviewing skills.

- What are your strengths and weaknesses? Work on correcting your weaknesses, such as speaking rapidly, talking too loudly or softly and nervous habits such as shaking hands or inappropriate facial expressions.

- Learn the questions that are commonly asked and prepare answers to them. Examples of commonly asked interview questions are provided later in this chapter. Career centers and libraries often have books which include interview questions. Practice giving answers which are brief but thorough.

- Decide what questions you would like to ask and practice politely interjecting them at different points in the interview.

Evaluate your strengths

- Evaluate your skills, abilities and education as they relate to the type of job you are seeking.

- Practice tailoring your answers to show how you meet the Postal Service's needs, if you have details about the specific job before the interview.

Assess your overall appearance.

- Find out what clothing is appropriate for your job series. Acceptable attire for most professional positions is conservative.

- Have several sets of appropriate clothing available since you may have several interviews over a few days.

- Your clothes should be clean and pressed and your shoes polished.

- Make sure your hair is neat, your nails clean and you are generally well groomed.

Research the Postal Service. The more you know about the Postal Service and the job you are applying for, the better you will do on the interview. Get as much information as you can before the interview.

Professional applicants and applicants for positions that do not require entrance exams should have extra copies of their resume or application available to take on the interview. The interviewer may ask you for extra copies. Make sure you bring along the same version of your resume or application that you originally provided them. You can also refer to your resume to complete applications that ask for job history information (i.e., dates of employment, names of former employers and their telephone numbers, job responsibilities and accomplishments.) A blank application form is provided in Appendix B for your use.

Arrive early at the interview. Plan to arrive 10 to 15 minutes early. Give yourself time to find a restroom so you can check your appearance.

It's important to make a good impression from the moment you enter the reception area. Greet the receptionist cordially and try to appear confident. You never know what influence the receptionist has with your interviewer. With a little small talk, you may get some helpful information about the interviewer and the job opening. If you are asked to fill out an application while you're waiting, be sure to fill it out completely and print the information neatly. Prepare the sample application in Appendix B.

Don't make negative comments about anyone or anything, including former employers.

DURING THE INTERVIEW

The job interview is usually a two-way discussion between you and a prospective employer. The interviewer is attempting to determine whether you have what the Postal Service needs, and you are attempting to determine if you would accept the job if offered. Both of you will be trying to get as much information as possible in order to make those decisions.[2]

The interview that you are most likely to face is a structured interview with a traditional format. It usually consists of three phases. The introductory phase covers the greeting, small talk and an overview of which areas will be discussed during the interview. The middle phase is a question-and-answer period. The interviewer asks most of the questions, but you are given an opportunity to ask questions as well. The closing phase

---

[2] Postal Service Handbook EL-311, Exhibit 533.5 page 178

gives you an opportunity to ask any final questions you might have, cover any important points that haven't been discussed and get information about the next step in the process.

Introductory Phase. This phase is very important. You want to make a good first impression and, if possible, get additional information you need about the job and the company.

■ Make a good impression. You only have a few seconds to create a positive first impression which can influence the rest of the interview and even determine whether you get the job.

The interviewer's first impression of you is based mainly on non-verbal clues. The interviewer is assessing your overall appearance and demeanor. When greeting the interviewer, be certain your handshake is firm and that you make eye contact. Wait for the interviewer to signal you before you sit down.

Once seated, your body language is very important in conveying a positive impression. Find a comfortable position so that you don't appear tense. Lean forward slightly and maintain eye contact with the interviewer. This posture shows that you are interested in what is being said. Smile naturally at appropriate times. Show that you are open and receptive by keeping your arms and legs uncrossed. Avoid keeping your briefcase or your handbag on your lap. Pace your movements so that they are not too fast or too slow. Try to appear relaxed and confident.

■ Get the information you need. If you weren't able to get complete information about the job in advance, you should try to get it as early as possible in the interview. Be sure to prepare your questions in advance. Knowing the following things will allow you to present those strengths and abilities that the employer wants.

✎ Why does the Postal Service need someone in this position?

✎ Exactly what would they expect of you?

✎ Are they looking for traditional or innovative solutions to problems?

■ When to ask questions. The problem with a traditional interview structure is that your chance to ask questions occurs late in the interview.

How can you get the information you need early in the process without making the interviewer feel that you are taking control?

Deciding exactly when to ask your questions is the tricky part. Timing is everything. You may have to make a decision based on intuition and your first impressions of the interviewer. Does the interviewer seem comfortable or nervous, soft spoken or forceful, formal or casual? These signals will help you to judge the best time to ask your questions.

The sooner you ask the questions, the less likely you are to disrupt the interviewer's agenda. However, if you ask questions too early, the interviewer may feel you are trying to control the interview.

Try asking questions right after the greeting and small talk. Since most interviewers like to set the tone of the interview and maintain initial control, always phrase your questions in a way that leaves control with the interviewer. Perhaps say, "Would you mind telling me a little more about the job so that I can focus on the information that would be most important to the Postal Service?" If there is no job opening but you are trying to develop one or you need more information, try saying, "Could you tell me a little more about where the Postal Service is going so I can focus in those areas of my background that are most relevant?"

You may want to wait until the interviewer has given an overview of what will be discussed. This overview may answer some of your questions or may provide some details that you can use to ask additional questions. Once the middle phase of the interview has begun, you may find it more difficult to ask questions.

Middle Phase. During this phase of the interview, you will be asked many questions about your work experience, skills, education, activities and interests, You are being assessed on how you will perform the job in relation to the agency objectives.

All your responses should be concise. Use specific examples to illustrate your point whenever possible. Although your responses should be prepared in advance so that they are well-phrased and effective, be sure they do not sound rehearsed. Remember that your responses must always be adapted to the present interview. Incorporate any information you obtained earlier in the interview with the responses you had prepared in advance and then answer in a way that is appropriate to the question.

Below are frequently asked questions and some suggested responses:

"Tell me about yourself."

Briefly describe your experience and background. If you are unsure what information the interviewer is seeking, say, "Are there any areas in particular you'd like to know about?"

"What is your weakest point?" (A stress question)

Mention something that is actually a strength. Some examples are:

"I'm something of a perfectionist."

"I'm a stickler for punctuality."

"I'm tenacious."

Give a specific situation from your previous job to illustrate your point.

"What is your strongest point?"

"I work well under pressure."

"I am organized and manage my time well,"

If you have just graduated from college you might say,

"I am eager to learn, and I don't have to unlearn old techniques."

Give a specific example to illustrate your point.

"What do you hope to be doing five years from now?"

"I hope I will still be working here and have increased my level of responsibility based on my performance and abilities."

"Why have you been out of work for so long?" (A stress question)

"I spent some time re-evaluating my past experience and the current job market to see what direction I wanted to take."

"I had some offers but I'm not just looking for another job; I'm looking for a career."

"What do you know about the Postal Service? Why do you want to work here?'"

This is where your research will come in handy.

"The Postal Service is a leader in mail/package delivery and on the Fortune 500's list of successful businesses."

"The Postal Service has a superior reputation with generated income of over 24 billion dollars a year."

You might try to get the interviewer to give you additional information about the Postal Service by saying that you are very interested in learning more about the agency objectives. This will help you to focus your response on relevant areas.

"What is your greatest accomplishment?"

Give a specific illustration from your previous or current job where you saved the company money or helped increase their profits. If you have just graduated from college, try to find some accomplishment from your school work, part-time jobs or extra-curricular activities.

"Why should we hire you?" (A stress question)

Highlight your background based on the Postal Service's current needs. Recap your qualifications keeping the interviewer's job description in mind. If you don't have much experience, talk about how your education and training prepared you for this job.

"Why do you want to make a change now?"

"I want to develop my potential."

"The opportunities in my present company are limited."

"Tell me about a problem you had in your last job and how you resolved it."

The employer wants to assess your analytical skills and see if you are a team player. Select a problem from your last job and explain how you solved it.

Some Questions You Should Ask.

✎ "What are the Postal Service's current challenges?"

✎ "Could you give me a more detailed job description?"

✎ "Why is this position open?"

✎ "Are there opportunities for advancement?"

✎ "To whom would I report?"

Closing Phase. During the closing phase of an interview, you will be asked whether you have any other questions. Ask any relevant question that has not yet been answered. Highlight any of your strengths that have not been discussed. If another interview is to be scheduled, get the necessary information. If this is the final interview, find out when the decision is to be made and when you can call. Thank the interviewer by name and say goodbye.

ILLEGAL QUESTIONS

During an interview, you may be asked some questions that are considered illegal. It is illegal for an interviewer to ask you questions related to sex, age, race, religion, national origin or marital status, or to delve into your personal life for information that is not job-related. What can you do if you are asked an illegal question? Take a moment to evaluate the situation. Ask yourself questions like:

✎ How uncomfortable has this question made you feel?

✎ Does the interviewer seem unaware that the question is illegal?

✎ Is this interviewer going to be your boss?

Then respond in a way that is comfortable for you.

If you decide to answer the question, be succinct and try to move the conversation back to an examination of your skills and abilities as quickly as possible. For example, if asked about your age, you might reply, "I'm in my forties, and I have a wealth of experience that would be an asset to your company." If you are not sure whether you want to answer the question, first ask for a clarification of how this question relates to your qualifications for the job. You may decide to answer if there is a reasonable explanation. If you feel there is no justification for the question, you might say that you do not see the relationship between the question and your qualifications for the job and you prefer not to answer it.

AFTER THE INTERVIEW

You are not finished yet. It is important to assess the interview shortly after it is concluded. Following your interview you should:

- Write down the name, phone number, e-mail address, and title (be sure the spelling is correct) of the interviewer.

- Review what the job entails and record what the next step will be.

- Note your reactions to the interview; include what went well and what went poorly.

- Assess what you learned from the experience and how you can improve your performance in future interviews.

PHONE FOLLOW-UP

If you were not told during the interview when a hiring decision will be made, call after one week.

At that time, if you learn that the decision has not been made, find out whether you are still under consideration for the job. Ask if there are any other questions the interviewer might have about your qualifications and offer to come in for another interview if necessary. Reiterate that you are very interested in the job.

- If you learn that you did not get the job, try to find out why. You might also inquire whether the interviewer can think of anyone else who might be able to use someone with your abilities, either in another department or at another agency.

- If you are offered the job, you have to decide whether you want it. If you are not sure, thank the employer and ask for several days to think about it. Ask any other questions you might need answered to help you with the decision.

- If you know you want the job and have all the information you need, accept the job with thanks and get the details on when you start. Ask whether the Postal Service will be sending a letter of confirmation, as it is best to have the offer in writing.

Who Gets Hired?

In the final analysis, the Postal Service will hire someone who has the abilities and talents which fulfill their needs. It is up to you to demonstrate at the interview that you are the person they want.

Chapter Eight
Veterans Preference

There are several special emphasis civil service employment programs available to veterans. *Veterans Preference* and the *Veterans Readjustment Act (VRA)* are two of the better known programs.

When vacancies are announced by the Postal Service or a federal agency, the selecting official can fill the position by:

Over 28% of all federal employees are veterans.

- ✎   Internal promotions or reassignments of existing workers;
- ✎   Reemploying former employees;
- ✎   Using approved special purpose noncompetitive appointments such as the VRA program; and,
- ✎   Appointing a new employee who has successfully completed an examination. The examination can be either written or an extensive examination of your past work experience and education as listed on a Employment Application.

VETERANS PREFERENCE

When the Postal Service or agency advertises job vacancies they must select from the top rated eligible applicants. Government publication WEE-2 states; *"The official may not pass over a Veterans Preference eligible, however, and appoint a nonpreference eligible lower on the list unless the reasons for passing over the veteran are sufficient."*

Veterans preference gives special consideration to eligible veterans looking for federal or Postal Service employment. Veterans who are disabled or who served on active duty in the United States Armed Forces during certain specified time periods or in military campaigns are entitled to preference over nonveterans both in hiring into the federal civil service and in retention during *reductions in force*. There are two classes of preference for honorably discharged veterans:

Five Point Preference

Five-point preference is given to veterans who served on active duty:

• During the period 12/7/41 to 7/1/55; or
• For more than 180 consecutive days, any part of which occurred after 1/31/55 and before 10/15/76.
• Served in a campaign or expedition for which a campaign medal has been authorized, including Lebanon, Grenada, Panama, and Southwest Asia (Desert Shield/Storm). Medal holders who enlisted after September 7, 1980, or entered active duty on or after October 14, 1982, must have served continuously for 24 months or the full period called or ordered to active duty. This service requirement does not apply to veterans with compensable service-connected disabilities, or to veterans separated for disability in the line of duty, or for hardship.

Ten Point Preference

Ten-point preference is given to disabled veterans - **with a 30% rated disability** - who served on active duty at any time. The disability must be service-connected. Wives, husbands, widows, widowers and mothers of disabled veterans also receive preference in certain cases.

Ten points are added to the passing examination score of:

• A veteran who served at any time, and who (1) has a present service-connected disability; or (2) is receiving compensation, disability retirement benefits, or pension from the military or the Department of Veteran Affairs.
• An unmarried spouse of certain deceased veterans, a spouse of a veteran unable to work because of a service-connected disability, and a mother of a veteran who died in service or who is permanently and totally disabled.

Ten-point preference eligibles may apply for any job for which (1) a list of exam eligibles is (or is about to be) established, or (2) a non-temporary appointment was made in the last three years.

PURPLE HEART RECIPIENTS ARE
CONSIDERED TO HAVE A SERVICE
CONNECTED DISABILITY

WHAT DOES IT MEAN?

If you apply for a Postal Service or federal job, your knowledge, skills and abilities will be rated on a point system. You will receive points for related education, experience, special skills, awards, and written tests if required. The maximum points anyone can accumulate is 100. If an eligible five-point preference candidate accumulates 90 points, five additional points are awarded on preference for a total score of 95. A 10-point preference vet would have a total score of 100.

Qualified veterans with a compensable service-connected disability of 10 percent or more are placed at the top of most civil service examination registers, except for scientific and professional jobs at GS-9 or higher.

The Postal Service may not pass over a candidate with preference and select an individual without preference who has the same or lower score, unless OPM approves the agency's reasons.

SPECIAL CONSIDERATION

Veterans can file application with the Office of Personnel Management or the Postal Service after an examination has closed. *If a current list of eligibles exists the veteran can apply within 120 days before or after separation. Ten-point preference veterans can apply anytime to be placed on an existing eligibles list.*

All veterans, regardless of when they served on active duty, may file application for any examination which was open while he or she was in the armed forces or which was announced within 120 days before or after his or her separation, provided the veteran makes application within 120 days after an honorable discharge. A disabled veteran receives 10 points preference and may file an application at any time.

VETERANS READJUSTMENT APPOINTMENTS (VRAs)

VRA appointments were originally limited to Vietnam Era Vets. *Public Law 102-568 - OCT. 29, 1992* greatly expanded VRA appointments to millions of Post Vietnam Era Vets. You may be eligible for a non-competitive federal government job appointment. By law, federal agencies may hire qualified veterans of the Armed Forces directly under the Veteran's Readjustment Appointment (VRA) program. Successful completion of the VRA program leads to a permanent civil service appointment.

The features of the law are:

Between 1982 & 1991 the federal government hired over 136,000 veterans under VRA appointments.

- If you served on active duty between August 5, 1964, and May 7, 1975, you have either 10 years after the date of your last separation from active duty, or until December 31, 1995, whichever is later.

- If you first entered active duty <u>after</u> May 7, 1975, you have 10 years after the date of your last separation from active duty, or until December 31, 1999, whichever is later.
- Education restrictions were removed.
- Extension of the VRA program through December 31, 1999.

WHAT IS A VRA APPOINTMENT?

A vet can be hired by any federal agency without going through the Office of Personnel Management (OPM). An agency that identifies a hiring need can pick up a VRA candidate immediately. If an agency has to advertise an opening through OPM it can take up to six months before the position can be filled. The Postal Service hires mostly through competitive exams that eligible veterans can receive preference.

HOW TO APPLY

Call the Customer Service Center in your area that is listed in Chapter Four for specific instructions on how to apply. Agencies **do not have to hire through the VRA program**. Only if your education and work experience meets their requirements, they have openings, and like what they see will they make you an offer. Be tactful and don't be demanding.

ELIGIBILITY

You are an eligible veteran if you (A) served on active duty for a period of more than 180 days, all or part of which occurred after August 4, 1964, and have other than a dishonorable discharge, or (B) were discharged or released from active duty because of a service-connected disability.

The requirement for more than 180 days active service does not apply to (1) veterans separated from active duty because of a service-connected disability, or (2) reserve and guard members who served on active duty (under 10 U.S.C. 672 a, d, or g; 673 or 673 b) during a period of war, such as the Persian Gulf War, or in a military operation for which a campaign or expeditionary medal is authorized.

Compared to other sectors, the federal government employs two times the number of veterans and three times the number of disabled veterans. In 1993, 28% of all federal employees were veterans. The Department of Veterans Affairs, Army, Air Force, and Navy were the top employing agencies. Approximately 60% of all federal employees who retired from 1984 through 1990 were veterans.

Chapter Nine
Job Descriptions

There are over 2,000 jobs identified in the Postal Service's Position Directory,[1] all of which are listed in Chapter Ten. This Chapter features 28 job descriptions—a cross section of Postal Service occupations, from accountants and engineers to welders and custodians.

Mail carrier and clerk occupations are presented in Chapter Three. The job descriptions provided in this chapter were included to show the tremendous diversity that the U.S. Postal Service, a Fortune 500 company, offers. Many of these jobs are first offered to qualified postal employees. Anyone interested in these jobs should consider taking the 470 Battery Test or any one of the other tests administered by the Postal Service to get their foot in the door. Over half of all Postal Service workers began their career as a mail carrier or clerk after taking and passing an entrance exam.

For the majority of jobs, Postal Service employees get the first opportunity to bid (apply for) vacancies through what is called an internal merit promotion program. If the hiring manager determines that an insufficient pool of qualified applicants exists or no qualified bidders (applicants) are selected for a vacancy, the agency advertises the job to the general public through classified ads. They also post job announcements at hiring postal facilities. Not all jobs are filled through written exams. A number of jobs, including professional positions, are advertised direct to the public. Resumes and the PS Form 2591 (Application for Employment) are accepted.

To determine the number employed and pay for the listed occupations refer to Chapter Ten for a complete list, excluding manager and supervisory positions, of over 2,000 classified jobs.

---

[1] Postal Service OMSS Report $PD09 (7/3/95)

Standard position descriptions

ACCOUNTING TECHNICIAN, PS-06 Occupation Code: 0525-31XX

Ensures the proper completion of a designated major segment of accounting work in a district office; or serves as assistant to the Postmaster in performing accounting and clerical duties involved in the preparation, maintenance, and consolidation of accounts and related reports in a post office.

DUTIES AND RESPONSIBILITIES

1. Performs, with assistance of accounting clerks if needed, either duty 2 or 3, in combination with duty 3. In a smaller post office having characteristics like those in the basic function, and subject to the provisions of Postal Service directives concerning internal control and separation of duties, performs any combination of duties 5 through 8.

2. In the accounting area, receives daily cash reports from all reporting units of the post office, verifies and balances reports with supporting documents, consolidates the data in one cash report, and posts the daily financial report. Items which are questionable are taken up with the reporting unit or individual in order to determine the correct entries. Reporting units are debited or credited as necessary.

3. In the budget and cost control area, receives reports and data relating to mail volume, workload, and cost ascertainment from the various reporting units, examines reports for completeness and tabulates and posts data in accordance with daily and periodic reporting requirements. Discusses with supervisor data submitted by their units in order that further necessary information and explanation may be obtained. Documents explanatory information for subsequent analysis and inclusion in management reports.

4. In addition, works closely with the supervisor in preparing weekly, biweekly, accounting period, or other periodic reports. Gives guidance and instruction to and acts as group leader for any assigned clerical assistance. May maintain accounts, reflecting trust funds, suspense items and inventories of accountable paper, stamp stock, and fixed credits. Participates with the supervisor interpreting instructions and regulations in implementing procedures pertaining to accounting. May be required to research, compile and record data for special studies and reports on various phases of postal activities as desired by the postmaster or higher authority.

5. Receives daily cash reports from all reporting units of the post office, verifies and balances reports with supporting documents, consolidates into one cash report, and post the cashbook. Items which are questionable are taken up with the reporting unit or individual to determine the correct entries.

6. Receives reports and data relating to mail volume, workload, and cost ascertainment from the various reporting units, examines reports for completeness and accuracy, makes the necessary computations, consolidates the information in accordance with daily and periodic reporting requirements. Discusses with supervisors figures submitted by them to obtain further information and explanation as required. Prepares explanatory comments for inclusion in the reports.

7. Works closely with the postmaster in preparing required accounting period reports including operating report, financial statement, workload and mail volume reports.

8. May maintain stamp stock and fill requisitions - for window clerks, stations and branches.

ARCHITECT/ENGINEER, EAS-20 Occupation Code: 0808-3020

Performs design work and assists in administering design and construction contracts within a District office.

DUTIES AND RESPONSIBILITIES

1. Provides architect/engineering consulting services, evaluates technical problems, and surveys technical alternatives for construction projects within a District office.

2. Participates in the analysis, evaluation, and determination of feasibility, costs, and technical problems related to the planning, design, installation, test, and operation of advanced engineered systems and equipment in support of construction projects.

3. Oversees construction term contracts to ensure compliance with contract requirements and adherence to established policies and procedures.

4. Participates in the activities related to the design, construction, testing, start-up, and operation of facilities, systems, and/or equipment.

5. Participates in the preparation of requests for proposal, including specifications and drawings; participates in the evaluation of contractor bids.

6. Reviews contractor specifications and drawings for technical accuracy and compliance with contract requirements.

7. Attends preconstruction and final acceptance meetings for progress review; makes on-site inspections during installation and test, and reports discrepancies in contract work.

8. Works with architects, engineers, contractors, construction representatives, and others involved in the design and construction of postal facilities.

9. Provides technical assistance to employees and others in the development of facility projects.

AREA MAINTENANCE TECHNICIAN, PS-08 Occupation Code: 4801-20XX

Installs, maintains, repairs, removes, and disposes of postal equipment as appropriate at post offices (offices not having maintenance capability) within the geographic area served by the area maintenance office to which assigned. Installs, moves, or repairs post office screen-line equipment, lock boxes, furniture, and mechanical equipment, supervising such additional help as projects may require.

DUTIES AND RESPONSIBILITIES

1. At regional direction, moves and sets up offices in new or remodeled postal quarters; assembles, installs screen-lines, workroom, lobby, and operating equipment. Supervises carpenters and/or helpers as projects may require. Classifies or assists postmasters in classification of postal equipment for disposal or refurbishing. Under postmaster's authority, purchases materials and employs helpers as warranted.

2. Makes major and minor repairs to postal operating equipment in offices without maintenance capabilities; conducts maintenance inspections and provides operating, minor repair, and maintenance instruction to postal employees in the offices served. Whenever possible, conducts

maintenance inspection and the instruction of postal employees in conjunction with emergency service trips to installations.

3. Troubleshoots, repairs, overhauls, and installs postal operating equipment such as, but not limited to, stamp vending machines, canceling machines, scales, print punch money order machines, tying machines, conveyors, safe and vault locks and other components, protective systems and devices, time clocks, and money changers. Keeps abreast of current maintenance criteria and effects service accordingly.

4. Maintains inventory of all postal operating equipment in the offices served by the area maintenance office. Makes recommendations to supervisors and/or obtains stock of operating equipment repair parts, maintaining inventories at levels prescribed by the region or the Department. Maintains record of parts in stock; ships parts to territory offices as required to meet respective office needs. Keeps records of parts used, frequency of replacements, and submits reports to the regional office at prescribed intervals.

5. Installs and maintains protective systems and devices on safes and vaults in post offices. Opens safes and vaults, changes and repairs combinations, and disarms systems and devices.

6. Provides emergency service and makes minor repairs to air conditioning systems at government owned buildings not under service contracts. Prepares report of needs for the postmaster if the lessor has maintenance responsibility or the manufacturer if the system is under warranty.

7. Initiates reports to the regional office on major work assignments, shortages of equipment, and completed screen line installations. Makes reports of unsatisfactory conditions relating to equipment damage, classification, and deficiencies. Makes written recommendations for equipment improvements, operations, and fabrication changes.

8. Drives motor vehicle to respective offices to effect on-the-scene repairs and screen line installation or modifications. Communicates with postmasters by phone, correspondence, and personal visits to investigate reports of malfunctions, disorders, or other needs within the area maintenance office territory.

9. Performs other maintenance duties as instructed by the postmaster at the area maintenance office when not engaged in area maintenance duties.

10. Uses various hand and power tools and testing devices incident to the mechanical, electrical and electronic, and carpentry trades.

11. Observes established safety practices and procedures and instructs helpers accordingly.

AUTOMOTIVE MECHANIC, PS-06 Occupation Code: 5823-03XX
Repairs vehicles, including the removal and installation of complete motors, clutches, transmissions, and other major component parts.

DUTIES AND RESPONSIBILITIES

1. Diagnoses mechanical and operating difficulties of vehicles, repairing defects, replacing worn or broken parts.

2. Adjusts and tunes up engines, cleaning fuel pumps, carburetors, and radiators; regulates timing, and makes other necessary adjustments to maintain in proper operating condition trucks that are in service.

3. Repairs or replaces automotive electrical equipment such as generators, starters, ignition systems, distributors, and wiring; installs and sets new spark plugs.

4. Conducts road tests of vehicles after repairs, noting performance of engine, clutch, transmission, brakes, and other parts.

5. Operates standard types of garage testing equipment.

6. Performs other duties as assigned, such as, removing, disassembling, reassembling, and installing entire engines; overhauling transmission, rear end assemblies, and braking systems; straightening frames and axles, welding broken parts where required; making road calls to make emergency repairs; and making required truck inspections.

BUDGET AND FINANCIAL ANALYST (DISTRICT), EAS-19 Occupation Code: 0504-5022

Performs all activities for the development and control of district operating and capital budgets; performs research and analysis of district financial operations.

DUTIES AND RESPONSIBILITIES

1. Develops, prepares, allocates, implements, monitors, and controls the district operating and capital budgets; includes current estimates of future financial performance; and integrates planning assumptions into operating budget plans.

2. Integrates all district functions into the planning process and validates budget and financial forecasts developed by managers.

3. Provides-ongoing analyses to support-operations management and improve overall financial and work hour performance, including the analysis and validation of major capital, facility, and program expenditures and packages.

4. Develops and implements business planning and forecasting techniques and monitors effectiveness; analyzes operating results to identify improvement opportunities and evaluate the effectiveness of cost reduction program implementation.

5. Develops and presents training for operating managers to increase their understanding of the budget process and the financial analysis techniques used for performance measurement.

6. Provides technical guidance to financial and operating employees in the development of capital investment strategies and operating expense budgets; maintains an effective financial planning and forecasting process for all district organizations.

BUILDING EQUIPMENT MECHANIC, PS-07 Occupation Code: 5306-07XX

Performs involved trouble shooting and complex maintenance work on Building and Building Equipment systems, and preventive maintenance and preventive maintenance inspections of building, building equipment and building systems, and maintains and operates a large automated air conditioning system and a large heating system.

DUTIES AND RESPONSIBILITIES

1. Performs, on building and building equipment, the more difficult testing, diagnosis, maintenance, adjustment and revision work, requiring a thorough knowledge of the mechanical, electrical, and electronic, pneumatic, or hydraulic control and operating mechanisms of the equipment. Performs trouble shooting and repair of complex supervisory group control panels, readout and feedback circuits and associated mechanical and electrical components throughout the installation; locates and corrects malfunctions in triggering and other electromechanical and electronic circuits.

2. Observes the various components of the building systems in operation and applies appropriate testing methods and procedures to insure continued proper operation.

3. Locates the source of and-rectifies trouble in involved or questionable cases, or in emergency situations where expert attention is required to locate and correct the defect quickly to avoid or minimize interruptions.

4. Installs or alters building equipment and circuits as directed.

5. Reports the circumstances surrounding equipment and failures, and recommends measures for their correction.

6. Performs preventive maintenance inspections of building equipment to locate incipient mechanical malfunctions and the standard of maintenance. Initiates work orders requesting corrective actions for conditions below standard; assists in the estimating of time and materials required. Recommends changes in preventative maintenance procedures and practices to provide the proper level of maintenance; assists in the revision of preventive maintenance checklists and the frequency of performing preventive maintenance routes. In instances of serious equipment failures, conducts investigation to determine the cause of the breakdown and to recommend remedial action to prevent recurrence.

7. Uses necessary hand and power tools, specialized equipment, gauging devices, and both electrical and electronic test equipment.

8. Reads and interprets schematics, blue- prints, wiring diagrams and specifications in locating and correcting potential or existing malfunctions and failures.

9. Repairs electromechanically operated equipment related to the building or building systems. Repairs, installs, modifies, and maintains building safety systems, support systems and equipment.

10. Works off ladders, scaffolds, and rigging within heights common to the facility. Works under various weather conditions out doors.

11. Completes duties and tasks related to building equipment maintenance as required.

12. Observes established safety practices and requirements pertaining to the type of work involved; recommends additional safety measures as required.

13. In addition, may oversee the work of lower level maintenance employees, advising and instructing them in proper and safe work methods and checking for adherence to instructions; make in-process and final operational checks and tests of work completed by lower level maintenance employees.

14. Performs other job related tasks in support of primary duties.

CARRIER (CITY), PS-05 Occupation Code: 2310-01XX

Delivers and collects mail on foot or by vehicle under varying conditions in a prescribed area within a city. Maintains pleasant and effective public relations with route customers and others, requiring a general familiarity with postal laws, regulations, and procedures commonly used, and with the geography of the city. (Refer to Chapter Three for a complete description of Clerk and Mail Carrier occupations.)

CASUAL, EAS-07 Occupation Code: 5201-1001

Performs mail handling, mail processing, mail delivery, mail collection, mail transportation, and custodial functions, or a combination of such duties on a supplemental basis. (Refer to Chapter Three for a complete description of Clerk and Mail Carrier occupations.)

CLERK STENOGRAPHER, PS-05 Occupation Code: 0312-01XX

Performs miscellaneous office clerical, stenographic, and typing work.

DUTIES AND RESPONSIBILITIES

1. Takes dictation, in shorthand or on a shorthand writing machine, of letters, memorandums, reports, and other materials and transcribes it on the typewriter or wordprocessor; sets up the material transcribed in accordance with prescribed format and assembles it for required initialing, signing, routing, and dispatch.

2. Types similar materials from handwritten and other drafts, and from dictating machine-records.

3. Makes up file folders, keeps them in prescribed order, and places in and withdraws from them papers relating to the business of the office.

4. Makes and keeps routine records of the office.

5. Composes routine memorandums and letters relating to the business of the office, such as acknowledgments and transmittals.

6. Examines the incoming and outgoing mail of the office, routes it to the appropriate persons, and controls the time allowed for preparation of replies to incoming correspondence.

7. Receipts for and delivers salary checks and fills out various personnel forms.

8. Acts as receptionist and answers telephone calls, taking and relaying messages and furnishing routine information requested.

9. Relieves office clerks, typists, clerk typists or other clerk-stenographers during periods of their absence.

10. Operates copy machine and calculators.

COMPUTER SYSTEMS ANALYST/PROGRAMMER (PDC), DCS-20 Occupation Code: 0334-3056

Analyzes and evaluates existing and proposed systems and develops computer programs, systems, and procedures to process data.

DUTIES AND RESPONSIBILITIES

1. Translates user requirements to automate problem analysis and record keeping activities into detailed program flowcharts.

2. Prepares programming specifications and diagrams and develops coding logic flowcharts.

3. Codes, tests, debugs, and installs computer programs and procedures.

4. Reviews and updates computer programs and provides the necessary documentation for the computer operations function.

5. Prepares charts and diagrams to assist in problem analysis.

6. Prepares detailed program specifications and flowcharts and coordinates the system's installation with the user.

7. Provides technical advice and guidance to programmers assigned on a project basis; provides advice and assistance to managers involved in installing an automated system.

8. Has regular contact with contract employees and computer equipment vendors

CUSTODIAN, PS-02 Occupation Code: 3566-04XX
Performs manual laboring duties in connection with custody of an office or building.

DUTIES AND RESPONSIBILITIES

1. Performs any one or a combination of the duties listed below.

2. Moves furniture and equipment.

3. Uncrates and assembles furniture and fixtures, using bolts and screws for assembly.

4. Loads and unloads supplies and equipment.

5. Removes trash from work areas, lobbies, and washrooms.

6. Tends to lawns, shrubbery, and premises of the post office and cleans ice and snow from the sidewalk s and-driveways.

7. Stacks supplies in storage rooms and on shelves, and completes forms or records as required.

8. May perform cleaning duties as assigned.

DATA COLLECTION TECHNICIAN, PS-06 Occupation Code: 0301-69XX
Collects, records, and analyzes a variety of statistical data on selected operating and financial activities. Performs relief assignments for PSDS Technicians.

DUTIES AND RESPONSIBILITIES

1. Collects, records, & analyzes statistical data under any number of national data collection systems.

2. Operates computer equipment to enter data; recognizes diagnostic messages and takes appropriate actions; and performs data transfer functions through telecommunications systems.

3. Reviews input and output data to determine accuracy and compliance with national programs. Analyzes and edits data to detect and correct errors.

4. Updates national data bases; maintains and updates records and files.

5. Participates in data collection activities in support of special studies or national programs.

6. Reads and interprets reference manuals and other written materials.

7. May drive a vehicle to other facilities when work assignments require.

8. Performs other job related tasks in support of primary duties.

DISTRIBUTION CLERK, PS-05 Occupation Code: 2315-04XX

Separates mail in a post office, terminal, airport mail facility or other postal facility in accordance with established schemes, including incoming or outgoing mail or both. (Refer to Chapter Three for a complete description of Clerk and Mail Carrier occupations.)

ELECTRONICS TECHNICIAN, PS-10 Occupation Code: 0856-01XX

Carries out all phases of maintenance, troubleshooting, and testing of electronic circuitry used in equipment and systems requiring a knowledge of solid state electronics. Instructs and provides technical support on complex systems and on combinational (hardware/software) or intermittent problems.

DUTIES AND RESPONSIBILITIES

1. Performs the testing, diagnosis, maintenance, and revision work requiring a knowledge of solid state electronics.

2. Observes the various equipment and systems in operation and applies appropriate testing and diagnostic methods and procedures to ensure proper- operation.

3. Locates source of equipment and system failures, rectifies trouble in involved cases, or provides instructions to be used by maintenance employees performing repair work.

4. Makes-or participates with contractor representative or electronic technician in installing or altering equipment and systems as required.

5. Makes reports of equipment and system failures which require corrective action by contractor and follows up to see that appropriate action is taken.

6. Makes preventive maintenance inspections to discover incipient malfunctions and to review the standards of maintenance. Recommends changes in preventive maintenance procedures and practices as found to be necessary.

7. Programs scheme and/or scheme changes into memory units as requested by management.

8. Furnishes pertinent data to superiors and contract employees on operation and testing problems.

9. Participates in training programs: classroom, on-the-job, and correspondence, at postal facilities, trade schools, and manufacturer's plants as required. May assist in developing and implementing training programs. Instructs equal or lower level employees as required.

10. Observes established safety regulations pertaining to the type of work involved.

11. May drive vehicle or utilize other available mode of transportation to work site when necessary.

12. Provides technical support to other electronic technicians to resolve complex, combinational (hardware/software), and/or intermittent failures.

13. Performs such other duties as may be assigned.

FINANCIAL SERVICES COORDINATOR, EAS-18 Occupation Code: 0510-5050
Coordinates, analyzes, and monitors district wide financial accounting programs and processes; coordinates the implementation of new accounting and timekeeping policies and procedures; provides technical guidance to post offices and field units in the resolution of daily accounting problems.

DUTIES AND RESPONSIBILITIES

1. Analyzes, evaluates, and determines the need for changes to district financial accounting programs and processes; identifies deficiencies and problems; and recommends and implements corrective actions to improve quality and reduce errors.

2. Provides guidance and training to post office and field unit employees concerning financial accounting procedures, including the proper recording of statements of accounts and adjustments of daily unit financial statements.

3. Resolves accounting problems, including those associated with banking, payables, and payroll adjustments.

4. Monitors revenue reporting and performs audits of financial activities to ensure financial integrity.

5. Coordinates district accounting programs and processes with the Postal Data Center and other functional areas.

6. Implements national, area, and district accounting and timekeeping policies and procedures.

7. Provides technical advice, guidance, assistance, and training to post offices and field units throughout the district area on the full range of accounting and timekeeping programs and processes.

FLAT SORTING MACHINE OPERATOR, PS-05 Occupation Code: 2315-20XX
Operates a single or multi-position, electromechanical operator paced flat sorting machine in the distribution of flats requiring knowledge and application of approved machine distribution of directs, alphabetical or geographic groupings, by reading the ZIP Code on each flat. (Refer to Chapter Three for a complete description of Clerk and Mail Carrier occupations.)

HUMAN RESOURCES SPECIALIST, EAS-15 Occupation Code: 0201-5117
Performs technical staff work in support of the implementation and administration of one or more human resources programs.

OPERATIONAL REQUIREMENTS

In addition to the following program responsibilities, oversees and coordinates the activities of a small size group of lower level employees, including making assignments, monitoring and reviewing work, providing continuing technical guidance, approving leave, and taking disciplinary action.

DUTIES AND RESPONSIBILITIES

1. PERSONNEL SERVICES: Implements and administers employee compensation and benefits programs, including wage and salaries, pay procedures and rules, performance evaluations, merits, suggestions, incentive and superior accomplishment awards, quality step increases, retirements, and insurance.

2. Provides information to and processes requests from state unemployment compensation agencies for separated employees; testifies in unemployment compensation hearings.

3. Administers employment and selection policies, procedures, and processes for bargaining, initial level supervisor, non-bargaining, and postmaster positions.

4. Coordinates entrance and in-service examination programs; oversees all procedures and processes related to examination scheduling, conducting, processing, grading, notification, and forwarding of test data.

5. SAFETY AND HEALTH: Monitors compliance with safety and health standards and regulations; conducts periodic inspections; ensures accurate accident reporting; analyzes accident rates and trends; and provides for improvement of safety awareness and accident prevention through training and promotional activities.

6. Implements Wellness Program by coordinating programs, services, and activities that promote employee health efforts.

7. Administers procedures under which employees with substance abuse and other personal problems are referred to external providers contracted under the Employee Assistance Program.

8. INJURY COMPENSATION: Provides comprehensive case management in the review and processing of injury compensation claims, including authorization and control of continuation of pay; controversion of claims; identification of possible fraud and abuse; third party claims and recovery; assignment to limited duty; and referral to the rehabilitation program, or for second opinions or fitness for duty exams.

9. TRAINING: Plans, schedules, implements, administers, coordinates, evaluates, and performs employee training, career planning and development, diagnostic testing, and counseling services; conducts workshops, orientations, and demonstrations; coordinates managerial and supervisory training; and provides guidance to employees, job trainers, and management regarding training and instructional processes.

MAINTENANCE MECHANIC, PS-05

Independently performs semiskilled preventive, corrective and predictive maintenance tasks associated with the upkeep and operation of various types of mail processing, buildings and building equipment, customer service and delivery equipment.

DUTIES AND RESPONSIBILITIES

1. Independently performs preventive maintenance and minor repairs on plumbing, heating, refrigeration, air-conditioning, low-voltage electrical systems, and other building systems and equipment.

2. Performs preventive maintenance and routine repairs on simple control circuitry, bearings, chains, sprockets, motors, belts and belting, and other moving parts or wearing surfaces of equipment.

3. Assembles, installs, replaces, repairs, modifies and adjusts all types of small operating equipment such as letter boxes, mechanical scales, stamp vending equipment, building service equipment, manhandling equipment and related equipment.

4. Under the direction of skilled maintenance employees, or clearly written instructions from either hard copy or electronic format, performs specific tasks related to disassembling equipment, replacing parts, relocating and reassembling equipment; assists higher level workers in locating and repairing equipment malfunctions.

5. Maintains an awareness of equipment operation, especially excessive heat, vibration, and noise, reporting malfunctions, hazards or wear to supervisor.

6. Uses a variety of hand and power tools, gauging devices and test equipment required, or as directed, to perform the above tasks.

7. May drive a vehicle to transport tools, equipment, employees, materials or in the normal performance of assigned duties.

8. Completes or initiates work record sheets, as required. Takes readings from meters, gauges, counters and other monitoring and measuring devices. Maintains logs and other required records; reports on breakdowns and equipment being tested.

9. Follows established safety practices and requirements while performing all duties.

10. May serve as a working leader over a group of lower level employees assigned to a specific task.

11. Performs other duties as assigned.

MECHANICAL ENGINEER, EAS-24 Occupation Code: 0830-4012

Plans, organizes, and executes the design, construction, installation, and implementation of new systems, equipment, or controls of major magnitude and scope, in support of the mail processing objectives of the Postal Service.

DUTIES AND RESPONSIBILITIES

Translates operating objectives for mail processing into functional requirements for facilities, or equipment, oversees the reporting, analysis, and evaluation of data from field operating units related to mail volume, productivity, or costs; integrates this information with technical data to determine functional specifications.

2. Oversees the preparation and justification of engineering proposals and alternatives for complex mechanized systems equipment; evaluates engineered systems and related costs to determine

alternatives to support mail processing objectives; provides program costs estimates; develops and recommends plans for program implementation.

3. Oversees engineering activities related to the design, construction, installation, test, and start-up of mechanized systems and equipment; provides technical management of contracts; evaluates contractor bids; makes recommendations affecting the selection of contractors; determines criteria for performance evaluation of prototype equipment; controls program costs; certifies contractor requests for payment.

4. Coordinates planning and implementation of mechanization systems and equipment programs with headquarters and field employees.

5. Provides mechanical engineering consulting services, as required.

6. Has frequent contact with contractors, professional consultants, officials of government agencies, and equipment manufacturers.

NURSE, OCCUPATIONAL HEALTH PNS-01 Occupation Code: 0610-4001
Provides professional nursing services to employees under the general direction of a medical officer. Implements and participates in programs to provide preventative medical care and health maintenance services in support of Postal Service safety and health goals and objectives.

DUTIES AND RESPONSIBILITIES

1. Implements, monitors, and participates in occupational health programs and services within a postal facility.

2. Provides professional nursing care to employees; administers medications at the direction of a physician; and makes arrangements for physicians' care.

3. Provides continuous health or injury care, under physicians' instructions, to employees with prolonged illnesses or injuries.

4. Assists Medical Officer in conducting reemployment or fitness-for-duty physical examinations; performs routine examinations for items such as vision, hearing, and blood pressure; and makes recommendations regarding suitability for employment and/or referral for additional testing and evaluation.

5. Advises or counsels employees regarding general and/or mental health care; assists employees with doctor and/or community service referrals, when necessary.

6. Prepares, updates, and maintains confidential health records for employees using the health and medical unit; compiles and analyzes various medical data and reports; and prepares regular summary reports.

7. Requisitions appropriate quantities and types of medical supplies and maintains security of supplies and equipment.

8. Regularly checks first aid boxes to ensure an adequate supply of necessary items.

9. Maintains the health/medical unit in a sanitary and orderly condition.

10. Provides continuous medical monitoring of workers exposed to potentially harmful substances.

11. Reports on-the-job injuries and other safety and health matters to appropriate postal officials.

12. Maintains familiarity with Workers Compensation and safety and personnel practices and procedures relative to occupational health programs.

13. Serves as liaison with employees, supervisors, physicians, PAR and safety employees; refers employees for participation in the PAR and other health related programs.

14. Performs related clerical duties.

15. Makes frequent contact with private physicians and representatives of hospitals and health clinics. Has occasional contact with customers, contractors' employees, and representatives of emergency services and social agencies.

16. Provides professional advice and guidance to supervisors regarding administrative procedures; provides health care advice and counseling to employees.

17. Exercises a normal regard for the safety of self and others.

PERSONNEL CLERK, PS-05 Occupation Code: 0203-14XX
Performs specialized clerical work involved in providing the central personnel services of a postal installation.

DUTIES AND RESPONSIBILITIES

1. Performs any one or a combination of the duties listed below.

2. Examines, documents, and otherwise processes official personnel actions.

3. Inducts new employees by taking their fingerprints, providing them with, and instructing them in filling out forms, administering oaths, and performing related operations.

4. Examines applications for leave by employees when the type or durations of leave desired fall within the categories required to be acted on centrally; compares the justification with the criteria for approval, and drafts memorandums or notifications of the action to be taken on the applications.

5. Examines for completeness or composes reports of personnel injuries sustained by employees in the performance of their duties and examines for completeness claims by such employees for compensation due to time lost from work because of such injuries; makes these reports and claims ready for forwarding to the appropriate government agency and composes notification to the employees or their supervisors of additional information needed and of decisions made on claims.

6. Furnishes information to employees and applicants about personnel regulations and practices, including employment in the postal installation, by personal conversations, telephone conversations, and composition of letters and memorandums.

7. Maintains various personnel records by performing such operations as posting actions taken concerning employees, adding names to and removing them from registers and rosters, and filing official papers in personnel folders.

8. Compiles various recurring and special statistical reports on personnel subjects, such as numbers of actions of various types, numbers of employees of various titles and salaries, numbers of vacancies of various titles and organizational locations.

9. In addition, may perform any of the following duties: document and otherwise process official personnel actions originating on the basis of personnel records; record the receipt of employee suggestions and initiate action for their review by appropriate supervisors; assist employees in filling out applications for retirement and documenting these forms for submission to appropriate organizations; process bids for position openings on seniority basis; and accept employment applications, and forward them to appropriate organizations.

POLICE OFFICER, POSTAL (B), PPO-06

Performs a variety of duties pertaining to the security of postal buildings, personnel, property, mail, and mail-in-transit in support of the postal security program.

DUTIES AND RESPONSIBILITIES

1. Performs a variety of duties pertaining to the security of postal buildings, personnel, property, mail, and mail-in-transit.

2. Carries a firearm and exercises standard care required by the Inspection Service on firearms and use of reasonable force. Maintains assigned firearms in good condition.

3. Maintains incidents reported and daily logs of orders and basic in formation for the security force.

4. Answers the office telephone and responds to reports and inquiries.

5. Performs patrol duty, as assigned, on foot or by motor vehicle to maintain order and safeguard the facility, property, and personnel; ensures the application of security measures in manhandling areas.

6. Maintains contact with other security force personnel; responds to emergencies and other conditions, including burglaries and hold-ups, requiring immediate attention.

7. Controls access to building at an assigned post; enforces the regulations requiring identification.

8. Makes arrests and testifies in court on law violations within assigned authority.

9. Performs other job related tasks in support of the primary duties.

POSTAL INSPECTOR (PROJECTS COORDINATOR), EAS-24

Oversees and coordinates the most complex and sensitive criminal, civil, administrative, and audit investigations, programs, projects, and studies; oversees task forces and teams of Postal Inspectors in the accomplishment of investigative objectives; oversees and coordinates the planning, development, implementation, and monitoring of projects, and studies within assigned area.

OPERATIONAL REQUIREMENTS

Carries firearms when engaged in official business and for self-defense; maintains established physical requirements necessary to perform law enforcement assignments; maintains eligibility to operate a motor vehicle when engaged in official business; and maintains mental and emotional standards necessary to perform law enforcement assignments.

DUTIES AND RESPONSIBILITIES

1. Oversees and coordinates the most complex-and sensitive criminal, civil, administrative, and audit investigations, programs, projects, and studies. Investigates violations of postal laws and apprehends and arrests postal offenders.

2. Oversees and supervises the activities of task forces and teams of Postal Inspectors, and a small group of technical and support employees. Evaluates performance and takes the necessary action to correct deficiencies, including discipline or remedial training. Provides training for new or less experienced Inspection Service employees.

3. Assists U. S. Attorneys and other criminal justice employees in preparing court cases involving postal laws. Independently prepares comprehensive case presentation letters to the U. S. Attorney. Serves as a witness in court and administrative proceedings.

4. Coordinates the development, planning, and implementation of new programs and projects to improve methods, techniques, and skills of Inspection Service employees.

5. Ensures that all regularly scheduled and standard inspections are properly monitored and carried out by assigned personnel.

6. Analyzes, reviews, and initially approves investigation reports, correspondence, case history information, and other documentation prepared for management review; prepares special reports and correspondence.

7. Maintains liaison with law enforcement agencies to coordinate record exchanges, case development, suspect apprehension, jurisdiction definition, security checks, and joint training.

8. Provides technical guidance and advice to postal management. Conducts conferences with postal management on the results of major audit projects and makes recommendations for service improvements, operational economies, and other areas included in the review.

9. Recommends policies and procedures that are not covered by established Inspection Service methods or guidelines.

10. Oversees and coordinates the investigation into the misconduct of postal employees and the presentation of evidence to Postal management for consideration in disciplinary cases.

11. Represents the Inspection Service by providing supporting information or participating in the development, implementation, and administration of technology, automation, service, operations, and training programs.

12. Reacts in emergencies to protect mail and postal assets where use of firearms and defensive techniques may be required. May work in undesirable neighborhoods and in adverse and hazardous situations.

13. Has frequent contact with the general public, witnesses, victims, complainants, suspects and offenders, informants, postal customers and contractors, federal and private attorneys, and representatives of the business community, law enforcement agencies, government agencies, armed services, and the courts. Represents the Inspection Service at law enforcement, security, and civic conferences and meetings.

14. Exercises normal protective care for the use of facilities and equipment, including vehicles, weapons, and communications and technical equipment.

15. Exercises a normal regard for the safety of self and others when investigating criminal cases and apprehending or maintaining surveillance of those suspected of violating postal laws. Exercises the standard of care required by Inspection Service policies on firearms and use of reasonable force when apprehending and restraining suspects.

RURAL CARRIER, RCS-00

Cases, delivers, and collects mail along a prescribed rural route using a vehicle; provides customers on the route with a variety of services. (Refer to Chapter Three for a complete description of Clerk and Mail Carrier occupations.)

SECRETARY, EAS-11 Occupation Code: 0318-2041

Provides secretarial support for a manager and his/her staff. Processes information in accordance with established organizational and functional area administrative practices and procedures.

DUTIES AND RESPONSIBILITIES

1. Produces reports, letters and other documentation using word processing equipment, and monitors peripheral equipment.

2. Accesses, retrieves and/or updates files and other data maintained on computers.

3. Sends and receives electronic messages, files and other documentation via the local area network.

4. Produces charts, tables and other documentation using various graphics packages.

5. Compiles information on a variety of subjects; reviews periodicals, publications, and industry related documents, bringing those of interest to manager's attention.

6. Reviews materials prepared for accuracy and proper format; ensures compliance with established collective bargaining policies.

7. Performs routine clerical duties such as, answering telephones, operating office equipment, requisitioning supplies, and coordinating printing, maintenance, and other service requests.

8. Screens, logs, and routes office mail.

9. Performs other administrative duties, such as maintaining a variety of reports, such as: time and attendance records, correspondence control, training plans, etc. , and maintains office files.

TELECOMMUNICATIONS SPECIALIST, EAS-17 Occupation Code: 0393-5001

Provides analysis, coordination, and technical support for the voice and data telecommunications activities in a district.

DUTIES AND RESPONSIBILITIES

1. Analyzes voice and data telecommunications requirements, including networks and hardware; recommends new and improved services; and coordinates acquisition/implementation.

2. Prepares recommendations for system changes to improve effectiveness and reduce telecommunications costs; coordinates with national telecommunications network program specialists, and implements approved changes.

3. Coordinates the acquisition and installation of new telecommunications hardware; performs preacceptance tests to verify proper operations; makes changes to telecommunications control systems to activate or restrict specific services to designated lines, and oversees equipment repair projects.

4. Monitors all aspects of the telecommunications system, including line traffic and overall system usage; oversees the verification and certification of monthly billings, and prepares analyses and reports for management review.

5. Prepares and implements training for telecommunications system users throughout the district.

6. Troubleshoots network & equipment problems & resolves or coordinates resolution with vendors.

7. Has regular contact with representatives of local telecommunication services vendors.

8. Provides technical guidance to employees on telecommunications system operations.

WELDER, PS-06
Fabricates or repairs metal items in forge and on anvil; performs welding and brazing operations.

DUTIES AND RESPONSIBILITIES

1. Forges and fabricates or repairs tools and metal parts for building and equipment; heats metal to proper temperature in forge, hammers and bends metal to specified size and shape; hardens and tempers metals.

2. Does acetylene and electric welding on building equipment and such items as machine parts, hand truck frames, pouch racks, and conveyor equipment; also does brazing work; sets up job to be welded or brazed; sets up and adjusts proper type of welding equipment and selects proper type of rod according to the needs of the work; performs metal cutting and burning with torch.

3. Works from drawings, sketches and general instructions.

4. Uses required hand and power tools.

5. In addition, oversees helpers as assigned & may perform work incident to other trades as required.

WINDOW CLERK, PS-05

Performs a variety of services at a public window of a post office or post office branch or station. maintains pleasant and effective public relations with customers and others requiring a general familiarity with postal laws, regulations, and procedures commonly used. (Refer to Chapter Three for a complete description of Clerk and Mail Carrier occupations.)

Chapter Ten
Occupation Directory

The Postal Service employs workers in approximately 2,000 job classifications. This USPS Position Directory will assist job seekers in several ways. First, it provides a comprehensive resource for job seekers to identify all potential occupations for which they may qualify. Second, it lists the pay (refer to the pay charts in Chapter One), the total number employed for each position, and the USPS Occupational Code (OCC-CODE). Occupations featured in Chapter Nine are marked with an arrow symbol (➤).

This directory presents a pandoras box of opportunities from custodial, maintenance, and general labor trades to accountants, engineers, and computer specialists. The majority of manager's positions were excluded from this list because they are generally not entry level positions.

After reviewing this list and identifying various occupations as potential job sources, go to the "Job Hunter's Checklist" in Appendix A. This checklist will guide you step-by-step through the USPS hiring maze.

OCCUPATION DIRECTORY

OCCUPATION	OCC-CODE	PAY	TOTAL
ACCOUNT REPRESENTATIVE	2345 5031	EAS-15	436
ACCOUNT REPRESENTATIVE	2345-5032	EAS-18	62
ACCOUNTABLE CLERK ML RECOVERY CTR	2345-69XX	PS-06	4
ACCOUNTABLE PAPER CONTROL SPECLST	200l 5008	EAS-17	2
ACCOUNTABLE PAPER CONTROL SPECLST	2001-5020	EAS-19	
ACCOUNTABLE PAPER DISTRIBUTION SPC	2003-5022	EAS-23	3
ACCOUNTABLE PAPER MANUFCTRNG SPCLS	2003-6021	EAS-25	2
ACCOUNTABLE PAPER SPEC (PFSC)	0530-2009	EAS-13	in
ACCOUNTANT	0510-4055	EAS-21	11
ACCOUNTANT	0510-4056	EAS-25	11
ACCOUNTANT	0510-4057	EAS-23	1
ACCOUNTANT JR PDC	0510-3002	DCS-16	20
ACCOUNTANT POSTAL FACILITIES (A)	0510-3020	EAS-16	3
ACCOUNTING ASSOCIATE	0540-5009		2
ACCT PPR SUPP CLK	0530-05XX	PS-05	151
ACCTG ASST	0525 6003	EAS-14	I
ACCTG CLERK PDC	0520-2020	DCS-09	21
ACCTG CLK	0520-01XX	PS-05	72
ACCTG SPEC SP PDC	0525-5015	DCS-17	11

OCCUPATION	OCC-CODE	PAY	TOTAL
➤ ACCTG TECH	0525-3iXX	PS-06	1,193
ACCTG TECH COST MES	0525-2026	EAS-13	I
ACCTG TECH PDC	0525-5019	DCS-11	46
ACCTG&BUDGET TECH	0525-3010	EAS-14	2
ACCTNG SPEC PDC	0525-5018	DCS-14	83
ACCTNT PDC	0510-3014	DCS-18	26
ACCFNT PSTL FAC C	0510-6023	EAS-20	
ACCTS PAYABLE ASST CENTER SPEC	0540-5016	DCS-14	7
ACCTS PAYABLE ASST CTR ANALYST	0540-5017	DCS-18	1
ACQUISITIONS LIBRARIAN	1411-5003	EAS-16	I
ADDRESS MANAGEMENT SYSTEMS SPCLST	2310-4014		425
ADDRESS MGMT SYSTEMS SPECIALIST	2310-4013	EAS-17	9
ADM CLK EXPRESS ML	2340-81XX	PS-05	226
ADMIN COORDINATOR - PMG OFFICE	0301-5362	EAS-19	1
ADMIN SERVICES COORDINATOR	0301-5365	EAS-14	1
ADMIN SERVICES TECH	0301-5364	EAS-11	1
ADMIN SUPPORT SPEC (IS)	2335-6011	EAS-18	6
ADMIN SUPPORT SPECIALIST	2335-6010	EAS-21	6
ADMIN SUPPORT SPECIALIST	2335-6012	EAS-16	20
ADMINISTRATIVE CLERK (NISSC)	0301-2108	EAS-07	1
ADMINISTRATIVE COORDINATOR	0301-5248	EAS-19	2
ADMINISTRATIVE JUDGE	0935-4003	EAS-30	2
ADMINISTRATIVE LAW JUDGE	0935-4004		1
ADMINISTRATIVE SPEC (LAW DEPT)	0341-5046	EAS-18	2
ADMINISTRATIVE SPECIALIST (EPD)	0341-5051	EAS 14	1
ADMINISTRATIVE SPECIALIST (MTSC)	0341-5025	EAS-15	1
ADMN CLK PDC	0301-2073	DCS-07	12
ADMN CLK VMF	0301-09XX	PS-06	135
ADMN SERVICES COORDINATOR	0342-5029	EAS-14	10
ADP PLANNING SPECIALIST	0340-4002	EAS-24	1
ADP RESOURCES ANALYST	0301-5341	EAS-23	1
ADP RESOURCES ANALYST	0301-5342	EAS-21	1
ADVERTISING SPECIALIST	1081-5032		1
ADVERTISING SPECIALIST	1081-5034	EAS-23	9
ADVERTISING SPECIALIST	1081-5046	EAS-25	1
ADVISORY RESOURCES SPECIALIST	1081-5056	EAS-23	1
AIR RECORDS PROCESSOR	2330-46XX	PS-05	504
AIR TRANSPORTATION SPECIALIST (B)	2330-6012	EAS-17	35
AIR TRANSPTN SPEC A	2330-5016	EAS-15	26
ANALYST SCHEMES&SCHD	2350-4003		24
APPEALS INFORMATION SYSTEMS SPCLST	0335-5002	EAS-19	1
APPEALS REVIEW EXAMINER/ANALYST	0954-4015	EAS-21	13
APPEALS REVIEW SPECIALIST	0954-4012	EAS-23	21
APPEALS REVIEW SPECIALIST	0954-5001	EAS-25	2
APPEALS TECHNICIAN	0301-5350	EAS-14	1
APPEALS TECHNICIAN	0335-3019		5
APPLIED TECHNOLOGY PLANNER	0334-4111	EAS-24	3
APPRAISER	1171-4003	EAS-25	1
APPRAISER	1171-4004	EAS-23	2
ARBITRATION SCHED COORD	0303-5001	EAS-13	5
ARCHITECT/ENGINEER	0808-3017	EAS-21	9
ARCHITECT/ENGINEER	0808-3018	EAS-23	46
ARCHITECT/ENGINEER	0808-3019	EAS-25	34
➤ ARCHITECT/ENGINEER	0808-3020	EAS-20	103
AREA COORD EI/QWL PROCESSES	0230-5064	EAS-18	39
AREA MAIL TRANSPORT EQUIPMENT SPEC	2330-4028	EAS-19	10
AREA MAINT SPEC	4801-21XX	PS-07	150
➤ AREA MAINT TECH	4801-20XX	PS-08	323
AREA MGR STAMP DISTRIBUTION NETWK	2003-7021	EAS-19	2
ASSIGNMENT CLK	0212-05XX	PS-06	12
ASSOC JUDICAL OFFICER	0905-5030	PCES-I	1
ASSOC MEDICAL DIRECTOR AREA OFFICE	0602-7006	EAS-26	29
ASST PSTL INSP-P-IN-CHG	2335-7032	EAS-26	19

ASST SECRETARY TO THE BOG	0301-5563	PCES-1	
ASST SUPT NGHT TOUR WHT HSE	2315-6039	EAS-16	1
ASST SUPT WHT HSE ML SEC	2305-6039	EAS-18	1
ASST SUPV REC SEC CTR WHT HSE	2340-6016	EAS-16	1
ASST TREASURER BANKING	0505-7070	PCES-I	1
ASST TREASURER FINANCING/INVESTMENT	0505-7069		1
ATTORNEY	0905-4034	APS-01	123
AUDIOVISUAL PRODUCER	1071-5014	EAS-18	5
AUDIOVISUAL TECHNICIAN	1071-3018	EAS-16	2
AUTOMATED OPRNS SOFTWARE SPEC	0334-4116	EAS-20	3
AUTOMATION INTEGRATION ANALYST	0301-5366	PCES-I	I
AUTOMATION INTEGRATION ANALYST	0301-5367	EAS-25	1
AUTOMATION INTEGRATION ANALYST	0301-5368	EAS-23	1
AUTOMOTIVE MECH	5823-03XX	PS-07	6
➤ AUTOMOTIVE MECH	5823-03XX	PS-06	2,762
AUTOMOTIVE MECHANIC JUNIOR	5823-02XX		
AUTOMOTIVE MECHANIC JUNIOR	5823-02XX	PS-05	87
AUTOMOTIVE PAINTER	415S-OIXX	PS-06	33
AUTOMOTIVE TECHNICIAN ASSOCIATE	5823-11XX	PS-05	
AUTOMOTIVE TECHNICIAN ASSOCIATE	5823-11XX		3
AUX RURAL CARRIER	2325-03XX	RAUX-05	177
BANKING OFFICER	0505-4035	EAS-23	2
BANKING SYSTEMS OFFICER	0505-4040	EAS-25	
BLDG SVC MECH	5306-OBXX	OSD-07	3
BODY AND FENDER REPAIRMAN	3809-02XX	PS-07	289
BUDGET & FINANCIAL ANALYST	0560-5022	EAS-20	3
BUDGET AND FINANCIAL ANALYST	0560-5023	EAS-23	I
BUDGET ASSOCIATE	0560-5021	EAS-16	1
BUDGET SPECIALIST	0560-4027	EAS-25	4
BUDGET SPECIALIST	0560-4028	EAS-23	7
BUDGET SPECIALIST	0560-4029	EAS-21	3
BUDGET&COST ANALYST	0560-4025	EAS-20	1
BUDGET/COST ANALYST	0560-4018	EAS-22	6
BUDGET/COST ANALYST	0560-4019	EAS-24	3
BUDGET/COST ANALYST	0560-4030	EAS-20	1
BUDGET/FINANCIAL ANALYST(AREA OFC)	0504-5019	EAS-21	56
➤ BUDGET/FINANCIAL ANALYST(DIST)	0504-5022	EAS-19	146
BUDGET/PERSONNEL COORDINATOR	0301-5346		1
BUILDING CUSTODIAN	4749-06XX	PS-04	2
➤ BUILDING EQUIPMENT MECH	5306-07XX	PS-07	1,928
BUILDING MAINTENANCE CUSTODIAN	4749-10XX	PS-04	1,004
BUILDING SERVICES SPECIALIST	1601-4004	EAS-19	2
BUILDING SERVICES SPECIALIST	1601-4026	EAS-21	I
BULK MAIL DOCK CLK	2315-99XX	PS-06	403
BULK ML CLK	2320-15XX		4
BULK ML CLK	2320-15XX	PS-05	1,350
BULK ML TECH	2320-28XX	PS-06	1,864
BUSINESS MAIL ENTRY ANALYST	2345-4019	EAS-15	76
BUSINESS PROJECT			42
LEADER	0334-4131	EAS-24	
BUSINESS REENGINEERING ANALYST	0334-4123	EAS-25	4
BUSINESS SYSTEMS ANALYST	0334-4129	EAS-23	62
BUSINESS SYSTEMS ENGINEER	0334-4132	EAS-24	9
BUSINESS SYSTEMS MANAGER	0334-6045	EAS-25	26
CABINETMAKER/CARPENTER	4605-OIXX	OSD-07	I
CAPITAL INVESTMENT SPECIALIST	0505-4037	EAS-25	2
CAPITAL INVESTMENT SPECIALIST	0505-4036	EAS-23	
CAPITAL INVESTMENT SPECIALIST	0505-4039	EAS-21	1-
CAPITAL MARKETS ASSOCIATE	0505-4033	EAS-23	1
CAREER PLANNING SPECIALIST	0212-5049	EAS-25	
CAREER PLANNING SPECIALIST	0212-5050	EAS-23	
CAREER PLANNING SPECIALIST	0212-5051	EAS-21	I
CARPENTER	4607-02XX	PS-06	145
CARRIER (CITY)	2310-2009	?Q?-05	
➤ CARRIER CITY OR SPEC	2310-01XX	PS-05	223,562

CARRIER TECH	2310-02XX	PS-06	28,240
CARRIER TECHNICIAN	2310-2010	?Q?-06	
CASH MANAGER	0505-4031	EAS-23	1
➤ CASUAL	5201-1001	EAS-07	27,854
CASUAL SEVERLY HANDICAPPED	5201-1005		1
CHAUFFEUR	5703-2010	EAS-11	5
CHF COUNS CLASS & CUSTOMER SERVICE	0905-7037	PCES-I	1
CHF COUNS CONSUMER PROTECTION LAW	0905-7038		1
CHF COUNS EMPLOYEE RELATIONS LAW	0905-7039		1
CHF COUNS LABOR RELATIONS LAW	0905-7040		1
CHF COUNS LITIGATION & PROG SUPP	0905-7042		1
CHF COUNSEL ETHICS & INFO LAW	0905-7032		1
CHF COUNSEL STATE & LOCAL POLICIES	0905-7047		1
CHIEF CAPITAL MARKETS ASSOCIATE	0505-4032	EAS-25	1
CHIEF COUNSEL APPELLATE	0905-7041	PCES-I	1
CHIEF COUNSEL CLAIMS LAW	0905-7044		1
CHIEF COUNSEL ENFORCEMENT LAW	0905-7043		1
CHIEF COUNSEL FACILITIES LAW	0905-7034		1
CHIEF COUNSEL LEGISLATIVE	0905-7035		1
CHIEF COUNSEL PURCHASING LAW	0905-7033		1
CHIEF COUNSEL RATEMAKING	0905-7036		1
CHIEF FIELD COUNSEL	0905-7045		a
CHIEF INSPECTOR	0301-7036	PCES-IL	1
CHIEF INVESTMENT OFFICER	0505-4028	EAS-25	1
CLAIMS & INQUIRY CLK	2345-15XX	PS-05	395
CLAIMS SPECIALIST	0992-5006	EAS-15	4
CLASSIFICATION SPECIALIST	2345-4016	EAS-25	3
CLASSIFICATION SPECIALIST	2345-4017	EAS-23	2
CLASSIFICATION SUPPORT SPEC SR	2345-4010		16
CLASSIFICATION SUPPORT SPEC STF	2345-4013	EAS-19	1
CLASSIFICATION SUPPORT SPECIALIST	2345-4011	EAS-21	41
CLASSIFICATION SUPPORT TECHNICIAN	2345-3002	EAS-15	1
CLEANER	3565-OIXX	PS-03	
CLEANER	3565-01XX	PS-02	2
CLEANER	3565-01XX	PS-01	48
CLEANER EXECUTIVE AREAS	3565-06XX	OSD-02	1
CLERK ADP EQUIPMENT	0301-2105	MESC-05	10
CLERK FINANCE ST	2320-05XX	PS-06	1,137
CLERK RECOVERY CENTER LETTERS	2345-07XX	PS-05	168
CLERK RECOVERY CENTER PARCELS	2345-09XX		33
➤ CLERK STENOGRAPHER	0312-01XX		673
CLERK TYPIST	0322-02XX	PS-04	313
CLK VEHICLE DISPATCHING	0301-47XX	PS-05	118
CLK-INCHG SPCLL DLVY SVC	2310-24XX	PS-06	1
CLMS&VCHER EXAM SPEC SR PDC	0540-5007	DCS-17	3
CLMS&VCHR EXAM SPEC PDC	0540-5011	DCS-14	57
CLMS&VCHR EXAM TECH PDC	0540-5012	DCS-11	34
COMMUN CNTRL TECH	0394-2003	EAS-11	1
COMMUN SPEC STAFF	0391-4006	EAS-18	4
COMMUNICATIONS ENGINEER	0855-4029	EAS-25	1
COMMUNICATIONS ENGINEER	0855-4031	EAS-23	4
COMMUNICATIONS EQUIPMENT SPEC	0392-3003	EAS-21	4
COMMUNICATIONS EQUIPMENT SPECIALST	0391-4005		22
COMMUNICATIONS PROGRAMS SPECIALIST	1081-5055	EAS-23	40
COMMUNICATIONS RESOURCES SPECIALST	1081-5057		1
COMMUNICATIONS SOFTWARE SPECIALIST	0334-4035	EAS-22	2
COMMUNICATIONS SPECIALIST	0391-4003	EAS-24	2
COMMUNICATIONS SPECIALIST	1081-5013	EAS-16	11
COMMUNICATIONS SPECIALIST	1081-5036	EAS-18	4
COMMUNICATIONS TECHNICAL COORD	0393-4001	EAS-23	I
COMMUNICATIONS TECHNOLOGY SPECLST	0801-4067	EAS-25	1
COMP PRINT LN PROD OPER	4401-02XX	MH-05	8
COMP PROGMR	0334-3023	EAS-19	1
COMP SYS OPER	0332-3009	EAS-11	1
COMP SYS OPER LEAD	0332-4002	EAS-17	3

COMPENSATION SPECIALIST	0201-5099	EAS-23	5
COMPENSATION SPECIALIST	0201-5100	EAS-21	2
COMPENSATION SPECIALIST (BENEFITS)	0201-5098	EAS-25	
COMPENSATION SPECIALIST (PAY)	0201-5097		1
COMPLAINTS & INQUIRY CLK	2345-23XX	PS-06	396
COMPUTER ANALYSIS TECHNICIAN	0301-5535	EAS-14	
COMPUTER OPERATIONS SUPPORT SPCLST	0332-3025	EAS-17	4
COMPUTER OPERATIONS SUPPORT SPEC	0332-3026	EAS-15	3
COMPUTER PERFORMANCE SPECIALIST	0334-4084	EAS-24	3
COMPUTER PROGRAMMER	0334-3021	EAS-21	4
COMPUTER PROGRAMMER	0334-3035	EAS-16	I
COMPUTER PROGRAMMER/ANALYST	0334-3026	EAS-18	1
COMPUTER PROGRAMMER/SOFTWARE SPCLS	0334-4040	EAS-23	37
COMPUTE SYS ANLST/PRGMR ASSOC PDC	0334-3061	DCS-18	84
➤ COMPUTER SYS ANLST/PRGMR PDC	0334-3056	DCS-20	125
COMPUTER SYS ANLST/PRGMR SR PDC	0334-3057	DCS-22	128
COMPUTER SYS OPR LEAD PDC	0332-3013	DCS-17	10
COMPUTER SYS OPR SR PDC	0332-3012	DCS-14	18
COMPUTER SYS SPEC (JCL) SR (PDC)	0335-4005	DCS-18	15
COMPUTER SYS SPEC JCL (PDC)	0335-4008	DCS-16	18
COMPUTER SYSTEM OPERATOR JR (PDC)	0332-3005	DCS-08	2
COMPUTER SYSTEM SCHEDULER SR (PDC)	0330-5003	DCS-20	6
COMPUTER SYSTEMS ADMIN	0334-4020	EAS-21	6
COMPUTER SYSTEMS ADMIN JR PDC	0334-3031	EAS-19	1
COMPUTER SYSTEMS ADMINISTRATOR	0334-4055	EAS-24	2
COMPUTER SYSTEMS ADMNSTR PDC	0330-4008	EAS-23	4
COMPUTER SYSTEMS ANALYST	0334-4017	EAS-22	4
COMPUTER SYSTEMS ANALYST	0334-4022	EAS-23	13
COMPUTER SYSTEMS ANALYST	0334-4026	EAS-19	24
COMPUTER SYSTEMS OPERATOR	0332-4003	EAS-14	134
COMPUTER SYSTEMS OPERATOR (MDC)	0332-3018	MESC-09	2
COMPUTER SYSTEMS OPERATOR PDC	0332-3006	DCS-11,	22
COMPUTER SYSTEMS SCHEDULER PDC	0330-4021	DCS-17	6
COMPUTER SYSTEMS SPECIALIST	0335-3010	EAS-18	12
COMPUTER SYSTMS ANALYST/PROG ASSOC	0334-3060		14
COMPUTER SYSTMS ANALYST/PROGRAM SR	0334-3045	EAS-22	20
COMPUTER SYSTMS ANALYST/PROGRAMMER	0334-3044	EAS-20	15
CONFIDENTIAL SECTRY FLD	0318-2030		
CONSOLE OPERATOR	2315-64XX	PS-07	28
CONSOLE OPERATOR	2315-64XX	PS-06	2
CONSOLE OPERATOR	2315-65XX	MH-07	4
CONSOLE OPERATOR	2315-65XX	MH-06	I
CONSUMER AFFAIRS REPRESENTATIVE	2345-6008	EAS-15	1
CONTRACT PRICE ANALYST	1102-5033	EAS-23	3
CONTRACT PRICE ANALYST	1102-5034	EAS-20	2
CONTRACT PRICE ANALYST	1102-5052	EAS-25	2
CONTRACT TECHNICIAN	1102-01XX	PS-06	346
CONTRACT TRANSPORTATION SPECIALIST	2330-4033	EAS-21	41
CONTRACT TRANSPORTATION SPECIALIST	2330-4034	EAS-19	50
CONVEYOR MECH	5343-02XX	PS-06	2
COORD TERMINAL HANDLING FACILITY	2330-2011	EAS-14	2
CORRESPONDENCE CONTROL COORD	0301-5195	EAS-16	1
COST ACCOUNTANT (MES)	0510-4058	EAS-20	
CPTR PERF SPEC	0334-4086	EAS-21	9
CPTR PERF SPEC SR	0334-4085	EAS-23	1
CPTR PROGMR SOFTWARE SPEC	0334-4019	EAS-22	25
CPTR SYS ANLST SR (MINI/MICRO)	0334-4074	EAS-23	9
CPTR SYS SPEC PDC	0335-3009	DCS-18	23
CRIMINAL ELECTRONICS ENGINEER	0802-4012	EAS-23	1
CURRICULUM DEVELOPMENT SPECIALIST	1710-5020		5
CURRICULUM DEVELOPMENT SPECIALIST	1710-5021	EAS-25	1
CURRICULUM DEVELOPMENT SPECIALIST	1710-5025	EAS-21	6
CURRICULUM PLANNING SPECIALIST	1710-5012	EAS-25	1
CURRICULUM PLANNING SPECIALIST	1710-5014	EAS-23	2
CURRICULUM PLANNING SPECIALIST	1710-5015	EAS-21	1

CURRICULUM PLNG & DEVELOP SPEC	1710-5026	EAS-23	5
CUST LABORER A	3566-05XX	OSD-01	12
CUST LABORER B	3566-06XX	OSD-02	12
CUST LABORER C	3566-07XX	OSD-03	a
CUST LABORER D	3566-08XX	OSD-04	3
CUST SUPPT SPEC PDC	0335-3008	DCS-15	26
CUST SUPPT TECH PDC	0335-3007	DCS-13	45
CUSTODIAL MGMT SPEC	3502-5001	EAS-14	1
CUSTODIAN	3566-04XX	PS-04	5
CUSTODIAN	3566-04XX	PS-03	58
➤ CUSTODIAN	3566-04XX	PS-02	1,844
CUSTOMER PROGRAMS SPECIALIST	0301-5336	EAS-25	
CUSTOMER PROGRAMS SPECIALIST	0301-5337	EAS-23	I
CUSTOMER RELATIONS COORDINATOR	2345-5035	EAS-17	198
CUSTOMER RESPONSE SPECIALIST	0301-5168	EAS-20	11
CUSTOMER RESPONSE SPECIALIST	0301-5335	EAS-23	2
CUSTOMER SERVICE ANALYST	0301-5332	EAS-25	8
CUSTOMER SERVICE ANALYST	0301-5333	EAS-23	4
CUSTOMER SERVICE ANALYST	0301-5334	EAS-21	1
CUSTOMER SERVICE REPRESENTATIVE	2345-401B	EAS-13	2B9
CUSTOMER SERVICE REPRESENTATIVE	2345-5034	EAS-16	86
CUSTOMER SERVICE SPECIALIST	0301-5352	EAS-23	1
CUSTOMER SERVICE SPECIALIST	0301-5353	EAS-20	1
CUSTOMER SERVICES ANALYST	2310-5027	EAS-16	442
CUSTOMER SERVICES CLERK (PFSC)	0530-2015	PS-06	26
CUSTOMER SUPPORT CENTER SPECIALIST	2050-5005	EAS-25	1
CUSTOMER SUPPORT PROG SPEC (NCSC)	1140-6021		2
CUSTOMER SUPPORT TECHNICIAN	0335-4081	EAS-13	
CUSTOMER SUPPT SPEC	0335-3011	EAS-15	9
CUSTOMER SVC PRGM ANALYST(AREA OF)	2340-5041	EAS-21	19
CUSTOMER SVC PRGM ANALYST(AREA OF)	2340-5042	EAS-23	19
CUSTOMER SVC SUPPORT ANLYST	1140-5042	EAS-21	9
CUSTOMER SVC SUPPORT ANLYST	1140-5043	EAS-23	23
CUSTOMER SVC SUPPORT ANLYST	1140-5044	EAS-25	20
DATA ADMINISTRATOR	0334-4094	EAS-22	4
DATA ADMINISTRATOR	0334-4095	EAS-23	1
DATA BASE MANAGEMENT SPECIALIST	0334-4110	EAS-25	4
DATA CNTRL TECH JR PDC	0335-2008	DCS-08	11
DATA CNTRL TECH SR PDC	0335-4007	OCS-13	3
➤ DATA COLL TECH	0301-69XX	PS-06	1,183
DATA CONTROL TECHNICIAN (MDC)	0335-3020	MESC-07	1
DATA CONVERSION GROUP LEADER PDC	0356-2004	DCS-09	1
DATA CONVERSION OPERATOR	0356-09XX	PS-04	8,078
DATA CONVERSION OPERATOR (MES)	0356-2019		2
DATA CONVERSION OPERATOR GROUP LDR	0356-2020	MESC-05	1
DATA CONVERSION OPERATOR PDC	0356-2003	DCS-06	16
DATA SYSTEMS TECHNICIAN SR	0335-4003	EAS-13	3
DATABASE ADMINISTRATOR	0334-4134	EAS-23	19
DATABASE SPECIALIST	0334-4089	EAS-21	5
DECISION SUPPORT SPECIALIST	0505-5018	EAS-25	1
DELIVERY AND RETAIL ANALYST	2310-5003	EAS-15	I
DELIVERY/CUSTOMER SVCS EQUIPMT SPC	0801-5020	EAS-25	3
DELIVERY/RETAIL ANALYST	2310-5026	EAS-17	74
DEPUTY CHIEF FIELD COUNSEL	0905-6014	PCES-I	7
DEPUTY CHIEF INSPECTOR	2335-7040		3
DEPUTY GENERAL COUNSEL	0905-7046	PCES-I	1
DEPUTY POSTMASTER GENERAL	0340-7011	PCES-IL	1
DIGITAL SYSTEMS SPECIALIST	0855-4024	EAS-25	I
DIRECTIVES & FORMS SPECIALIST	0343-5061	EAS-21	2
DIRECTIVES/FORMS SPECIALIST	0343-5053	EAS-23	2
DIRECTIVES/FORMS SPECIALIST	0343-5056	EAS-25	I
DIRECTORY ANALYSIS SPECIALIST	2340-5029	EAS-15	263
DISBURSING SPEC POC	0530-5007	DCS-14	3
DISBURSING SPEC SR PDC	0530-5006	DCS-17	5
DISBURSING TECH PDC	0530-5008	DCS-11	5

DIST CLK MACH MPLSM	2315-13XX	PS-06	29,851
DIST CLK MACH MPLSM TRNEE	2315-17XX		80
DIST CLK MACH MPLSM TRNEE	2315-17XX	PS-05	6,163
DIST CLK MACH SPLSM	2315-14XX	PS-06	973
DIST CLK MACH SPLSM TRNEE	2315-18XX		I
DIST CLK MACH SPLSM TRNEE	2315-18XX	PS-05	225
DIST WINDOW CLK	2340-02XX	PS-05	58,930
DISTANCE LEARNING SYSTEMS COORD	1710-4029	EAS-21	3
DISTRIBUTION CLERK	2315-04XX	PS-06	257
DISTRIBUTION CLERK	2315-04XX	PS-05	90,394
DISTRIBUTION SPECIALIST	2330-4036	EAS-21	20
DISTRIBUTION WINDOW & MARK UP CLK	2340-80XX	PS-05	5,312
DISTRICT MANAGER	0340-7118	PCES-I	16
DISTRICT MANAGER	0340-7121		14
DISTRICT MANAGER	0340-7122		53
DIVERSITY DEVELOPMENT EDUCTN PSYCH	0180-4016	EAS-23	1
DIVERSITY DEVELOPMENT INFO SYS SPC	0334-4128		1
DIVERSITY DEVELOPMENT SPEC (FLD)	0160-5056	EAS-19	38
DIVERSITY DEVELOPMENT SPECIALIST	0160-5053	EAS-25	1
DIVERSITY DEVELOPMENT SPECIALIST	0160-5054	EAS-23	8
DIVERSITY DEVELOPMENT SPECIALIST	0160-5055	EAS-21	1
DIVERSITY DEVELOPMENT SPLST(AREA)	0160-5057		17
DIVERSITY STRATEGIC PROGRAMS SPEC	0160-5061	EAS-25	I
DIVERSITY VENDOR PROGRAMS SPECLST	1102-5056		1
DRAFTING CLK	0818-01XX	PS-05	59
DRAFTING/DESIGN SPECIALIST	0802-4010	EAS-21	1
DRAFTSMAN	0818-3002	EAS-11	2
DRIVER INSTRUCTOR & EXAMINER	5752-01XX	PS-06	113
DUPLICATOR OPERATOR	0301-2089	EAS-09	3
EAP ANALYST	0301-5343	EAS-23	I
EAP COORDINATOR	0301-5363	EAS-21	83
ECONOMIST	0110-4016	EAS-25	20
ECONOMIST	0110-4017	EAS-23	8
ECONOMIST	0110-4018	EAS-21	2
EDITOR	1081-5004	EAS-25	2
EEO COMPLIANCE/APPEALS COORDINATOR	0954-4016	EAS-24	5
EEO COUNSELOR/INVESTIGATOR	0160-5050	EAS-17	1
EEO COUNSELOR/INVESTIGATOR	0160-5060		238
EEO COUNSELOR/INVESTIGATOR	1810-5001	EAS-19	4
ELCT ENGN TECHNLST	0856-3019	EAS-20	1
ELCT-MECH ENGN TECH	0802-3009	EAS-19	4
ELECTRICAL ENGINEER	0850-4007	EAS-25	3
ELECTRICAL EQUIP/POWER ENGINEER	0850-3009	EAS-21	1
ELECTRICAL LEADER	2805-05XX	OSD-08	I
ELECTRICIAN	2805-02XX	PS-07	1
ELECTRICIAN	2805-09XX	OSD-07	5
ELECTRICIAN HELPER	2805-06XX	OSD-04	
ELECTRO-OPTICS ANALYST	0855-4014	EAS-25	1
ELECTRO-OPTICS SYSTEMS SPEC	0855-4025		2
ELECTRONIC ENGINEER	0855-3005	EAS-22	I
ELECTRONIC ENGINEER	0855-4009	EAS-23	10
ELECTRONIC ENGINEER	0855-4010	EAS-24	5
ELECTRONIC ENGINEER	0855-4011	EAS-25	5
ELECTRONIC ENGINEER	0855-4034	EAS-21	
➤ ELECTRONIC TECHNICIAN	2604-01XX	PS-09	5,896
ELECTRONICS TECH	0856-01XX	PS-10	119
ELECTRONICS TECH	0856-01XX	PS-09	452
ELEVATOR & BOILER INSPECTION COORD	5401-5002	EAS-21	2
ELEVATOR ELECTRONIC TECH	5313-05XX	OSD-09	2
ELEVATOR MECH	5313-03XX	PS-07	30
ELEVATOR MECHANIC	5313-04XX	OSD-08	
ELEVATOR OPER	5438-01XX	PS-03	224
ELEVATOR/BOILER INSPECTOR	5401-3001	EAS-17	41
EMPLMT&PLACMT SPEC	0212-5025	EAS-21	4
EMPLOYEE FEEDBACK PROCESS COORD	0301-5539	EAS-18	

EMPLOYEE RELATIONS PROGRAMS SPCLST	0201-5081	EAS-23	1
EMPLOYEE RELATIONS SPECIALIST	0018-5029	EAS-23	1
EMPLOYEE TRANSPORTATION COORD	0301-5360	EAS-15	14
EMPLOYMENT & PLACEMENT SPECIALIST	0212-5023	EAS-23	2
EMPLOYMENT/PLACEMENT SPECIALIST	0212-5047	EAS-19	2
EMPLOYMENT/PLACEMENT SPECIALIST	0212-5052	EAS-25	
ENGINEERING TECHNICIAN	0802-3025	EAS-18	2
ENGINEERING TECHNICIAN	0802-4011	EAS-20	2
ENGINEMAN	5309-02XX	PS-06	1
ENGINEMAN	5309-1001	MESC-06	6
ENVIRONMENTAL COMPLIANCE COOR DIST	0819-5004	EAS-21	
ENVIRONMENTAL SPECIALIST	0819-4001	EAS-25	6
ENVIRONMENTAL COMPL COORD (DIST)	0819-5003	EAS-19	3
ENVIRONMENTAL COMPLIANCE COORD(AO)	0819-5001	EAS-25	6
ENVIRONMENTAL COMPLIANCE COORD(AO)	0819-5002	EAS-23	11
ENVIRONMENTAL PROGRAMS ANALYST	0819-4003	EAS-21	
ENVIRONMENTAL PROGRAMS ANALYST	0819-4005	EAS-25	1
ENVIRONMENTAL SPECIALIST	0819-4002	EAS-23	6
EQUIP HAND	3502-12XX	OSD-03	
EQUIP HAND TRUCK DRIVER	3502-11XX	OSD-05	1
ERGONOMIST	0896-4053	EAS-24	1
ESTIMATOR	0828-4001	EAS-23	2
EXAMINATION SPECIALIST	0203-19XX	PS-06	2
EXAMINATIONS ASST	0203-5004	EAS-14	3
EXAMINATIONS PROC CLK SR	0301-2097	EAS-11	5
EXAMINATIONS PROCESSING CLERK	0301-2060	EAS-09	5
EXAMINATIONS SUPPLY CLERK	2005-2008	EAS-08	3
EXEC DIR INTERNATIONAL POSTAL REL	0345-7051	PCES-I	1
EXECUTIVE CAREER DEVELOPMENT SPEC	0235-5059	EAS-25	1
EXECUTIVE CAREER DEVELOPMENT SPEC	0235-5060	EAS-23	2
EXECUTIVE DEVELOPMENT SPECIALIST	0235-5051	EAS-25	1
EXECUTIVE DEVELOPMENT SPECIALIST	0235-5052	EAS-23	1
EXECUTIVE DEVELOPMENT SPECIALIST	0235-5053	EAS-21	1
EXECUTIVE VICE PRESIDENT	0340-7098	PCES-IL	1
EXHIBITS SPECIALIST	1010-5003	EAS-22	2
EXPEDITED SERVICE SPECIALIST	2345-6056	EAS-15	170
EXPRESS MAIL SERVICE CLK	2330-77XX	PS-06	233
EXPRESS ML TECH	2340-82XX		73
EXTRACTION CODE CLERK	2315-63XX	PS-05	52
FACILITIES CONTRACT SPECIALIST	1102-5020	EAS-21	1
FACILITIES CONTRACT SPECIALIST	1102-5032	EAS-18	8
FACILITIES CONTRACT TECHNICIAN	1106-5005	EAS-15	34
FACILITIES ENGINEER	1601-4016	EAS-19	47
FACILITIES PLANNING SPECIALIST	0345-5085	EAS-21	
FACILITIES PLANNING SPECIALIST	0345-5086	EAS-23	1
FACILITIES PLANNING SPECIALIST	0345-5087	EAS-25	3
FACILITIES PROGRAMS ANALYST	0345-5088		2
FACILITIES PROGRAMS ANALYST	0345-5089	EAS-23	5
FACILITIES PROGRAMS ANALYST	0345-5090	EAS-21	2
FACILITIES REQUIREMENTS SPECIALIST	0801-4050	EAS-25	2
FACILITIES SPECIALIST	1601-3008	EAS-17	84
FACILITY ACTIVATION COORDINATOR	0345-5119	EAS-18	
FACILITY ACTIVATION COORDINATOR	0345-5120	EAS-20	1
FACILITY ACTIVATION COORDINATOR	0345-5121	EAS-22	1
FACILITY ACTIVATION SPECIALIST	0345-5095	EAS-25	2
FACILITY ACTIVATION SPECIALIST	0345-5096	EAS-23	4
FACILITY ACTIVATION SPECIALIST	0345-5097	EAS-21	2
FACILITY COMMUNICATIONS TECH	0332-3023	OCS-17	17
FACILITY COMMUNICATIONS TECH SR	0332-3027	DCS-19	3
FACILITY MGMT AND SERVICES COORD	0301-5240	EAS-19	1
FACILITY REQUIREMENTS SPECIALIST	0801-5015	EAS-23	2
FIELD COORDINATOR, QWL PROCESS	0230-5074	EAS-18	
FIELD HUMAN RESOURCES POLICY SPCLS	0201-5103	EAS-25	I
FIELD LIAISON COMMUNICATIONS	1081-5048		2
FILE CLERK	0305-03XX	PS-04	6

FINANCIAL ANALYST	0345-5098	EAS-25	5
FINANCIAL ANALYST	0345-5099	EAS-23	2
FINANCIAL ANALYST	0345-5100	EAS-21	1
FINANCIAL PLANNING SPECIALIST	0345-5107	EAS-25	2
FINANCIAL PLANNING SPECIALIST	0345-5108	EAS-23	2
➤ FINANCIAL SERVICES COORDINATOR	0510-5050	EAS-18	85
FINANCIAL SPECIALIST	0505-5107	EAS-25	1
FINANCIAL SVCS/SYSTEMS COORDINATOR	0510-5052	EAS-18	6
FINANCIAL SYSTEMS ANALYST	0505-4014	EAS-21	1
FINANCIAL SYSTEMS ANALYST	0505-5012	EAS-23	1
FINANCIAL SYSTEMS ANALYST	0505-5013		1
FINANCIAL SYSTEMS ANALYST	0505-5019		28
FINANCIAL SYSTEMS COORDINATOR	0505-5051	EAS-18	77
FINANCIAL SYSTEMS SPECIALIST	0505-5015	EAS-25	4
FINANCIAL SYSTEMS SPECIALIST	0505-5016	EAS-23	4
FINGERPRINT TECH	0072-3007	EAS-14	
FIREMAN	5402-01XX	PS-04	3
FIREMAN LABORER	5402-02XX		467
FLAT SORTING MACHINE OPERATOR	2315-20XX	PS-05	13,195
FLAT SORTING MACHINE OPERATOR	2315-21XX	PS-06	6,745
FORENSIC ANALYST	0802-3041	EAS-23	33
FORENSIC ANALYST	0802-3042	EAS-19	
FORENSIC ANALYST	0802-3043	EAS-17	
FORENSIC ANALYST	0802-3044	EAS-21	1
FORENSIC LATENT PRNT ANALYST IS	0072-3005		
FORENSIC LATENT PRNT ANALYST STAFF	0072-3004	EAS-19	
FORENSIC LATENT PRNT ASSOCIATE IS	0072-3003	EAS-17	
FORENSIC PHOTOGRAPHER	1060-3002		2
FORENSIC PHOTOGRPHR/EVIDENCE TECH	1060-3011	EAS-19	3
FORFEITURE PROGRAM ADMINISTRATOR	2335-5025	EAS-24	1
FORFEITURE SPECIALIST	2335-5020	EAS-16	42
FORKLIFT OPERATOR	5704-1001	MTEC-05	41
FORKLIFT OPERATOR	5704-1003	MESC-05	32
FRNSC DOC ANALYST (INSP SRV)	1397-3008	EAS-21	
FRNSC DOC ANALYST ASSOC (IS)	1397-3006	EAS-17	
FRNSC DOC ANALYST SR (INSP SRV)	1397-3009	EAS-23	4
FRNSC DOC ANALYST STAFF (IS)	1397-3007	EAS-19	
FRNSC LATENT PRT ANLST SR (INSP)	0072-3006	EAS-23	
GARAGEMAN	6955-02XX	PS-04	333
GEN CLERK	0301-2106	MESC-05	I
GEN CLK	2340-01XX	PS-06	42
GEN CLK	2340-OIXX	PS-05	3,350
GEN ENGINEER	0801-3005	EAS-23	17
GEN MECHANIC	4749-02XX	PS-05	56
GEN MECHANIC (MES)	4749-1002	MESC-05	3
GEN SERVICE MECHANIC	4749-1001	MTEC-05	3
GEN SUPV BLDG SVC	3501-6011	EAS-13	3
GEN SUPV COMPUTERIZED MARK-UP UNIT	0301-6103	EAS-17	31
GEN SUPV MTEC	6951-6003		1
GEN SUPV PSDS OPERATIONS (A)	0301-7174	EAS-15	37
GEN SUPV PSDS OPERATIONS (S)	0301-7175	EAS-17	56
GEN SUPV PSDS OPERATIONS ©	0301-7176	EAS-19	30
GEN SUPV REPAIRS (MTEC)	4801-6004	EAS-17	2
GENERAL CLERK VMF	0301-48XX	PS-05	266
GENERAL EXPEDITOR	2315-11XX	PS-06	3,747
GENERAL OFC CLK FOREIGN MAILS	2340-16XX		42
GRAPHICS PRODUCTION SPECIALIST	1084-5009	EAS-24	1
GRAPHICS PRODUCTION SPECIALIST	1084-5010	EAS-21	1
GROUP LEADER ADMINIST CLERK (PDC)	0301-5320	DCS-10	I
GROUP LEADER CUSTODIAL	3501-01XX	PS-04	497
GROUP LEADER, INTERNATIONAL ACCTS	0540-5005	DCS-16	3
GROUP LEADER, WAREHOUSING	6960-1001	MESC-05	11
GRP LDR CUSTODIAL	3501-1001	MESC-04	1
GRP LDR DATA CONVERSION OPERATOR	0356-10XX	PS-05	11
GRP LDR MAIL EQUIP REPAIR	3105-1001	MTEC-05	9

GRP LDR MAIL EQUIPMENT HANDLERS	3501-1002		8
GRP LDR MAILBAG EXAMINATION	3152-1001		1
GRP LDR ML HANDLER	2315-02XX	MH-05	1,230
GRP LDR SEWING MACHINE OPERS (MES)	3111-1004	MESC-05	I
GRP LEADER SACK SORT MCH OPER	2315-28XX	MH-06	3
HEADQUARTERS INJURY COMPENSTN ASOC	0230-5065	EAS-15	1
HEAVY TRUCK DRIVER	5755-01XX	OSD-04	2
HIGHWAY TRANSPORTATION CLK	2330-13XX	PS-06	35
HR SPECIALIST (INSPECTION SERVICE)	0201-5121	EAS-17	4
HR STRATEGIC PLANNING SPEC	0201-5125	EAS-23	
HRIS COORDINATOR	0201-5128	EAS-16	
HRIS SPECIALIST	0201-5091	EAS-19	14
HRIS SPECIALIST	0201-6054	EAS-21	4
HRIS TECHNICIAN	0201-5092	EAS-17	2
HUMAN FACTORS SPECIALIST	0896-4044	EAS-24	1
HUMAN RES ADMNR	0235-5029	EAS-16	2
HUMAN RESOURCE ASSOCIATE IS	0201-5123	EAS-11	66
HUMAN RESOURCE SPECIALIST	0201-5122	EAS-15	6
HUMAN RESOURCES ANALYST	0201-5102	EAS-25	1
HUMAN RESOURCES ANALYST (AREA OFC)	0201-5116	EAS-23	47
HUMAN RESOURCES ASSOCIATE	0201-5111	EAS-16	4
HUMAN RESOURCES ASSOCIATE	0201-5112	EAS-11	750
HUMAN RESOURCES ASSOCIATE (HFU)	0201-5109		2
HUMAN RESOURCES ASSOCIATE (HFU)	0201-5110	EAS-14	1
HUMAN RESOURCES INITIATIVES SPEC	0201-5124	EAS-21	
HUMAN RESOURCES PROGRAMS ASSISTANT	0201-5126	EAS-13	1
HUMAN RESOURCES SPECIALIST	0201-5101	EAS-23	I
HUMAN RESOURCES SPECIALIST	0201-5106	EAS-21	5
➤ HUMAN RESOURCES SPECIALIST	0201-5117	EAS-15	1,288
HUMAN RESOURCES SPECIALIST	0201-5118	EAS-17	323
HUMAN RESOURCES SPECIALIST	0201-5119	EAS-19	2
HUMAN RESOURCES SPECIALIST (HFU)	0201-5127	EAS-15	I
HUMAN RESOURCES SPECIALIST (HQ)	0201-5129	EAS-19	
ILLUSTRATOR	1020-OIXX	PS-07	25
ILLUSTRATOR TECHNICAL	1020-5010	EAS-16	2
INDUSTRIAL ENG	0896-9007	EAS-26	1
INDUSTRIAL ENGINEER (FLD)	0896-4036	EAS-19	105
INDUSTRIAL ENGINEER (HDQS)	0896-4035	EAS-23	4
INDUSTRIAL ENGINEER (HDQS)	0896-4039	EAS-25	3
INDUSTRIAL ENGINEER SR (FLD)	0896-3020		29
INDUSTRIAL EQUIPMENT MECHANIC	5828-01XX	PS-06	52
INDUSTRIAL HYGIENIST	0690-4003	EAS-24	1
INFO SYS SPEC	0334-4083	EAS-21	16
INFO SYSTEMS COORDINATOR	0334-4044	EAS-22	1
INFORMATION CLK	2320-12XX	PS-06	122
INFORMATION DEVELOPMENT COORDINATR	1529-5002	EAS-25	1
INFORMATION DISCLOSURE SPEC	0343-5036	EAS-23	1
INFORMATION DISCLUSURE TECHNICIAN	0343-5054	EAS-17	2
INFORMATION SCIENCES SPECIALIST	0330-4013	EAS-25	8
INFORMATION SERVICES SPECIALIST	0334-4118		4
INFORMATION SPECIALIST (INSP SRVC)	1081-5058	EAS-21	2
INFORMATION SPECIALIST INSP SRVC	1081-5038	EAS-19	2
INFORMATION SYSTEMS COORDINATOR	0330-5017	EAS-15	94
INFORMATION SYSTEMS COORDINATOR	0334-4043	EAS-19	6
INFORMATION SYSTEMS COORDINATOR	0334-4045	EAS-23	19
INFORMATION SYSTEMS COORDINATOR	0334-4058	EAS-16	10
INFORMATION SYSTEMS COORDINATOR	0334-4125	EAS-25	3
INFORMATION SYSTEMS COORDINATOR	0334-4127	EAS-21	17
INFORMATION SYSTEMS PROGRAMS COORD	0334-6018	EAS-25	5
INFORMATION SYSTEMS SECURITY SPEC	0334-5002	EAS-23	7
INFORMATION SYSTEMS SECURITY SPEC	0334-5003	EAS-21	2
INFORMATION SYSTEMS SECURITY SPEC	0334-5014	EAS-24	5
INFORMATION SYSTEMS SECURITY SPEC	0334-5021	EAS-16	2
INFORMATION SYSTEMS SPECIALIST	0330-5016	EAS-17	110
INFORMATION SYSTEMS SPECIALIST	0334-4082	EAS-23	14

INFORMATION SYSTEMS SPECIALIST	0334-4090	EAS-19	3
INFORMATION SYSTEMS SPECIALIST	0334-4108	EAS-25	8
INFORMATION TECHNOLOGY PLANNER	0334-4109		4
INFORMATION TECHNOLOGY SPEC	0334-3065	EAS-18	19
INFORMATION TECHNOLOGY SPEC	0334-3066	EAS-20	18
INJURY COMPENSATION SPECIALIST	0230-5066	EAS-23	2
INJURY COMPENSATION SPECIALIST	0230-5067	EAS-21	1
INJURY COMPENSATION SPECIALIST	0230-5068	EAS-25	1
INSPECTION SERVICE OPERATIONS COOR	0341-5055	EAS-14	47
INSPECTION SERVICE OPERATIONS SPEC	0345-5116	EAS-15	9
INSPECTION SERVICE PROGRAM SPEC	0345-5117	EAS-19	12
INSPECTION SERVICE PROGRAM SPEC	0345-5118	EAS-23	7
INTEGRATED SUPPORT PLANNING SPCLST	2001-5017	EAS-25	1
INTERCONNECTION/INFO SYS SPECLST	0334-4119		2
INTERN	0301-2109	EAS-17	2
INTERN HEADQUARTERS	0301-2110	EAS-07	
INTERNATIONAL POSTAL AFFAIRS SPCLS	0345-5109	EAS-21	3
INTERNATIONAL POSTAL AFFAIRS SPCLS	0345-5110	EAS-23	3
INTERNATIONAL POSTAL AFFAIRS SPCLS	0345-5111	EAS-25	4
INTERNATIONAL RECORDS UNIT COORD	2340-6030	EAS-18	1
INTL CVL/MLTRY MAIL COORD	2330-4026	EAS-21	4
INTL SURFACE ML REP	2330-4011	EAS-15	2
INTRNL CLAIMS CLK, PAY OFC	2345-16XX	PS-07	6
INVENTORY CONTROL CLERK	2040-2009	MESC-05	11
INVENTORY PROGRAMS SPECIALIST	2003-5029	EAS-25	1
INVENTORY SPECIALIST	2010-5007	EAS-23	7
INVENTORY SPECIALIST	2010-5008	EAS-20	6
IS BUSINESS AREA SPECIALIST	0334-5019	EAS-25	7
IS OPERATIONS TECH	0301-2234	EAS-11	443
JR CLERK	0301-2023	EAS-04	2
JR STENO	0312-2007	EAS-07	1
JUDICIAL OFFICER	0905-7008	PCES-II	1
LABEL MACH OPER	4401-05XX	MH-04	5
LABEL PRINTING TECH	4401-06XX	MH-05	12
LABEL PRINTING TECH (EASC)	4401-1013	PS-05	3
LABOR ECONOMIST	0110-4015	EAS-25	2
LABOR RELATIONS ANALYST IS	0230-5073	EAS-21	1
LABOR RELATIONS PROGRAMS COORD	0233-5013	EAS-19	1
LABOR RELATIONS REP PDC	0230-5030		1
LABOR RELATIONS SPEC (AREA OFFICE)	0233-5019	EAS-23	35
LABOR RELATIONS SPECIALIST	0230-5012	EAS-21	4
LABOR RELATIONS SPECIALIST	0230-5013	EAS-23	10
LABOR RELATIONS SPECIALIST	0230-5014	EAS-25	10
LABOR RELATIONS SPECIALIST	0233-5016	EAS-19	356
LABOR RELATIONS SPECIALIST	0233-5017	EAS-17	
LABOR RELATIONS SPECIALIST (FIELD)	0233-5021	EAS-24	6
LABOR RELATIONS SPECLST(AREA OFC)	0233-5018	EAS-21	32
LABOR RELATIONS SPECLST(AREA OFC)	0233-5020	EAS-25	10
LABOR RELATIONS SYSTEMS SPECIALIST	0301-5351	EAS-21	1
LABOR RELATIONS TECHNICIAN	0301-5348	EAS-16	2
LABOR RELATIONS TECHNICIAN	0301-5349	EAS-14	2
LABORATORY TECHNICIAN	2335-4001	EAS-11	1
LABORER	3502-07XX	OSD-02	3
LABORER CUSTODIAL	3502-03XX	PS-06	6
LABORER CUSTODIAL	3502-03XX	PS-05	15
LABORER CUSTODIAL	3502-03XX	PS-04	13
LABORER CUSTODIAL	3502-03XX	PS-03	13,134
LABORER CUSTODIAL	3502-03XX	PS-02	13
LABORER CUSTODIAL	3502-1019	MESC-03	12
LABORER CUSTODIAL (MES)	3502-1022		6
LABORER CUSTODIAL (MTEC)	3502-1024	MTEC-03	
LABORER LEADER	3502-08XX	OSD-06	
LABORER MATERIALS HANDLING (MES)	3502-1023	MESC-03	8
LABORER MTL HNDLNG	3502-14XX	PS-03	2
LAN SPECIALIST	0334-3063	EAS-21	

LAN SPECIALIST	0334-3064	EAS-23	1
LBR REL ASST FLD	0230-5028	EAS-16	1
LEAD AUTOMOTIVE MECHANIC	5823-10XX	PS-07	444
LEATHER WORKER (MES)	3102-1002	MESC-05	
LEGAL ADVISOR OFC OF LEGAL ADV	0905-9021	EAS-35	I
LEGAL INTERN	0301-2111	EAS-16	6
LEGAL SECRETARY	0986-3005	EAS-11	19
LEGAL SECRETARY	0986-3008	EAS-14	22
LEGAL SYS SPEC	0950-5004	EAS-18	1
LEGISLATIVE AFFAIRS ANALYST	0301-5356	EAS-17	2
LEGISLATIVE AFFAIRS ANALYST	0301-5358	EAS-21	4
LEGISLATIVE AFFAIRS ANALYST	0301-5359	EAS-23	1
LEGISLATIVE AFFAIRS REPRESENTATIVE	0301-5354		8
LETTER BOX MECHANIC (MES)	3843-02XX	PS-06	195
LIBRARIAN	1410-5009	EAS-20	3
LIBRARIAN	1410-5011	EAS-25	1
LIBRARY TECHNICIAN	1411-5002	EAS-14	2
LIBRARY TECHNICIAN	1411-5004	EAS-16	2
LOCAL AREA NETWORK ADMINISTRATION	0334-4136	EAS-21	2
LOCAL AREA NETWORK ADMINISTRATION	0334-4137	EAS-19	
LOCK AND SAFE MECHANIC	5311-06XX	PS-06	1
LOCK BOX EQUIPMENT REPAIRER (MES)	5311-1004	MESC-05	
LOCKMAKER	5311-02XX	PS-05	1
LOCKMAKER (MES)	5311-1002	MESC-05	4
LOCKSMITH CARPENTER	5311-04XX	OSD-07	2
LOGISTICS REQUIREMENTS PLANNG SPC	2003-5030	EAS-25	I
LOGISTICS SUPPORT SPECIALIST	2003-5037	EAS-16	2
LOGISTICS TECHNICAL DATA SPECIALST	2003-5034	EAS-25	I
MACHINE OPER PHILATELIC FULFILLMNT	2340-05XX	PS-05	12
MACHINE OPERATOR (MES)	3401-1002	MESC-04	44
MACHINE OPERATOR (MES)	3401-1003	MESC-03	33
MACHINE OPERATOR A (MES)	3401-1001	MESC-06	1
MACHINE OPERATOR B (MES)	3401-1004		2
MACHINIST	3414-02XX	PS-07	22
MACHINIST	3414-1002	EAS-13	I
MACHINIST HELPER	3414-1001	EAS-10	1
MAIL ACCEPTANCE SPECIALIST	2345-6057	EAS-16	103
MAIL CLASS CLK MSC	2345-52XX	PS-07	44
MAIL CLASS CLK MSC	2345-52XX	PS-06	30
MAIL CLERK	0305-2001	EAS-06	5
MAIL EQUIPMENT HANDLER	3502-01XX	MH-04	67
MAIL EQUIPMENT HANDLER	3502-1020	MTEC-04	197
MAIL EQUIPMENT SHOP TECHN (MES)	6753-1001	MESC-09	I
MAIL HANDLER	2315-OIXX	MH-05	219
➤ MAIL HANDLER	2315-01XX	MH-04	46,390
MAIL HANDLER LEADMAN	2315-8OXX	MH-05	3
MAIL MESS COORDINATOR	0305-04XX	OSD-05	1
MAIL MESS DRIVER	2340-09XX	OSD-04	1
MAIL MGMNT SPECIALIST	0305-2010	EAS-12	I
MAIL ORDER CLERK (PFSC)	0530-26XX	PS-05	12
MAIL PROCESSING MACHINE OPERATOR	2340-45XX	MH-05	1,599
MAIL PROCESSOR	2315-55XX	PS-04	22,719
MAIL REWRAPPER	2340-27XX	MH-04	32
MAILING REQUIREMENTS CLK	2345-32XX	PS-07	4
MAILING REQUIREMENTS CLK	2345-32XX	PS-06	350
MAILING REQUIREMENTS CLK	2345-32XX	PS-05	188
MAILPIECE DESIGN ANALYST	2345-5033	EAS-15	168
MAIN TECH	4749-08XX	OSD-06	4
MAINT CNTL CLK	0301-16XX	PS-06	3
MAINT CNTL CLK	0301-16XX	PS-05	560
MAINT CNTL TECH	0301-07XX	PS-06	416
MAINT ELECTRICIAN	2805-03XX		217
MAINT MECH MPE	5342-01XX	PS-07	5,482
MAINT SOFTWR SPEC	0334-3046	EAS-21	10
MAINT SUPPORT CLERK	0303-02XX	PS-06	1

MAINTENANCE CONTROL AND STOCK CLK	0301-19XX	PS-05	378
MAINTENANCE ELECTRICIAN	2805-1010	MESC-06	1
MAINTENANCE ENGINEERING ANALSYT	1670-4017	EAS-21	43
MAINTENANCE ENGINEERING SPECIALIST	1641-5004	EAS-18	108
MAINTENANCE ENGINEERING SPECIALIST	1670-4025	EAS-25	3
MAINTENANCE FIELD SUPPORT SPECLST	1641-4024		3
MAINTENANCE HELPER	4701-02XX	OSD-04	1
MAINTENANCE INFORMATION SPECIALIST	1641-4019	EAS-16	4
MAINTENANCE MAN	4749-05XX	PS-04	2
MAINTENANCE MANAGEMENT SPECIALIST	1601-4018	EAS-23	14
MAINTENANCE MECH GEN (SPLY CTR)	5301-1008	MESC-06	4
➤ MAINTENANCE MECHANIC	4749-03XX	PS-05	2,386
MAINTENANCE MECHANIC	4749-11XX	PS-04	353
MAINTENANCE MECHANIC GENERAL	5301-1007	MTEC-06	9
MAINTENANCE MECHANIC MACHINIST	3414-1003	EAS-12	1
MAINTENANCE PROGRAMS/POLICY SPCLST	1641-5003	EAS-25	1
MAINTENANCE REQUIRE/PLANNING SPCLS	1641-5002		1
MAINTENANCE SUPPORT CLERK	0303-01XX	PS-05	
MAINTENANCE SUPPORT PLANNING SPCLS	0801-4038	EAS-24	2
MANAGEMENT ANALYST	0343-3012	EAS-19	13
MANAGEMENT ANALYST	0343-3013	EAS-17	10
MANAGEMENT ANALYST	0343-5021	EAS-22	2
MANAGEMENT ANALYST PDC	0343-3014	EAS-19	6
MANAGEMENT ASSOCIATE	0301-5504	SMD-04	12
MANAGEMENT ASSOCIATION RELTNS SPEC	0341-5052	EAS-21	2
MANAGEMENT ASSOCIATION RELTNS SPEC	0341-5053	EAS-23	1
MANAGEMENT DEVELOPMENT SPECIALIST	0235-5054	EAS-25	1
MANAGEMENT DEVELOPMENT SPECIALIST	0235-5055	EAS-23	2
MANAGEMENT DEVELOPMENT SPECIALIST	0235-5056	EAS-21	I
MANAGEMENT INTERN	0301-5501	SMD-01	17
MANAGEMENT TRAINEE	0301-5505	SMD-05	5
MANAGEMENT TRAINING SPECIALIST	1710-5022	EAS-21	8
MANAGEMENT TRAINING SPECIALIST	1710-5023	EAS-23	3
MARKET RESEARCH SPECIALIST	1140-5045	EAS-25	5
MARKET RESEARCH SPECIALIST	1140-5046	EAS-23	3
MARKET RESEARCH SPECIALIST	1140-5047	EAS-21	I
MARKETING SPECIALIST	1140-5009		8
MARKETING SPECIALIST	1140-5011	EAS-23	24
MARKETING SPECIALIST	1140-5025	EAS-25	35
MARKTING SERVICES SPECIALIST (BMC)	2345-5036	EAS-19	2
MARKTING SERVICES SPECIALIST (BMC)	2345-5037	EAS-18	19
MARKUP CLK AUTOMATED	0301-41XX	PS-04	6,124
MARKUP CLK MANUAL	0301-40XX		5
MASON	3603-02XX	PS-06	1
MATERIAL CLERK	2005-2019	MESC-05	is
MATERIAL HANDLING EQUIP OPER (MES)	5704-1002		3
MATERIALS ENGINEER	0806-4001	EAS-25	2
MATERIALS ENGINEER	0806-4005	EAS-24	2
MATERIALS HANDLING SYSTEMS SPEC	0801-4044	EAS-25	I
MATERIALS HANLDING EQUIP OPER	5704-01XX	PS-04	90
MATERIALS TECHNICIAN	0802-3023	EAS-19	2
MATERIEI DISTRIBUTION SYSTEMS SPCL	2030-5003	EAS-25	1
MATERIEL LOGISTICS SPECIALIST	2003-5031	EAS-21	17
MATERIEL LOGISTICS SPECIALIST	2003-5032	EAS-23	11
MATERIEL MANAGEMENT SPEC (MES)	2003-5038	EAS-15	2
MATERIEL MANAGEMENT SPECIALIST	2003-5021	EAS-25	3
MATERIEL MANAGEMENT SPECIALIST	2003-5023	EAS-23	10
MATERIEL MANAGEMENT SPECIALIST	2003-5024	EAS-20	33
MATERIEL MANAGEMENT SPECIALIST	2003-5036	EAS-15	85
MATHEMATICAL STATISTICIAN	1529-4011	EAS-21	2
MATHEMATICAL STATISTICIAN	1529-4012	EAS-23	4
MATHEMATICAL STATISTICIAN	1529-5001	EAS-25	9
MEASUREMENT/EVALUATION SPCLST	1710-5017		1
MEASUREMENT/EVALUATION SPCLST	1710-5018	EAS-23	6
MEASUREMENT/EVALUATION SPCLST	1710-5019	EAS-21	

MECH HLPR	4701-01XX	PS-04	8
MECHANIC HELPER (MES)	4701-1001	MESC-04	
MECHANICAL'ENGINEER	0830-3008	EAS-23	10
MECHANICAL ENGINEER	0830-4010	EAS-21	3
MECHANICAL ENGINEER	0830-4011	EAS-23	3
➤ MECHANICAL ENGINEER	0830-4012	EAS-24	12
MECHANICAL ENGINEER	0830-4013	EAS-25	6
MECHANICAL EQUIP/SERVICE ENG (FLD)	0830-3016	EAS-21	1
MECHANIZATION ESTIMATE/PLAN SPCLST	0801-4056	EAS-25	1
MEDIA RELATIONS REP, INSP SRVC	1081-5045	EAS-23	1
MEDIA RELATIONS REPRESENTATIVE	1081-5001	EAS-24	4
MEDICAL DIRECTOR	0602-7004	PCES-I	1
MEDICAL OFFICER	0602-6001	EAS-26	1
MEDICAL OFFICER FIELD DIVISION	0602-6009		16
MESSENGER/WAREHOUSEMAN	5703-1013	MESC-04	
MGMT ANALYST INSPECTION SERVICE	0343-5062	EAS-21	5
MGR ACCOUNTING OPERATIONS	0510-7078	PCES-I	1
MGR ACCOUNTING SERVICE CENTER	0510-7076		3
MGR., DIST. OPRNS (CAREER LADDER)	2315-7147	EAS-22	
MGR., DIST. OPRNS (CAREER LADDER)	2315-7148	EAS-20	
MICROMATION SPEC POC	0301-3014	EAS-14	1
MICROMATION TECHNICIAN PDC	0301-3009	DCS-12	1
ML FLOW CNTLR	2315-2011	EAS-14	254
ML HANDLER TECH	2315-62XX	MH-05	1,155
MLHDLR EQUIP OPER	5704-03XX		4,620
MO ACCTG SPEC PDC	0525-5014	DCS-16	7
MODEL MAKER	3403-3001	EAS-18	
MODEL MAKER	3403-3002	EAS-17	I
MOTOR VEH OPER	5703-02XX	PS-06	14
MOTOR VEH OPER	5703-02XX	PS-05	3,475
NATIONAL ACCOUNTS REPRESENTATIVE	1101-5042		82
NATIONAL ACCOUNTS REPRESENTATIVE	1101-5043	EA'S-23	22
NATIONAL ACCOUNTS REPRESENTATIVE	1101-5044	EAS-25	21
NATIONAL LAB MAINTENANCE ENGINEER	1601-3009	EAS-15	1
NETWORK PERFORMANCE SPECIALIST	0391-4009	EAS-21	1
NETWORK PERFORMANCE SPECIALIST PR	0391-4007	EAS-24	1
NETWORK PERFORMANCE SPECIALIST SR	0391-4008	EAS-23	1
NETWORK PLANNING SPECIALIST	2330-4032	EAS-21	48
NETWORK PLANNING SPECIALIST	2330-4038	EAS-19	102
NETWORKS SPECIALIST	2150-5010	EAS-15	278
OCCUP HEALTH NURSE ADMINISTRATOR	0610-4002	EAS - 17	67
➤ OCCUP HLTH NURSE	0610-4001	PNS-01	183
OCCUPATION SAFETY/HEALTH SPECIALST	0018-5022	EAS-25	1
OCCUPATION SAFTY/HEALTH SPECIALIST	0018-5015	EAS-23	2
OFC STAFF ASST (TYPIST)	0318-07XX	PS-05	1
OFF CLK-CUSTODIAL	0301-05XX		95
OFF MACH OPER	0350-OIXX	MH-05	14
OFF MACH OPER	0350-02XX	PS-05	22
OFFICE AIDE	0001-1001	EAS-01	3
OFFICE APPLIANCE REPAIRMAN	4806-04XX	PS-05	2
OFFICE CLERK	0301-OIXX		4
OFFICE CLERK	0301-OIXX	PS-04	89
OFFICE CLERK (MTEC)	0301-2104	MTEC-05	7
OFFICE CLERK (SUPPLY CENTER)	0301-2102	MESC-05	
OFFICE CLK VEHICLE OPERATIONS	0301-04XX	PS-05	92
OFFICE MACHINE OPERATOR	0350-OIXX	MH-04	1
OFFICE SERVICES ASSISTANT (AREA)	0342-2003	EAS-10	6
OFFICE SERVICES ASSISTANT PDC	0301-2034	DCS-10	4
OFFICE SERVICES CLERK	0301-2103	MESC-04	1
OFFICE SERVICES CLERK (AREA)	0301-2100	EAS-10	9
OFFICE SYSTEMS COORDINATOR ASSOC	0342-5028	EAS-14	2
OFFSET PRESS OPER	4417-OIXX	PS-05	3
OLYMPICS SPECIALIST	2340-5047	EAS-23	5
OLYMPICS SPECIALIST, PCES	2340-5048	PCES-I	
OPERATING ENGINEER	5415-02XX	OSD-06	6

OPERATING ENGINEER HELPER	5415-03XX	OSD-04	
OPERATIONAL REQUIREMENTS SPECIALST	0345-5112	EAS-23	18
OPERATIONS PERFORMANCE ANALYST	2305-5027	EAS-25	2
OPERATIONS PERFORMANCE ANALYST	2305-5028	EAS-23	1
OPERATIONS PERFORMANCE ANALYST	2305-5029	EAS-21	4
OPERATIONS PRGMS ANALYST(AREA OFC)	2310-5023	EAS-23	20
OPERATIONS PRGMS ANALYST(AREA OFC)	2310-5024	EAS-21	18
OPERATIONS QUALITY IMPROVEMENT SPC	1910-4015	EAS-17	247
OPERATIONS QUALITY IMPROVEMENT SPC	1910-5005	EAS-25	1
OPERATIONS QUALITY IMPROVEMENT SPC	1910-5006	EAS-23	3
OPERATIONS QUALITY IMPROVEMENT SPC	1910-5007	EAS-21	2
OPERATIONS QUALITY IMPROVEMT ANLST	1910-3001	EAS-15	32
OPERATIONS REDESIGN SPECIALIST	2305-5031	EAS-21	1
OPERATIONS REDESIGN SPECIALIST	2305-5032	EAS-23	4
OPERATIONS REDESIGN SPECIALIST	2305-5033	EAS-25	5
OPERATIONS REDESIGN SPECIALIST	2305-5037	EAS-19	1
OPERATIONS RESEARCH ANALYST	1515-4014	EAS-23	10
OPERATIONS RESEARCH ANALYST	1515-4015	EAS-21	7
OPERATIONS RESEARCH ANALYST	1515-4024	EAS-25	9
OPERATIONS RESEARCH ANALYST	1515-4025	EAS-23	9
OPERATIONS RESEARCH ANALYST	1515-5001	EAS-25	8
OPERATIONS.RESEARCH SPECIALIST	1515-4027		1
OPERATIONS SPECIALIST	2305-5023		29
OPERATIONS SPECIALIST	2305-5024	EAS-23	31
OPERATIONS SPECIALIST	2305-5025	EAS-21	13
OPERATIONS SPECIALIST	2305-5026	EAS-19	
OPERATIONS SUPPORT SPECIALIST	0345-5114	EAS-21	38
OPERATIONS SUPPORT SPECIALIST	0345-5115	EAS-23	42
OPERATIONS SUPPORT SPECIALIST	2340-5043	EAS-20	90
OPERATIONS SUPPORT SPECIALIST	2340-5044	EAS-18	215
OPERATIONS SUPPORT SPECIALIST	2340-5045	EAS-16	338
OPERATIONS SUPPORT SPECIALIST	2340-5046	EAS-14	54
OPERATIONS/SYSTEMS ENGINEER	0801-4058	EAS-25	3
OPERATIONS/SYSTEMS ENGINEER	0801-4059	EAS-23	2
OPERATOR COMPUTRIZD LABEL PRINTING	4401-10XX	PS-05	2
OPERATOR-VARITYPER	4401-1012	MESC-05	
OPERATOR, SEWING MACHINE	3111-1001	MTEC-04	4
OPRNS MGR CLASS STA AA	2305-7097	EAS-22	1
OPRNS MGR CLASSD STA (A)	2305-7055	EAS-21	18
ORGANIZATION/JOB EVALUATION ANALYS	0201-5094	EAS-25	1
ORGANIZATION/JOB EVALUATION ANALYS	0201-5095	EAS-23	1
ORGANIZATION/JOB EVALUATION ANALYS	0201-5096	EAS-21	2
ORGANIZATION/JOB EVALUATION ASSOC	0201-5105	EAS-14	I
OVERHAUL SPECIALIST	5342-11XX	PS-08	12
PACKER SHIPPER	7002-03XX	MH-04	14
PACKER/WAREHOUSEMAN	6907-1002	MESC-04	47
PAINTER	4102-02XX	PS-06	166
PAINTER	4102-03XX	OSD-06	1
PAINTER/PLASTERER LDR	4740-OIXX	OSD-07	1
PARALEGAL SPECIALIST	0950-5003	EAS-16	12
PARALEGAL SPECIALIST, SR	0950-5005	EAS-18	1
PARCEL POST DIST-MACHINE	2315-06XX	PS-06	59
PARCEL POST DIST-MACHINE	2315-06XX	PS-05	9,572
PAYROLL PROCESSING SPEC (POC)	0544-5003	DCS-14	36
PAYROLL PROCESSING SPEC SR (PDC)	0544-5004	DCS-16	13
PAYROLL PROCESSING SUPV	0544-6008	EAS-20	7
PAYROLL PROCESSING TECH (PDC)	0544-5006	DCS-11	72
PCES EXEC IN TRNG	0301-7141		3
PCES EXEC SPEC ASGNMT	0301-7142		27
PCES EXEC SPEC ASNGMT INSPTN SRVC	2335-7030		3
PERS ASST 8	0201-5025	EAS-14	3
PERSNL ASST ASF	0201-2004	EAS-11	5
➤ PERSONNEL CLK	0203-14XX	PS-05	179
PERSONNEL MANAGEMENT SPECIALIST	0230-5069	EAS-19	2
PEST CONTROLLER	5026-01XX	PS-06	5

PHIL CLK	2345-02XX	PS-05	95
PHIL STMP STOCK EXMR	0525-4008	EAS-13	4
PHILATELIC CONTROL SPECIALIST	2003-5015	EAS-22	1
PHILATELIC DESIGN SPECIALIST	1001-5030	EAS-24	I
PHILATELIC PROCUREMENT SPECIALIST	2003-5033	EAS-23	1
PHILATELIC PROGRAM SPECIALIST	1001-5014	EAS-17	2
PHILATELIC SALES PROGRAM ANALYST	1101-5040	EAS-20	2
PHOTOGRAPHER	1060-4002	EAS-21	I
PLANT MAINTENANCE ENGINEER	601-5004	EAS-19	6
PLANT MAINTENANCE ENGINEER (HFU)	1601-5005	EAS-17	
PLUMBER	4206-02XX	PS-06	60
PLUMBER	4206-05XX	OSD-07	2
PLUMBER HELPER	4206-04XX	OSD-04	1
PLUMBER LEADER	4206-03XX	OSD-08	I
PM RELIEF/REPLCMNT	2305-6100	PMLR-55	1,905
PM RELIEF/REPLCMNT	2305-6111	PMLR-09	5,161
PM RELIEF/REPLCMNT	2305-6113	PMLR-11	4,915
PM RELIEF/REPLCMNT	2305-6115	PMLR-13	970
PM/US VIRGIN ISLANDS COORDINATOR	2301-7140	EAS-22	1
POST OFFICE CLK	2340-04XX	PS-03	844
POSTAGE DUE CLK	2340-06XX	PS-05	350
POSTAGE DUE TECHN	2340-24XX	PS-06	280
POSTAL INSPECTOR (PROGRAM MGR)	2335-5018	EAS-24	95
➤ POSTAL INSPECTOR (PROJECT COORD)	2335-3004		352
POSTAL MAINTENANCE SPECIALIST	0801-4020	EAS-25	7
POSTAL OPER ASSOC	2340-5016	EAS-15	1
POSTAL OPER TECH	2340-2010	EAS-11	2
POSTAL OPERATIONS ANALYST	2340-3001	EAS-21	4
POSTAL OPERATIONS ANALYST	2340-3002	EAS-23	24
➤ POSTAL POLICE OFFICER (8)	2335-24XX	PPO-06	1,108
POSTAL POLICE OFFICER IN CHARGE(A)	2335-6009	EAS-15	40
POSTAL POLICE OFFICER IN CHARGE(B)	2335-7008	EAS-17	12
POSTAL POLICE OFFICER IN CHARGE©	2335-7009	EAS-20	3
POSTAL POLICE SUPERVISOR	2335-6008	EAS-14	150
POSTAL SYSTEMS COORDINATOR	0525-5020	EAS-15	204
POSTMASTER	2301-5103	EPM-52	20
POSTMASTER	2301-6104	EPM-53	721
POSTMASTER	2301-6105	EPM-54	44
POSTMASTER	2301-6106	EPM-55	987
POSTMASTER	2301-6111	EAS-11	5,307
POSTMASTER	2301-6113	EAS-13	6,013
POSTMASTER	2301-6115	EAS-15	2,643
POSTMASTER	2301-6118	EAS-18	3,877
POSTMASTER	2301-6120	EAS-20	2,127
POSTMASTER	2301-6213	EAS-13	279
POSTMASTER	2301-6215	EAS-15	3,024
POSTMASTER	2301-7121	EAS-21	975
POSTMASTER	2301-7122	EAS-22	675
POSTMASTER	2301-7139	PCES-I	26
POSTMASTER (F)	2301-7004	EAS-24	224
POSTMASTER (G)	2301-7005	EAS-26	49
POSTMASTER (I)	0340-7008	PCES-I	
POSTMASTER GENERAL	0340-7010	PCES-II	1
PREFERENTIAL MAIL CLERK	0305-2011	EAS-09	1
PRESENTATION SPECIALIST	1084-4001	EAS-20	2
PRESENTATION SPECIALIST	1084-4004	EAS-22	1
PRESS OPERATOR	3803-1001	MESC-05	2
PREVENTIVE MAINT ENGINEER	0802-3017	EAS-20	1
PRGM ANLST STAFF	0345-4038	EAS-18	3
PRGM MGR TELE	0334-4060		6
PRGMG LIBRARIAN	0335-2013	EAS-10	1
PRGMG LIBRN PDC	0335-2009	DCS-10	4
PRINCIPAL STATISTICIAN	1530-5002	EAS-25	2
PRINTING CONTR SPEC SR	1654-4003	EAS-21	1
PRIVATE SECRETARY TO THE PMG	0318-2024	EAS-23	1

PROC CLERK	1106-01XX	PS-05	62
PROCUR SPEC	1105-02XX	PS-06	I
PROCUREMENT & SUPPLY ASSISTANT PDC	1105-2002	DCS-13	6
PROCUREMENT & SUPPLY ASST (SMISC)	1105-2006	DCS-15	1
PROCUREMENT & SUPPLY ASST (SMISC)	1105-2007	DCS-17	1
PROCUREMENT SPECIALIST STAFF	1102-5010	EAS-17	1
PROCUREMENT/MATERIEL MGMT ASSIST	2003-09XX	PS-06	78
PROCUREMENT/SUPPLY ASSISTANT NISSC	1105-2004	EAS-13	1
PRODUCT PUBLICITY SPECIALIST	1081-5050	EAS-24	4
PRODUCTION PLANNING COORDINATOR	1152-6002	EAS-15	23
PROF/SPEC TRAINEE A	0301-5205	DCS-14	2
PROF/SPEC TRAINEE AA	0301-5264	EAS-13	12
PROF/SPEC TRAINEE 8	0301-5206	DCS-16	
PROF/SPEC TRAINEE B	0301-5213	EAS-15	
PROF/SPEC TRAINEE C'	0301-5202	EAS-16	
PROF/SPEC TRAINEE C	0301-5207	DCS-18	
PROF/SPEC TRAINEE D	0301-5214	EAS-17	
PROF/SPEC TRAINEE E	0301-5203	EAS-18	
PROF/SPEC TRAINEE F	0301-5247	EAS-19	I
PROG DIR OPERATIONS RESEARCH	1515-4023	EAS-26	
PROGRAM ANALYST	0345-4036	EAS-22	3
PROGRAM ANALYST	0345-4037	EAS-20	3
PROGRAM EVALUATION SPECIALIST	0345-5104	EAS-25	4
PROGRAM EVALUATION SPECIALIST	0345-5105	EAS-23	4
PROGRAM EVALUATION SPECIALIST	0345-5106	EAS-21	1
PROGRAM PERFORMANCE SPECIALIST	0345-5101	EAS-25	3
PROGRAM PERFORMANCE SPECIALIST	0345-5102	EAS-23	I
PROGRAM PERFORMANCE SPECIALIST	0345-5103	EAS-21	1
PROP INVN ASST	2001-2001	EAS-11	2
PROP MAINT&INV TECH	2001-2003	EAS-14	1
PROP SUP SPEC	2003-1OXX	OSO-06	
SPECIALIST POC	2003-2001	DCS-14	
PROPERTY CONTROL 3	0301-45XX	PS-06	1,344
PSO TECH			
PSTL INSP A	2335-2002	EAS-17	
PSTL INSP B	2335-3003	EAS-19	
PSTL INSP C	2335-3006	EAS-21	
PSTL INSP D	2335-3002	EAS-23	1,674
PSTL INSP-IN-CHG B	2335-7007	PCES-I	32
PSTL MACHS MECH	4801-06XX	PS-06	118
PSYCHOLOGIST	0180-4003	EAS-23	3
PSYCHOLOGIST	0180-4007	EAS-21	3
PSYCHOLOGIST	0180-4015	EAS-25	2
PURCHASING ASSISTANT	1105-5006	EAS-13	25
PURCHASING POLICIES SPECIALIST	1102-5029	EAS-23	4
PURCHASING POLICIES SPECIALIST	1102-5040	EAS-25	9
PURCHASING SPECIALIST	1102-5012	EAS-23	61
PURCHASING SPECIALIST	1102-5026	EAS-20	199
PURCHASING SPECIALIST	1102-5041	EAS-25	21
PURCHASING SPECIALIST	1102-5047	EAS-17	89
PURCHASING SPECIALIST	1102-5059		2
PURCHASING SPECIALIST	1102-5060	EAS-16	a
PURCHASING/MATERIEL COMPLIANCE SPC	1101-5041	EAS-23	I
PURCHASING/SUPPLY SYSTEMS SPCIALST	1101-5032	EAS-21	7
PURCHASING/SUPPLY SYSTEMS SPCIALST	1101-5033	EAS-23	5
PURCHASING/SUPPLY SYSTEMS SPCIALST	1101-5035	EAS-24	2
PURCHASING/SUPPLY TECHNICIAN	0301-5294	EAS-14	1
QUAL ASSUR ANLST PDC	1910-3011	0	
QUAL ASSUR ANLST SR PDC	1910-3010	OCS-18	11
QUAL ASSUR TECH PDC	1910-3012	D	
QUAL CNTL ANLST PDC	1910-4014	EAS-17	3
QUALITY ASSURANCE SPECIALIST	1910-3009	EAS-21	11
QUALITY ASSURANCE SPECIALIST	1910-4016	EAS-19	3
QUALITY ASSURANCE SPECIALIST	1910-4017	EAS-23	10
QUALITY ASSURANCE SPECIALIST	1910-4019	EAS-21	3

QUALITY ASSURANCE SPECIALIST	1910-4021	EAS-23	7
QUALITY ASSURANCE SPECIALIST	1910-5004	EAS-25	4
QUALITY CONTROL SPECIALIST	1910-3003	EAS-19	2
QUALITY FIRST CONSULTANT	0301-5331	EAS-25	8
QUALITY FIRST CONSULTANT	0301-7210	PCES-I	7
QUALITY FIRST TRAINER AD HOC	0301-5538	EAS-25	5
QUALITY SPECIALIST	0301-5326	EAS-24	1
QUALITY SPECIALIST	0301-5338	EAS-25	
QUALITY SPECIALIST	0301-5339	EAS-23	3
QUALITY SPECIALIST	0301-7211	PCES-I	1
QUALITY SPECIALIST	0343-5064	EAS-23	
QUALITY SPECIALIST	0343-5065	EAS-21	
QUALITY SPECIALIST (HQ)	0343-5063	EAS-25	
RAMP CLK AMF	2330-42XX	PS-06	476
REAL ESTATE SPECIALIST	1170-5017	EAS-21	29
REAL ESTATE SPECIALIST	1170-5019	EAS-23	60
REAL ESTATE SPECIALIST	1170-5018	EAS-25	37
RECEIVING AND SHIPPING CLERK	2040-2012	MESC-05	12
RECEIVING CLK FOREIGN AIR MAIL	2340-18XX	PS-06	57
RECEIVING&SHIPNG CLK	2040-20XX	OSD-05	1
RECEPTIONIST	0304-2008	EAS-09	1
RECEPTIONIST CORPORATE PERSNL OPRS	0304-2007	EAS-11	1
RECEPTIONIST OFC OF PMG	0304-2001		1
RECOGNITION SYSTEMS SPECIALIST	0855-4033	EAS-25	3
RECORDER	0986-3006	EAS-17	2
RECORDS CLK-INTERNATIONAL AIR MAIL	2340-10XX	PS-06	79
RECORDS MANAGEMENT CLERK	0301-2032	EAS-07	1
RECORDS SPECIALIST	0343-5057	EAS-25	1
RECORDS SPECIALIST	0343-5058	EAS-23	1
RECORDS SPECIALIST	0343-5059	EAS-21	3
REFERENCE LIBRARIAN	1410-4011	EAS-23	1
REGISTRAR	0301-5239	EAS-20	2
RELOCATION SPECIALIST	0303-5004	EAS-14	2
REPAIR PARTS CATALOGER	2050-5001	EAS-13	2
REQUIREMENTS ANALYST	0345-5091	EAS-25	2
REQUIREMENTS ANALYST	0345-5092	EAS-23	2
REQUIREMENTS ANALYST	0345-5093	EAS-21	2
ASSOCIATE POSTAL HISTORY	0170-5001	EAS-16	2
RESEARCH HISTORIAN	0301-6057		1
RESOURCE MANAGEMENT ANALYST	0343-4022	EAS-23	7
RESOURCE MANAGEMENT ANALYST	0343-5060	EAS-21	4
RESOURCES SPECIALIST	0301-5298	EAS-19	1
RETAIL SALES CLK POSTAL STORES	2320-39XX	PS-05	31
RETAIL SPECIALIST	2345-5030	EAS-16	173
RETIREMENT SPEC PDC	0501-5009	OCS-14	10
RETIREMENT SPEC SR PDC	0501-5008	DCS-16	2
RETIREMENT TECH PDC	0501-5010	DCS-11	13
REVIEW CLK	2315-26XX	PS-06	1,005
RURAL CARR ASSOC/SRV AUX RTE	2325-09XX	RAUX-05	4,700
RURAL CARR ASSOC/SRV REG RTE	2325-07XX		46,102
RURAL CARR ASSOC/SRV VAC RTE	2325-08XX		898
➤ RURAL CARRIER	2325-01XX	RCS-00	46,471
RURAL CARRIER RELIEF	2325-06XX	RAUX-05	2,934
SACK SORTING MACHINEOPR	2315-70XX	PS-06	136
SACK SORTING MACHINE OPR	2315-72XX	MH-05	1,618
SACK SORTING MACHINE OPR	2315-72XX	MH-04	71
SAFETY AND HEALTH ASSOCIATE	0018-5023	EAS-16	1
SAFETY ENGINEER	0803-4002	EAS-24	
SAFETY SPECIALIST	0018-5028	EAS-17	65
SALES SUPPORT SPECIALIST	1140-5048	EAS-23	10
SCALE MECH	3341-02XX	PS-05	2
SCHEDULE CLERK FOREGIN MAILS	2350-06XX	PS-06	2
SCHEDULE EXAMINER VEHICLE RUNS	2330-22XX	PS-07	16
SCHEMES & SCHEDULE CLK	2350-08XX	PS-06	36
SCHEMES EXAMNR	1712-04XX		9

SECRETARY	0318-2010	EAS-11	1
➤ SECRETARY	0318-2041		959
SECRETARY	0318-2042	EAS-14	123
SECRETARY	0318-2043	EAS-16	29
SECRETARY	0318-2045	EAS-18	4
SECRETARY TO THE DPMG	0318-2013	EAS-20	
SECRETARY TO THE EXECUTIVE VP	0318-2044		
SECRETARY-STENOGRAPHER	0318-04XX	PS-05	4
SECRETARY-TYPIST	0318-OSXX		5
SECURITY ENGINEERING TECH	0856-3013	EAS-16	7
SECURITY ENGINEERING TECHNICIAN	0856-3021	EAS-19	48
SECY USPS BD OF GOV	0301-5258	PCES-I	1
SELF SERVICE POSTAL CENTER TECH	2340-48XX	PS-06	828
SENIOR LOCKMAKER	5311-03XX		1
SERVICE REQ SPEC	0345-5021	EAS-18	1
SETUP PRESSMAN (MES)	3803-1002	MESC-06	1
SEWING MACHINE MECHANIC	5312-1001	EAS-11	2
SHEET METAL WORKER	3806-01XX	PS-07	1
SHIPPING COORD	2340-5011	EA -@14	1
SIGN PAINTER-ILLSTR	1020-OSXX	PS-06	29
SIGN PAINTER/LETTERER	4104-04XX	PS-05	33
SOFTWARE PROCESS ADMINISTRATOR	0334-4133	EAS-23	5
SOFTWARE SYSTEMS ADMINISTRATOR	0334-4046	EAS-24	12
SOFTWARE TEST ENGINEER	0854-4001	EAS-25	
SOFTWARE TEST ENGINEER	0854-4002	EAS-23	
SOFTWARE TEST ENGINEER	0854-4003	EAS-21	
SORTATION SYSTEMS SPECIALIST	0801-4063	EAS-25	2
SPACE & PROCUREMENT SPEC	0301-5010	EAS-21	1
SPACE MANAGEMENT SPECIALIST	0342-5013	EAS-17	1
SPACE MGMT SPEC	0342-5010	EAS-20	2
SPEC DEL MESSGR	2310-53XX	PS-05	1,555
SPEC POSTAL CLK	2315-08XX	PS-06	181
SPEC PSTL CLK	2320-31XX		31
SPEC TRANS CLERK	2330-02XX	PS-07	12
SPECIAL ASST - BOG	0318-2047	EAS-22	1
SPECIAL EVENTS COORDINATOR	1010-5002	EAS-25	1
SPECIAL TRANSFER CLERK AMF	2330-43XX	PS-07	9
SPECL SVC CUSTODIAN	5026-02XX	OSO-03	
SPEECHWRITER	1081-5052	EAS-25	2
SPEECHWRITER	1081-5053	EAS-23	2
SR BUDGET/FINANCIAL ANALYST (AREA)	0504-5020		29
SR BUDGET/FINANCIAL ANALYST(DIST)	0504-5021	EAS-21	78
SR CLERK PDC	0301-2072	DCS-06	11
SR COUNSEL	0905-4039	PCES-I	
SR DIRECTOR TECHNOLOGY INTEGRATION	0340-7128		
SR EEO COMPLAINTS PROCESSING SPCLS	0160-5058	EAS-21	2
SR EEO COMPLAINTS PROCESSING SPCLS	0160-5059	EAS-19	62
SR INJURY COMPENSATION SPEC	0230-5071	EAS-19	54
SR INJURY COMPENSATION SPEC	0230-5072	EAS-17	20
SR LABOR RELATIONS SPEC	0233-5015	EAS-21	73
SR LOCKMAKER (MES)	5311-1003	MESC-06	2
SR MAIL PROCESSOR	2315-56XX	PS-05	239
SR MARKUP CLK AUTOM	0301-49XX		81
SR MEDICAL DIRECTOR (AREA OFFICE)	0602-7005	EAS-26	9
SR MGR DISTRIBUTION OPERATIONS	2315-7138	EAS-25	39
SR OPERATIONS ANALYST	2310-5025	EAS-20	63
SR OPERATIONS ANALYST	2310-7039	EAS-22	14
SR PERSONNEL SERVICES SPECIALIST	0201-5115	EAS-21	72
SR PERSONNEL/TRAINING SPECIALIST	0201-5113		13
SR PSDS TECHNICIAN	0301-84XX	PS-07	6
SR SAFETY/HEALTH	0018-5026	EAS-19	60
SR SAFETY/HEALTH	0018-5027	EAS-17	12
SR SAFETY/INJURY COMP SPEC	0018-5024	EAS-19	11
SR SYS ACCT PDC	0510-4046	EAS-22	8
SR TRAINING SPECIALIST	0235-5058	EAS-19	67

SR VP CORPORATE/LEGISLATIVE AFFAIR	0340-7099	PCES-II	1
SR VP FINANCE	0340-7106		1
SR VP GENERAL COUNSEL	0905-7011		1
SR VP MARKETING	0340-7123		1
STAFF COUNSEL/HEARING OFFICER	0905-4038	APS-01	1
STAFF SECRETARY	0318-2039	EAS-09	102
STAFF SECRETARY (PDC)	0318-2040	DCS-09	9
STAMP DISTRIBUTION CLERK-SDN	2345-70XX	PS-06	
STAMP DISTRIBUTION TECHNICIAN	2003-4005	EAS-11	6
STAMP SUPP CLK	2320-03XX	PS-06	99
STATIONARY ENGINEER	5415-01XX	PS-07	71
STATIONARY ENGINEER'	5415-1001	MESC-07	1
STATISTICAL PROGRAMS COORDINATOR	1530-6005	EAS-18	84
STATISTICAL PROGRMS ANALYST (SPSC)	1530-5004	EAS-20	10
STOREKEEPER	2040-21XX	OSD-05	1
STOREKEEPER A (MES)	2040-1008	MESC-05	
STOREKEEPER B (MES)	2040-1009		1
STOREKPR AUTO PARTS	2040-11XX	PS-07	74
STOREKPR AUTO PARTS	2040-11XX	PS-06	111
STRATEGIC BUSINESS SYTEMS PLANNER	0334-4135	EAS-25	1
STRATEGIC PLANNING SPECIALIST	0345-4055	EAS-25	2
SUMMER INTERN	0301-2088	EAS-07	29
SUPPLY AND SERV CLK	2040-2002		1
SUPPLY ASST MES	2005-5006	EAS-15	1
SUPPLY CLERK	2005-2002	EAS-07	2
SUPPLY CLERK	2040-07XX	PS-05	4
SUPPLY CLERK	2040-07XX	PS-04	17
SUPPLY CLERK (MES)	2040-2015	MESC-04	
SUPPLY CLK B	2005-02XX	OSD-04	1
SUPPLY SYSTEMS CATALOGER SR	2050-5004	EAS-19	3
SUPPLY&RPR PTS TECH	2010-5003	EAS-17	7
SUPPORT SERVICES CLERK	0341-3001	EAS-07	5
SUPPORT SERVICES SPECIALIST	0341-5054	EAS-24	1
SUPPORT SERVICES TECHNICIAN	0341-3002	EAS-11	2
SUPPORT SERVICES TECHNICIAN	0341-3003	EAS-17	1
SUPT ACCTBL PAPER DISPOS	0530-6007		5
SUPT ENG A	4704-6007	EAS-11	3
SUPT ENG B	4704-6008	EAS-14	20
SUPT MAIL MTEC	6951-6011	EAS-18	6
TUPT SPECIAL DELIVERY	2310-6025	EAS-20	1
SUPT TRANSPORTATION EQUIP CNTR A	6951-6012	EAS-16	
SUPT WHITE HOUSE MAIL SECT	2305-6038	EAS-20	1
SUPV ACCOUNTING SECT	0540-6045	EAS-21	1
SUPV ACCOUNTING SERVICES	0510-6043	EAS-19	14
SUPV ACCOUNTING SERVICES	0510-6044	EAS-21	68
SUPV ACCOUNTS PAYABLE SECTION	0540-6043		2
SUPV ACCT PAPER	0530-6009	EAS-15	90
SUPV ACCT PAPER DPSTRY	0530-6008		1
SUPV ACCTG (CUSTOMER SERVICE)	0501-6046	EAS-18	1
SUPV ADMIN SERVICES	0341-6032		1
SUPV AREA STAMP DISTRIBUTOR	2003-6026		6
SUPV BUSINESS MAIL ENTRY	2345-6055	EAS-16	220
SUPV CANCELLATION SERVICES (PFSC)	0530-6012	EAS-15	1
SUPV CPTR MAINT LABL PRNTG	0356-6003	EAS-19	2
SUPV CPTR MRK-UP UNIT	0301-6079	EAS-15	308
SUPV CPTR OPER LASL PRNTG	0332-6009	EAS-20	1
SUPV CUST SUPPT	0334-6034	EAS-21	7
SUPV CUSTODIAL SERVICES	3502-6006	EAS-12	3
SUPV CUSTOMER CLAIMS SERV SECT	0540-6021	EAS-18	I
SUPV CUSTOMER SERVICE SUPPORT	0341-6031	EAS-17	206
SUPV CUSTOMER SERVICES	2305-6121	EAS-16	14,520
SUPV CUSTOMER SERVICES (PFSC)	0530-6022	EAS-15	I
SUPV DATA COLL&MAIL CNTRL	0301-6036		5
SUPV DATA CONV	0356-6006		1
SUPV DATA PROCESSING UNIT	0334-6044	EAS-23	1

SUPV DISBURSING	0501-6032	EAS-18	1
SUPV DISBURSING SECTION	0501-6044	EAS-22	1
SUPV DISTRIBUTION OPERATIONS	2315-6076	EAS - 1 6	8,659
SUPV DLVY&COLL	2310-6032	EAS-15	5
SUPV ELEV OPER	5438-6005	EAS-IT	3
SUPV EXAMINATIONS PROCESSING	0301-6101	EAS-18	I
SUPV FOREGN ML PLNG	2305-6028	EAS-17	I
SUPV GENERAL ACCOUNTING SECT	0501-6033	EAS-20	1
SUPV HQ PAYABLES/ASSET CONTROL SEC	0501-6043	EAS-21	1
SUPV INTERNATIONAL ACCOUNTS CENTER	0510-6045		1
SUPV INTL ACCTS	0501-6028	EAS-15	I
SUPV INTL AIRMAIL RECORDS UNIT (B)	2340-6009		4
SUPV INTL AIRML REC UNIT A	2340-6025	EAS-13	1
SUPV VEHICLE SUPPLIES (8)	2003-6024	EAS-16	58
SUPV VEHICLE SUPPLIES ©	2003-6025	EAS-17	13
SUPV WAREHOUSING	696O-6007	EAS-15	9
SUPV WHT HSE DISP UNIT	2315-6040	EAS-13	1
SYS LIAISON SPEC	0334-4073	DCS-21	4
SYSTEM/BUDGET SPECIALIST (DNO)	2330-4037	EAS-17	
SYSTEM/PROCESS ENGINEER	0801-4060	EAS-23	2
SYSTEM/PROCESS ENGINEER	0801-4061	EAS-21	1
SYSTEM/PROCESS ENGINEER	0801-4062	EAS-25	3
SYSTEMS ACCT PDC	0510-4052	EAS-20	4
SYSTEMS ANALYST (MIN/MICRO)	0334-4075	EAS-24	14
SYSTEMS ARCHITECT	0334-6016	EAS-25	1
SYSTEMS DEVELOPMENT SPECIALIST	0334-4107		6
SYSTEMS INTEGRATION ANALYST	0334-5023		1
TAPE LIBRARIAN PDC	0335-2007	DCS-09	9
TECHNICAL DOCUMENTATION SPECIALIST	1083-5003	EAS-24	1
TECHNICAL SERVICES MANAGER	0334-4130	EAS-25	6
TECHNICAL TRAINING SPECIALIST	1712-5021	EAS-17	
TECHNICAL TRAINING SPECIALIST	1712-5022	EAS-18	
TECHNICAL TRAINING SPECIALIST	1712-5023	EAS-20	96
TECHNICAL TRAINING SPECIALIST	1712-5024	EAS-25	5
TECHNICAL WRITER	1083-5002	EAS-19	6
TECHNOLOGY ACQUISITION SPECIALIST	0801-4064	EAS-25	11
TECHNOLOGY ACQUISITION SPECIALIST	0801-4065	EAS-23	9
TECHNOLOGY ACQUISITION SPECIALIST	0601-4066	EAS-21	2
TELE HARDWR TECH	0856-3016	EAS-17	10
TELECOMM HARDWARE TECHNICIAN SR	0334-3062	EAS-19	2
TELECOMMUNICATIONS HARDWARE SPCLST	0334-4041	EAS-21	16
➤ TELECOMMUNICATIONS SPECAILST(FLD)	0393-5001	EAS-17	82
TELEMARKETING ASSISTANTS	2005-2018	EAS-11	5
TELEPHONE OPERATOR	0382-01XX	PS-04	7
TELEPHONE OPERATOR	0382-2001	EAS-06	1
TELEPHONE OPERATOR	0382-2002	EAS-11	1
TELEPHONE OPERATOR	0382-2003	EAS-09	1
TELEPHONE SALES REPRESENTATIVE	1101-2001	EAS-11	2
TEXT&DATA SVC ASST	0332-2007	EAS-09	10
TIME AND ATTENDANCE CLK	0590-01XX	PS-05	427
TIME&ATTEND CLERK	0590-2006	EAS-08	1
TIRE REPAIRMAN	4504-01XX	PS-05	48
TOOL & PARTS CLK	6904-01XX	PS-06	2
TOOL & PARTS CLK	6904-OIXX	PS-05	838
TOOL AND DIE ENGINEER	3416-4001	EAS-18	1
TOOL AND PARTS CLERK (MES)	6904-1001	MESC-05	1
TOOL SPECIALIST (MES)	3416-3001	EAS-17	1
TOOL/DIE MAKER	3416-1002	EAS-14	3
TORT CLAIMS SPECIALIST (POC)	0540-5013	DCS-16	6
TORT CLAIMS SPECIALIST SR (PDC)	0540-5015	DCS-18	1
TOUR SUPT POSTAL OPERATIONS (A)	2305-6029	EAS-20	17
TRACTOR TRAILER OPER	5756-01XX	PS-06	4,633
TRAFFIC MANAGEMENT SPECIALIST	2330-4035	EAS-19	51
TRAINING TECHNICIAN	1702-5008	EAS-11	a
TRAINING TECHNICIAN	1702-5010		9

TRAINING TECHNICIAN, PEDC	1712-34XX	PS-06	580
TRANSFER CLK	2330-01XX		80
TRANSFER CLK AMF	2330-04XX		448
TRANSLATOR CORRESPONDENCE	1045-02XX	PS-07	7
TRANSPORTATION SPECIALIST	2330-5037	EAS-21	6
TRANSPORTATION SPECIALIST	2330-5038	EAS-23	11
TRANSPORTATION SPECIALIST	2330-5039	EAS-25	12
TREASURER	0505-7059	PCES-I	1
TYPIST	0322-2003	EAS-07	1
TYPIST	0322-2004	EAS-05	
TYPIST LABEL PRINTING	0322-04XX	MH-04	3
VEH OPER MAINT ASST	0341-06XX	PS-06	853
VEH OPNS ASST	2150-OBXX		9
VEH.TRAFFIC CONTROL TECHNICIAN-VCS	2330-75XX	PS-07	1
VEHICLE DISPATCHER	2151-01XX		15
VEHICLE DISPATCHER	2151-01XX	PS-06	4
VEHICLE MAINT PRGM ANALY(AREA OFC)	2150-5009	EAS-23	9
VEHICLE MAINTENANCE ANALYST	1601-08XX	PS-07	49
VEHICLE MAINTENANCE METHODS ANALYS	1601-4022	EAS-21	2
VEHICLE MAINTENANCE METHODS SPCLST	1601-4023	EAS-23	3
VEHICLE MAINTENANCE SPECIALIST	5823-5001	EAS-19	I
VEHICLE MAINTENANCE SPECIALIST(HQ)	1601-4021	EAS-25	
VEHICLE OPRNS ASST BULK MLS	2150-03XX	PS-06	267
VENDING MACHINES MECHANIC	4801-04XX		10
VIDEO PRODUCER	1071-5011	EAS-22	2
VIDEO PROGRAMMING SPECIALIST	1071-5013	EAS-24	1
VIDEOGRAPHER	1071-5012	EAS-21	1
VP AREA OPERATIONS	0340-7130	PCES-II	10
VP CONSUMER ADVOCATE	0301-7013		1
VP CONTROLLER	0505-7062		1
VP DIVERSITY DEVELOPMENT	0340-7102		1
VP ENGINEERING	0340-7104		1
VP FACILITIES	0340-7105		1
VP HUMAN RESOURCES	0340-7103		1
VP INFORMATION SYSTEMS	0340-7108		1
VP LABOR RELATIONS	0340-7109		1
VP LEGISLATIVE AFFAIRS	0340-7127		1
VP MARKETING SYSTEMS	0340-7126		1
VP OPERATIONS REDESIGN	0340-7136		1
VP OPERATIONS SUPPORT	0340-7111		1
VP PRODUCT MANAGEMENT	0340-7124		
VP PURCHASING	0340-7112		1
VP QUALITY	0340-7113	PCES-II	
VP RETAIL	0340-7138		
VP' SALES	0340-7134		1
VP TECHNOLOGY APPLICATIONS	0340-7125		1
VP WORKFORCE PLNG & SERVICE MGMT	0340-7135		1
WAREHOUSING SYSTEMS SPECIALIST	2030-5002	EAS-25	1
➤ WELDER	3704-02XX	PS-06	135
WINDOW CLEANER	3540-01XX	PS-04	5
WINDOW CLK	2320-01XX	PS-05	6,106
WINDOW SVC TECH	2320-29XX	PS-06	2,329
WLRS CONTROL CLERK	0301-94XX	PS-05	4
WORD PROCESSING OPERATOR	0322-2011	EAS-07	19
WORD PROCESSING OPERATOR	0322-2018	DCS-07	6
WORD PROCESSING OPERATOR SR	0322-2010	EAS-09	1
WORD PROCESSING OPERATOR SR	0322-2019	DCS-09	2
WORD PROCESSING TECHNICIAN	0301-4034	EAS-11	4
WORKFORCE PLANNING SPECIALIST	2305-5034	EAS-21	1
WORKFORCE PLANNING SPECIALIST	2305-5035	EAS-23	4
WORKFORCE PLANNING SPECIALIST	2305-5036	EAS-25	5
WORKING GP LDR DIST CLERKS	2315-25XX	PS-06	5
WRITER	1081-5023	EAS-21	1
WRITER/EDITOR	1082-5016	EAS-19	11
WRITER/EDITOR ASSISTANT	1081-5054		1

Appendix A
Job Hunter's Checklist

WHAT TO DO NOW

❑ Review the Postal Service occupations Listed in Chapter Three, Nine and Ten. These chapters provide complete lists of postal jobs that you may qualify for—including job descriptions for over 40 job categories.

❑ Call or write your local District office. See Chapter Four for a national list. Request the following information:

    ✔ Announcements for specific jobs.

    ✔ Exam test dates for your area.

    ✔ Sample tests and applications.

    ✔ A copy of "*You And The USPS*".

❑ Contact the Postal Services' "National Job Listings" web site at **http://www.usps.com/hrisp/**. This site lists national jobs and provides contact information for local jobs as well. Also, contact regional and local postal facilities including Customer Service District Offices, General Mail Facilities, Sectional Center Facilities, Management Sectional Centers, or Bulk Mail Centers in your area. Don't forget to talk with the Post Master at local Post Offices.

    ✔ National Vacancies Hotline: 1-800-JOB USPS

    ✔ Local Employment Hotline: 1-800-276-5627

✔ Obtain local postal facility office phone numbers from your phone directory. Look under "U.S. Government" in the Blue Pages. Look in the newspaper classified.

✔ Visit Federaljobs.net at (**http://federaljobs.net**). This web site provides information for finding federal jobs in all sectors and it offers over 200 links to federal agency employment web sites.

❑ Review Chapters One, Two and Three to fully understand the Postal Service job market, employee benefits, salary, and how they hire. Also review:

✔ Chapter Eight for Veteran's Hiring programs.

✔ Chapter Five and Six for sample postal exams and applications.

✔ The Occupation Directory in Chapter Ten.

❑ Locate your school transcripts, military records, awards, and professional licenses. Collect past employment history; salary, addresses, phone numbers, dates employed, for the application. Use the forms printed in Appendix B to draft your application.

APPLYING FOR A JOB

❑ When you receive requested job announcements, each announcement will be accompanied by all required application forms. You can use the blank application forms in Appendix B and Chapter Five to draft your application while waiting for the official forms from the Postal Service.

❑ If no vacancies exist for your specialty, call or write the District Office frequently to find out about new openings and read your local newspaper's help wanted section. Visit the web sites mentioned above and call the toll free numbers for local and national vacancies. Consider getting your foot in the door by taking the 470 Battery Test or any other written exam. Once hired you will have the opportunity to apply for vacancies in other occupations.

❑ Complete and sign **ALL** application forms received with the announcement including the Application/Admission Card, PS Form 2479-A/B. (Print or type them if possible). Follow all instructions.

❑ Retain a copy of your application and all other forms required in the announcement. These copies can be used for other bids.

✔ You can copy your application and use it for other jobs. You must have an original signature on the application and the correct job title and announcement number. Therefore, type your application and don't enter this data until after you have copied the completed form. Then, on the copy you are sending to the Postal Service, sign it, add the job number and name.

❑ Send in the completed forms to the address specified on the announcement. Applications must be post marked by no later than the closing date of the announcement for your application to be considered.

ADDITIONAL RESOURCES

NOTE: A computer, modem, and online or Internet access is required to contact the following services. You must have Internet access through a local provider or an online service such as America Online.

❑ **AMERICA ONLINE's** (AOL's) career center, created and directed by Gonyea and Associates, has a new FREE service called *"Government Jobs Central"* to help job seekers explore, find, and secure employment with the Federal government, including the US Postal Service. Dennis V. Damp, author of *Post Office Jobs* and *The Book Of U.S. Government Jobs* (1-800-782-7424)—a nationally recognized expert in federal employment—has written a comprehensive series of articles for this service covering many topics of value for people interested in securing federal jobs. AOL members can use the keyword **"Gonyea"** to go direct to the Career Center.

This service provides over 31 menu selections for job seekers, career counselors, and for those exploring career options. The service is loaded with up-to-date job information including current federal job vacancies, networking resources and job application guidance.

❑ **FEDERALJOBS.NET** (**http://federaljobs.net**) One of the most popular federal employment sites on the internet today with over

100,000 visitors each month. Visit this site to explore all federal job options including jobs with the USPS.

❑   **INTERNET CAREER CONNECTION (http://iccweb.com)** An on-line and interactive career center on the Internet.

❑   **FEDERAL EMPLOYEE NEWS DIGEST (http://www.fedforce.com)** Visit this site to find the latest news about what's going on in the Postal Service and Federal job sectors.

❑   **USPS Home Page (http://www.usps.gov)** This highly informative service offers general information about the USPS and includes all recent press releases. Also visit their new employment page.

❑   **FEDERAL RESEARCH SERVICE (http://www.fedjobs.com)** To find out about recent job openings in the federal sector and for updated information about employment opportunities.

RESULTS

❑   Your application will be processed and results returned to you within several weeks. You will receive a *Notice* informing you of your eligibility and scheduled testing date and location. If rated eligible, your name will be placed on the list of eligible applicants for that position. Selected applicants must:

   ✔ Meet Basic Qualifications
   ✔ Score Highest on the Exam, and
   ✔ Successfully Complete an Interview

THE INTERVIEW

❑   Prepare for the interview. Review chapter Seven for guidance on how to present yourself and prepare for the interview. Most Postal Jobs' books completely ignore the interview phase. If you don't impress the selecting officials, you may be passed over for the position.

Appendix B
Application Forms

There are two standard Postal Service job applications included in this Appendix, the *Application for Employment*, PS Form 2591, and the *Admission Card*, PS Form 2479-A. You should also refer to Chapter Six to review the sample application that you will encounter when taking any of the Postal Service's written exams.

The Postal Service will send a complete set of forms to applicants that call for information about a particular opening. Other forms may also be required depending on the type of job applied for.

A number of jobs are filled without a written test, generally professional or highly skilled positions. It is important to thoroughly complete all forms when applying for these positions. You will be examined and rated on a point system assessed through review of your knowledge, skills, and abilities that you submit on your resume and application forms. Your resume and application must be thorough and include all related experience, education and training that qualifies you for the position. Otherwise, you will loose points and others, who may be less qualified, will get the job.

Copy the forms that follow and use them to draft and refine your application prior to receipt of the official forms. This is an excellent time to compile your education, work, and military history. Draft concise work descriptions to place on your final application forms. You must provide your work history back at least 10 years. Go back further to include any work related experience that will help you qualify for this job, including military job experience. Take time to type these forms if possible and send a cover letter with the application package.

Application for Employment
(Shaded Areas for Postal Service Use Only)

The US Postal Service is an Equal Opportunity Employer

Rated Application			Veteran preference has been verified through proof that the separation was under honorable conditions, and other proof as required. (See Section D below.)	Check One:
Rated For	Rating	Date Rcvd.		☐ 10 pts. CPS
		Time Rcvd.	Type of Proof Submitted & Date Issued	☐ 10 pts. CP
				☐ 10 pts. XP
Signature & Date			Verifier's Signature, Title & Date	☐ 5 pts. TP

A. General Information

1. Name (First, MI, Last)	2. Social Security No. (SSN)	3. Home Telephone ( )
4. Mailing Address (No., Street, City, State, ZIP)	5. Date of Birth	6. Work Phone ( )
	7. Place of Birth (City & State or City & Country)	

8. Kind of Job Applied for and Postal Facility Name & Location (City & State)	9. Will You Accept: Temporary/Casual (Noncareer) Work ☐ Yes ☐ No	10. When Will You Be Available?	11. Are You Willing to Travel? (Complete only if you are applying for an executive or professional position.) ☐ Yes ☐ No

B. Educational History

1. Name and Location (City & State) of Last High School Attended	2. Are You a High School Graduate? Answer "Yes" if you expect to graduate within the next 9 months, or you have an official equivalency certificate of graduation. ☐ Yes - Month & Year: ____ ☐ No - Highest Grade Completed: ____

3a. Name and Location of College or University (City, State, and ZIP Code if known. If you expect to graduate within 9 months, give month and year you expect degree.)	Dates Attended		No. of Credits Completed		Type Degree (BA, etc.)	Year of Degree
	From	To	Semester Hrs.	Quarter Hours		

b. Chief Undergraduate College Subjects	Semester Hrs. Completed	Quarter Hours Completed	c. Chief Graduate College Subjects	Semester Hrs. Completed	Quarter Hours Completed

4. Major Field of Study at Highest Level of College Work

5. Other Schools or Training (For example, trade, vocational, armed forces, or business. Give for each: name, city, state, & ZIP Code, if known, of school; dates attended; subjects studied; number of classroom hours of instruction per week; certificates; & any other pertinent information.)

6. Honors, Awards, & Fellowships Received

7. Special Qualifications & Skills (Licenses; skills with machines, patents or inventions; publications - do not submit copies unless requested; public speaking; memberships in professional or scientific societies; typing or shorthand speed, etc.)

PS Form 2591, November 1993 (Page 1 of 4)

Name (First, MI, Last)	Social Security No.	Date

C. Work History

(Start with your present position and go back for 10 years or to your 16th birthday, whichever is later. You may include volunteer work. Account for periods of unemployment in separate blocks in order. Include military service. Use blank sheets if you need more space. Include your name, SSN, and date on each sheet.)

May the US Postal Service ask your present employer about your character, qualifications, and employment record? A "No" will not affect your consideration for employment opportunities.   ☐ Yes   ☐ No

1.

Dates of Employment (Month & Year) **Present**	Grade If Postal, Federal Service or Military	Starting Salary/Earnings $ per
From To		
Exact Position Title Average Hours per Week	Number & Kind of Employees Supervised	Present Salary/Earnings $ per
Name of Employer and Complete Mailing Address	Kind of Business (Manufacturing, etc.)	Place of Employment (City & State)
	Name of Supervisor	Telephone No. (If Known) ( )

Reason for Wanting to Leave

Description of Duties, Responsibilities, & Accomplishments

2.

Dates of Employment (Month & Year)	Grade If Postal, Federal Service or Military	Starting Salary/Earnings $ per
From To		
Exact Position Title Average Hours per Week	Number & Kind of Employees Supervised	Present Salary/Earnings $ per
Name of Employer and Complete Mailing Address	Kind of Business (Manufacturing, etc.)	Place of Employment (City & State)
	Name of Supervisor	Telephone No. (If Known) ( )

Reason for Wanting to Leave

Description of Duties, Responsibilities, & Accomplishments

3.

Dates of Employment (Month & Year)	Grade If Postal, Federal Service or Military	Starting Salary/Earnings $ per
From To		
Exact Position Title Average Hours per Week	Number & Kind of Employees Supervised	Present Salary/Earnings $ per
Name of Employer and Complete Mailing Address	Kind of Business (Manufacturing, etc.)	Place of Employment (City & State)
	Name of Supervisor	Telephone No. (If Known) ( )

Reason for Wanting to Leave

Description of Duties, Responsibilities, & Accomplishments

PS Form 2591, November 1993 (Page 2 of 4)

Name (First, MI, Last)	Social Security No.	Date

4.

Dates of Employment (Month & Year) From To	Grade If Postal, Federal Service or Military	Starting Salary/Earnings $ per
Exact Position Title Average Hours per Week	Number & Kind of Employees Supervised	Ending Salary/Earnings $ per
Name of Employer and Complete Mailing Address	Kind of Business (Manufacturing. etc.)	Place of Employment (City & State)
	Name of Supervisor	Telephone No. (If Known) ( )

Reason for Leaving

Description of Duties, Responsibilities, & Accomplishments

D. Veteran Preference

Answer all parts. If a part does not apply, answer "no".

	Yes	No
1. Have you ever served on active duty in the US military service? (Exclude tours of active duty for training as a reservist or guardsman.)		
2. Have you ever been discharged from the armed service under other than honorable conditions? You may omit any such discharge changed to honorable by a Discharge Review Board or similar authority. (If "Yes", give details in Section F.)		
3. Do you claim 5-point preference based on active duty in the armed forces? (If "Yes," you will be required to furnish records to support your claim.)		
4. Do you claim 10-point preference? If "Yes," check type of preference claimed and attach Standard Form 15, Claim for 10-Point Veteran Preference, together with proof called for in that form.		

☐ Compensable Disability (Less than 30%)   ☐ Compensable Disability (30% or more)   ☐ Non-compensable Disability (includes Receipt of the Purple Heart)   ☐ Wife/Husband

☐ Widow/Widower   ☐ Mother   ☐ Other:

5. List for all military service: (Enter N/A if not applicable)

Dates (From - To)	Serial/Service Number	Branch of Service	Type of Discharge

THE LAW (39 U.S. CODE 1002) PROHIBITS POLITICAL AND CERTAIN OTHER RECOMMENDATIONS FOR APPOINTMENTS, PROMOTIONS, ASSIGNMENTS, TRANSFERS, OR DESIGNATIONS OF PERSONS IN THE POSTAL SERVICE. Statements relating solely to character and residence are permitted, but every other kind of statement or recommendation is prohibited unless it either is requested by the Postal Service and consists solely of an evaluation of the work performance, ability, aptitude, and general qualifications of an individual or is requested by a Government representative investigating the individual's loyalty, suitability, and character. Anyone who requests or solicits a prohibited statement or recommendation is subject to disqualification from the Postal Service and anyone in the Postal Service who accepts such a statement may be suspended or removed from office.

Name (First, MI, Last)	Social Security No.	Date

E. Other Information

	Yes	No
1. Are you a United States citizen?		
2. Are you a citizen of American Samoa or any other territory owing allegiance to the United States?		
3. Are you an alien with permanent residence status. If "yes," be prepared to show Form I-151 or I-551.		

If you answer "yes" to question 4 and/or 5, give details in Section F below. Give the name, address (including ZIP Code) of employer, approximate date, and reasons in each case. ▶

	Yes	No
4. Have you ever been fired from any job for any reason?		
5. Have you ever quit a job after being notified that you would be fired?		
6. Do you receive or have you applied for retirement pay, pension, or other compensation based upon military, postal, or federal civilian service? (If you answer "yes," give details in Section F.)		

7a. Have you ever been convicted of a crime or are you now under charges for any offense against the Law? You may omit: (1) any charges that were dismissed or resulted in acquittal; (2) any conviction that has been set aside, vacated, annulled, expunged, or sealed; (3) any offense that was finally adjudicated in a juvenile court or juvenile delinquency proceeding; and (4) any charges that resulted only in a conviction of a non-criminal offense. **All felony and misdemeanor convictions and all convictions in state and federal courts are criminal convictions and must be disclosed. Disclosure of such convictions are required even if you did not spend any time in jail and/or were not required to pay a fine.**

7b. While in the military service were you ever convicted by special or general court martial?

If you answer "Yes" to question 7a and/or 7b, give details in Section F. Show for each offense:

(1) Date of conviction; (2) Charge convicted of; (3) Court and location; (4) Action taken.

Note: A conviction does not automatically mean that you cannot be appointed. What you were convicted of, and how long ago, are important. Give all of the facts so that a decision can be made.

8. Are you a former Postal Service or Federal Employee not now employed by the US Government? If you answer "Yes", give in Section F, name of employing agency(ies), position title(s), and date(s) employed.

9. Does the US Postal Service employ any relative of yours by blood or marriage?

Postal officials may not appoint any of their relatives or recommend them for appointment in the Postal Service. Any relative who is appointed in violation of this restriction can not be paid. Thus it is necessary to have information about your relatives who are working for the USPS. These include: mother, father, daughter, son, sister, brother, aunt, uncle, first cousin, niece, nephew, wife, husband, mother-in-law, father-in-law, daughter-in-law, sister-in-law, brother-in-law, stepfather, stepmother, stepdaughter, stepson, stepsister, stepbrother, half sister, and half brother.

If you answer "Yes" to question 9, give in section F for such relatives:

(1) Full name; (2) Present address and ZIP code; (3) Relationship; (4) Position title; (5) Name & location of postal installation where employed.

10. Are you now dependent on or a user of ANY addictive or hallucinogenic drug, including amphetamines, barbiturates, heroin, morphine, cocaine, mescaline, LSD, STP, hashish, marijuana, or methadone, other than for medical treatment under the supervision of a doctor?

F. Use This Space for Detailed Answers
(Use blank sheets if you need more space. Include your name, SSN, and date on each sheet.)

G. Certification

Enter number of additional sheets you have attached as part of this application: _____.

I certify that all of the statements made in this application are true, complete, and correct to the best of my knowledge and belief and are in good faith.	Signature of Applicant	Date Signed

Disclosure by you of your Social Security Number (SSN) is mandatory to obtain the services, benefits, or processes that you are seeking. Solicitation of the SSN by the USPS is authorized under provisions of Executive Order 9397, dated November 22, 1943. The information gathered through the use of the number will be used only as necessary in authorized personnel administration processes.

A false or dishonest answer to any question in this application may be grounds for not employing you or for dismissing you after you begin work, and may be punishable by fine or imprisonment. (US Code, Title 18, Sec. 1001). All the information you give will be considered in reviewing your application and is subject to investigation.

PS Form 2591, November 1993 (Page 4 of 4)   *U.S. Government Printing Office: 1993 — 342-723/83819

ADMISSION CARD
Do Not Write In This Space

Title of Examination	Social Security No.		
Date of Birth	Today's Date	Post Office Applied For	

If you have performed active duty in the Armed Forces of the United States and were separated under honorable conditions indicate periods of service

From (Mo., Day, Yr.) _____ to (Mo., Day, Yr.) _____

DO YOU CLAIM VETERAN PREFERENCE?   ☐ NO   ☐ YES   IF YES, BASED ON
☐ (1) Active duty in the Armed Forces of the U.S. during World War I or the period December 7, 1941, through July 1, 1955, (2) More than 180 consecutive days of active duty (other than for training) in the Armed Forces of the U.S. any part of which occurred between Jan. 31, 1955 and Oct. 14, 1976, or (3) Award of a campaign badge or service medal
☐ Your status as (1) a disabled veteran or a veteran who was awarded the purple heart for wounds or injuries received in action, (2) a veteran's widow who has not remarried, (3) the wife of an ex serviceman who has a service connected disability which disqualifies him for civil service appointment, or (4) the widowed, divorced or separated mother of an ex-service son or daughter who died in action or who is totally and permanently disabled

Print or Type Your Name and Address

Name (First, Middle, Last)

Address (House, Apt. No. & Street)

City, State, ZIP Code (ZIP Code must be included)

This card will be returned to you. Bring it, along with personal identification bearing your picture or description, with you when you report for the test. ID's will be checked, and a fingerprint or signature specimen may be required.

PS Form 2479-B, April 1987

APPLICATION CARD

Name (Last, First, Middle Initials)

Address (House/Apt. No. & Street)

City, State, ZIP Code

Birthdate (Month, Date, Year)

Telephone Number | Today's Date

Title of Examination

Post Office Applied For

Do Not Write In This Space

PS Form 2479-A, April 1987

Instructions to Applicants

Furnish all the information requested on these cards. The attached card will be returned to you with sample questions and necessary instructions, including the time and place of the written test.

TYPEWRITE OR PRINT IN INK. DO NOT SEPARATE THESE CARDS. FOLD ONLY AT PERFORATION.

Mail or Take This Form—Both Parts—to The Postmaster of the Post Office Where You Wish to Be Employed.

PS Form 2479-A, April 1987 (Reverse)

Final Eligibility in This Examination is Subject to Suitability Determination

The collection of information on this form is authorized by 39 U.S.C. 401.1001; completion of this form is voluntary. This information will be used to determine qualification, suitability, and availability of applicants for USPS employment, and may be disclosed to relevant Federal Agencies regarding eligibility and suitability for employment, law enforcement activities when there is an indication of a potential violation of law, in connection with private relief legislation (to Office of Management and Budget); to a congressional office at your request, to a labor organization as required by the NLRA, and where pertinent, in a legal proceeding to which the Postal Service is a party. If this information is not provided, you may not receive full consideration for a position.

Disclosure by you of your Social Security Number (SSN) is mandatory to obtain the services, benefits, or processes that you are seeking. Solicitation of the SSN by the United States Postal Service is authorized under provisions of Executive Order 9397, dated November 22, 1943. The information gathered through the use of the number will be used only as necessary in authorized personnel administration processes.

Applicant	Fingerprint
Make no marks on this side of the card unless so instructed by examiner.	
Signature of Applicant	

Political Recommendations Prohibited

The law (39 U.S. Code 1002) prohibits political and certain other recommendations for appointments, promotions, assignments, transfers, or designations of persons in the Postal Service. Statements relating solely to character and residence are permitted, but every other kind of statement or recommendation is prohibited unless it either is requested by the Postal Service and consists solely of an evaluation of the work performance, ability, aptitude, and general qualifications of an individual or is requested by a Government representative investigating the individual's loyalty, suitability, and character. Anyone who requests or solicits a prohibited statement or recommendation is subject to disqualification from the Postal Service and anyone in the Postal Service who accepts such a statement may be suspended or removed from office.

PS Form 2479-B, April 1987 (Reverse)

Have You Answered All Questions on the Reverse of This Form? *U.S. G.P.O.: 1993-342-723/83796

Index

215

POST OFFICE JOBS: *How To Get A Job With The U.S. Postal Service* by Dennis V. Damp
$17.95, 224 pages, 2000 - ISBN: 0-943641-19-5 *(Revised Second Edition)*

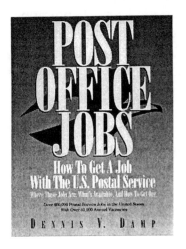

A one-stop-resource for those interested in working for the Postal Service. It presents what jobs are available, where they are, and how to get one. Includes a comprehensive 470 Battery Test study guide. "Post Office Jobs" dispels the myth that everyone in the postal service is a mail carrier or clerk. Over 200,000 workers are employed in hundreds of occupations; from janitors and truck drivers to accountants, personnel specialists, electronics technicians, and engineers. Many professional and administrative jobs do not require written examinations. An applicants background, work experience, and education is used to determine eligibility. Includes related Internet web site addresses and hundreds of contact numbers.

PRESENTS Eight steps to successfully landing a job:

❶ Identify job openings.
❷ Match skills to hundreds of jobs.
❸ Exam scheduling.
❹ Score between 90% - 100% on tests.

❺ Complete job applications.
❻ Prepare for the job interview.
❼ Apply for jobs without written tests.
❽ Pass the drug screening test.

This book includes sample exams for most job categories with study tips by Norman Hall for the 470 Battery Test's four key testing areas. Mr. Hall has scored 100% on the United States Postal Exam four times.

"Like the Postal Service, Damp delivers. His research shows."

— **Jim Pawlak**
"Career Moves" Columnist

THE BOOK OF U.S. GOVERNMENT JOBS: *Where They Are, What's Available, and How to Get One*, 7th Edition, by Dennis Damp.
$19.95, 2000, 256 pages, paperback , ISBN: 943641-18-7

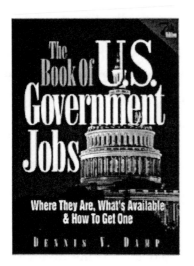

Damp, the author of 14 career books and the Associate Director of America Online's Career Center, guides readers through the federal employment system which has more employees that the top 16 Fortune 500 companies combined. You will discover what jobs are available, where they are, and how to get one. This **ALL NEW** *7th edition* covers the application process and resumes, testing criteria, Internet resources, professional and entry level jobs, handicapped employment, veterans preference, student hiring, overseas opportunities, Postal jobs, interviewing techniques, and over 1,000 job resources. An easy-to-use Job Hunter's Checklist is provided in Appendix A to guide readers step-by-step through the federal employment system.

Updated with the latest contact information including personnel office telephone numbers and Internet web site addresses.

Free updates for the 7th edition will be published on our web site:

http://federaljobs.net

"An updated, comprehensive how-to-guide. Written in a clear, readable style, this book is Recommended."   — **LIBRARY JOURNAL**

"A year ago you gave me pointers on finding a federal job. Well it all worked out and I'm a paralegal specialist in Oklahoma. I just wanted to say thanks."

— **JG, Tulsa, OK.**

"I just wanted to let you know that the information in your book helped me land a Congressional Summer Internship. After the internship, I would like to work in federal law enforcement. Thanks."

— **Gus**

"I just wanted to drop you a line to show my appreciation for the information you have provided. Before I ran across your publications I almost threw away $400 to a so called agency that "promised me a government job." So once again, thank you for your "civil service" from all of us hopeful civil service employees."

— **TomG,**

"Great book! Provided insight previously unknown. Comprehensive listing of all major government agencies, with complete addresses. Easy to read and understand. Resulted in my sending out an additional seven applications and resumes. Highly recommended!"

— **E.L. Testerman, USN (Ret)**

HEALTH CARE JOB EXPLOSION!: *High Growth Health Care Careers and Job Locator,* 2nd ed September 1998, by Dennis V. Damp. **$17.95, 320 pages,** ISBN: 0-943641-15-2

Explore high growth health occupations and use this book's 1,000 + resources to find job vacancies and networking contacts. This title presents detailed information for all major occupations. The health care job market is **EXPLODING.** The Department of Labor projects that jobs in health care will grow by 31 percent **(OVER 3,100,000 NEW JOBS)** by 2005.

This comprehensive **career guide** and **job finder** steers readers to where they can actually find job openings; periodicals with job ads, hundreds of Internet web sites, placement services, directories, associations, job fairs, and job hotlines. All major health care groups are explored including the nature of work for each occupation, describing:

- Typical working conditions
- Training/advancement potential
- Job outlook and earnings
- Employment opportunities
- Necessary qualifications
- Related occupations

PLUS more than 1,000 verified job resources

"...this book will be a boon to those seeking jobs. Well rounded... Recommended for general collections; this book will be in demand."   **— LIBRARY JOURNAL**

AIR CONDITIONING & REFRIGERATION TECHNICIAN'S EPA CERTIFICATION GUIDE: *Getting Certified, Understanding the Rules, & Preparing for EPA Inspections* by James Preston, $29.95, 1994, 192 pages.

Learn from an expert. The author, James Preston — certified universal technician — passed the **Type I, II, III, and Universal** exams on his first try using the techniques presented in this book. All air conditioning and refrigeration technicians now require certification by the EPA.

This certification and inspection primer teaches service technicians, those planning to enter the field, and business owners about the 1990 Clean Air Act's refrigerant recycling rules and prepares them for the certification test and on-site EPA inspections. This guide prepares technicians, students, and businesses for Clean Air Act implementation and includes:

- Certification Test Preparation
- Training Plan Development
- Freon Recovery/Recycling
- Labeling Requirements
- Complete References
- EPA Inspection Guidance
- Closed Book Practice Exams
- EPA Record Keeping Requirements
- Hundreds of Sample Test Questions
- The History Behind Ozone Depletion

HOW TO RAISE A FAMILY AND A CAREER UNDER ONE ROOF: A Parent's Guide to Home Business by Lisa Roberts.
$15.95, 224 pages, paperback, 1997, ISBN: 0-943-641-17-9.

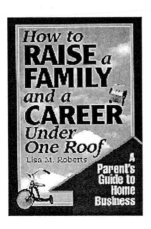

Join the 25 million Americans who have launched the Home Business Revolution. Learn how to start and nourish your business concurrently with the demands of your family, use valuable resources to get you started and how to use your hard-earned parenting skills to become a self-made entrepreneur. Hundreds of useful resources.

"...This book sends a positive and important message to parents who are struggling valiantly to balance work and family."
— **Paul & Sarah Edwards**
Authors of *"Working From Home"*

QUICK & EASY Version 4.0 FEDERAL JOBS KIT, Software (1999 Update) **$49.95 (Personal Version) WINDOWS 95, 98 and NT COMPATIBLE.**

During the past ten years, tens of thousands of people have used DataTech's Quick & Easy Federal Jobs Kit to get the Federal job they wanted.

This ALL NEW 1999 updated version 4.0 release, CD version, is compatible with all windows programs including Windows 98. The complete software package for getting a Federal job and completing your application. Contains everything you need including the SF 171, OF 612, and eight Federal resume formats, Also includes 7 new forms, the VA 10-2850, AID 1420-17, OPM 1170-17, SF-181, DA-3433, AD-779 and the SF-172.

As the Federal employment process has changed, Quick & Easy has changed with it. Now DataTech has updated the best-selling software to meet the needs of Federal job seekers in the twenty-first century.

Government Job Finder by Daniel Lauder
$16.95, 325 pages (1997-2000 3rd. Edition)

The perfect companion to The Book Of U.S. Government Jobs. A one-stop shopping center for federal, state, and local government positions in the U.S. and abroad. It shows you how to use over 2,002 specialty periodicals, job-matching services, Internet web sites, job hotlines, and directories to find the government vacancies in your specialty.

"Dynamite job hunting tool... the most complete compendium of resources for government jobs I've ever seen."
— **Joyce Lain Kennedy, careers columnist**

ORDERING INFORMATION

Use this order form to purchase the following titles. Include shipping charges and sales tax, if appropriate, in accordance with the instructions on the following pages and enclose your check or money order. Individuals must prepay before we can ship your order or you can order through our toll free number with all major credit cards by calling 1-800-782-7424. Purchase orders are accepted only from bookstores, libraries, universities, and government offices. Call or write for resale prices.

ORDER FORM

QTY.	TITLE	TOTAL
__ $17.95	Post Office Jobs (2nd edition)	_____
__ $19.95	Book of U.S. Government Jobs, 7th Edition (**Available 3/2000**)	_____
__ $17.95	Health Care Job Explosion! (2nd Edition)	_____
__ $29.95	EPA Certification Guide	_____
__ $16.95	Government Job Finder (3rd Edition)	_____
__ $15.95	How to Raise a Family and a Career Under One Roof	_____
__ $49.95	Quick & Easy Federal Jobs Kit (*CD Version 4.0*) (Personal Version - Unlimited files for one person)	_____

SUBTOTAL $____.____

☞ Shipping/handling: ($4.75 for first book.
   $1.25 for each additional book.) $ **4.75**

☞ Additional Books, __ x $1.25 $____.____

☞ Pennsylvania residents add 7% sales tax $____.____

☞   TOTAL $____.____

☞ *Please continue on the next page.*

SHIP TO:

(PLEASE PRINT)

First Name _____   Last Name _____

Company _____

Address _____   Apt # _____

City _____   State _____   Zip _____

Phone # _____   Ext _____   Fax # _____

Orders from individuals or private businesses must be prepaid. **Purchase orders** are accepted only from libraries, colleges and universities, bookstores, and government offices.

❑ Enclosed is a check or money order (made out to Bookhaven Press) for $ _____ . _____

(Send orders to Bookhaven Press LLC, P.O. Box 1243, Moon Township, PA 15108)

❑ **VISA/MASTER CARD** orders are accepted toll free at:

1-800-782-7424
<u>ORDERS ONLY</u>
WE ACCEPT ALL MAJOR CREDIT CARDS

BOOKHAVEN PRESS LLC
P.O. Box 1243
Moon Township, PA 15108

(412) 262-5578
FAX: (412) 262-5417

HOME PAGE: http://members.aol.com/bookhaven
FEDERAL CAREER CENTER: http://federaljobs.net
E-mail: Bookhaven@aol.com